Atlas of American Indian Affairs

Atlas of American Indian Affairs

Francis
Paul
Prucha

University of Nebraska Press: Lincoln & London

The paper in this book meets
the minimum requirements of
American National Standard for
Information Sciences — Perma-
nence of Paper for Printed Library
Materials, ANSI Z39.48 – 1984.

Library of Congress Cataloging
in Publication Data
Prucha, Francis Paul.
Atlas of American Indian affairs /
by Francis Paul Prucha.
p.   cm.
Includes bibliographical references.
isbn 0-8032-3689-1 (alk. paper)
1. Indians of North America — Maps.
2. Indians of North America —
Population — Maps.   3. Indians of
North America — History — Maps.
I. Title.
G1201.E1P7   1990   [G&M]   90-675000
912.7 — dc20   CIP   MAP

Second printing: 1991

Contents

Preface

I have long been fascinated by graphic display of statistical data, especially the presentation of geographical relationships on maps. Thus I was interested in the maps published by the Bureau of the Census showing the distribution of American Indian population by counties as enumerated in 1960 and in 1970. Because the Bureau of the Census did not make a comparable map for 1980, I undertook that task myself, plotting out the Indian population by counties and Standard Metropolitan Statistical Areas (SMSAs) for that census. The favorable reaction to my map from scholars with whom I shared it prompted me to make a series of such maps, as far back in time as useful statistics were available. That project led to a series of maps that showed the changes in urban Indian population, then to maps of land transfers from Indians to whites. I appropriated the maps of military posts in the West (largely Indian related) that I had made for an earlier publication on the military frontier, and soon I had a sizable group of maps, which in themselves made a small atlas. Piece by piece I augmented them with a historical series dealing with federal agencies that served Indians across the nation—trading houses, Indian agencies, schools, and hospitals—and with maps showing the Indian frontiers at various periods in United States history. To these I have added a selected portfolio of attractive and informative maps by the cartographer Rafael D. Palacios, which pertain to the history of the Indian wars in the post–Civil War decade.

Unlike other "Indian atlases," this one does not offer yet another survey of Indian-white relations in the United States, illustrated with a number of maps. I intend that the maps themselves in this atlas should convey useful and interesting information or at least (and perhaps most importantly) raise questions that will stimulate students to investigate further the material that appears on the maps.

I have limited the explanatory text to brief introductions to the sections of the atlas and to notes and references at the end of the atlas, which indicate the sources of my information, caution readers about the weaknesses in the data, and in a number of cases provide statistics for the information shown on the maps.

Many persons have helped me with the atlas, and I thank particularly the staff members who assisted me at the Cartographic Branch of the National Archives, the Geography and Map Division of the Library of Congress (especially Ralph E. Ehrenberg), the American Geographical Society Collection at the University of Wisconsin–Milwaukee, the Milwaukee Public Library, and the Marquette University Library. The Faculty Development Fund of the Graduate School, Marquette University, furnished financial aid for the project in its early stages.

The Cartographic Laboratory at the University of Wisconsin–Milwaukee gave me assistance on cartographic technique, and the Graphic Services of the Instructional Media Center, Marquette University, provided generous help. William Cronon advised and encouraged me along the way.

I am indebted to the following individuals and publishers for permission to use material:

The Macmillan Company for the Palacios maps from Andrist's *The Long Death*;

The State Historical Society of Wisconsin for the series of maps from *A Guide to the Military Posts of the United States, 1789–1895*;

Erwin Raisz and his estate for landform maps used as base maps;

The Department of Geography, University of Maryland Baltimore County, for outline base maps from *Historical U.S. County Outline Map Collection, 1840 to 1980*, Senior Editor: Thomas D. Rabenhorst; and

Sam Hilliard and the executive director of the Association of American Geographers for material from Indian land cession maps published in the *Annals of the Association of American Geographers*.

Note on Indian Tribal Names: The spelling of Indian tribal names is a problem for anyone using historical documents relating to Indians. This atlas follows the forms used in official documents and maps for the periods covered. Some variation in spelling results, but this seems better than to change historical designations to conform to present-day usage, as exemplified, for example, in the Smithsonian Institution's *Handbook of North American Indians.*

Marquette University   FRANCIS PAUL PRUCHA, S.J.

Maps

Indian-white relations in the United States rest on the culture of each society. The whites in what is now the United States had considerable diversity in the early years of contact—English, French, Spanish, and Dutch, to name only the national differences of the western Europeans who settled this part of the New World—but as the nation developed there came to be a greater homogeneity in language and other elements of culture. The Indians for their part had many distinct cultures, mutually unintelligible languages, differences in religious beliefs, and a variety of political structures. The European nations came to see the Indian entities as "tribes," with which they carried on diplomatic relations.

The three maps in this section show culture areas more or less agreed upon by anthropologists, general tribal locations, and land areas to which Indian groups had aboriginal or recognized title (as judicially established by the Indian Claims Commission). They provide a basis for later maps in the atlas.

I

Culture and Tribal Areas

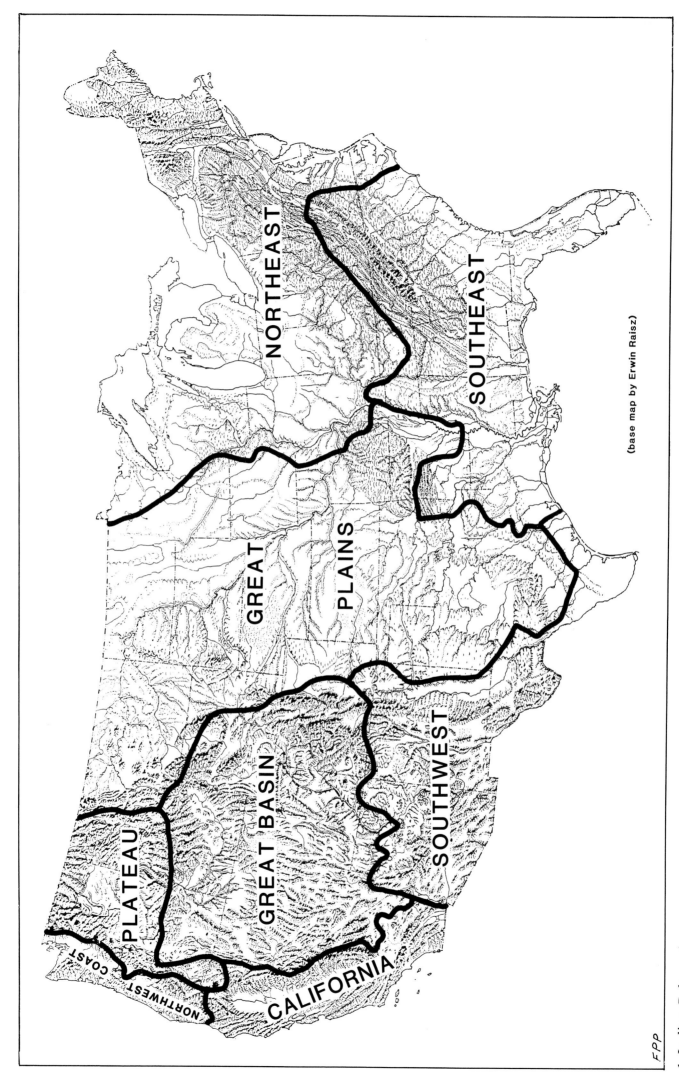

NORTHEAST

SOUTHEAST

GREAT

PLAINS

GREAT BASIN

PLATEAU

NORTHWEST COAST

CALIFORNIA

SOUTHWEST

(base map by Erwin Raisz)

F.P.P

1. Indian Culture Areas

4

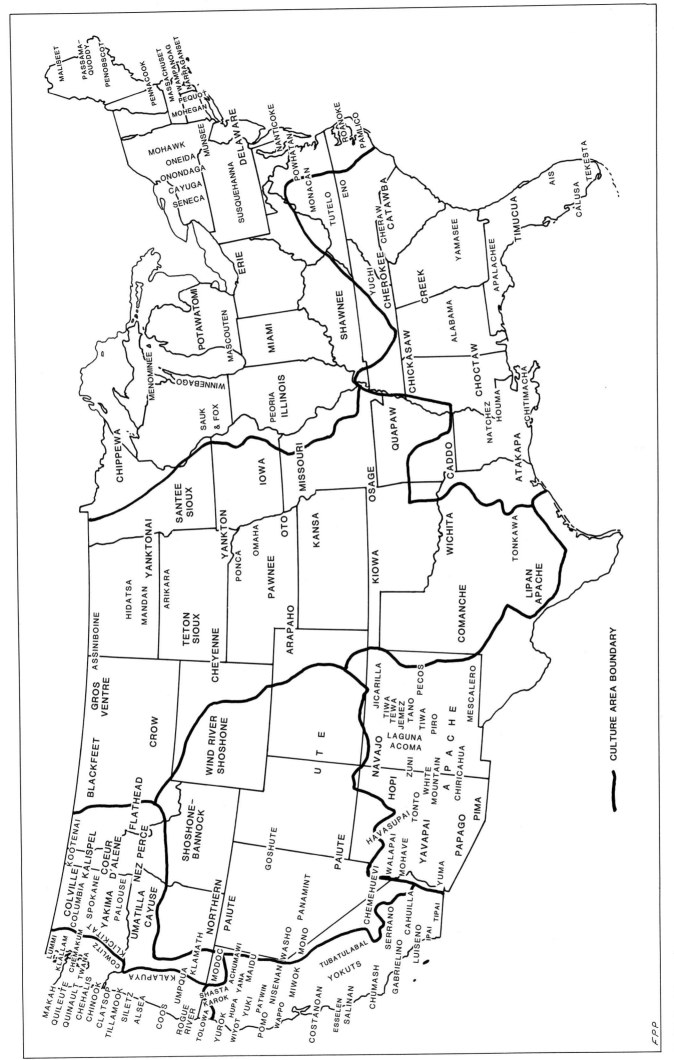

2. Tribal Locations

PASSAMAQUODDY
PENOBSCOT
IROQUOIS
SENECA 1
POWHATAN
LUMBEE
CATAWBA
SEMINOLE 41
CHEROKEE 37
CREEK
39
38
40
40

2
5
6
18 19
8
16
17
7 3 4 1
20 9
12 WATO
13 10 11
53 15
MENOMINEE
WINNE-BAGO
14 54
KICKAPOO
SAC & FOX
CHIPPEWA
42
43
44
45 46
47
49 48
50
51
52

CHOCTAW
CHICKASAW
ALABAMA COUSHATTA

21 22 23 24
25 26
30 27
31 28 32
29 35
33 34 36
55
56
59 60
61
IOWA 62
63
64
OMAHA 65
67
PONCA 66
PAWNEE 68
OSAGE 70
69 71
72
73

WICHITA
LIPAN APACHE 137

S I O U X
77
78
79
80
81
74
75
76
57
58

ARIKARA MANDAN HIDATSA 82
ASSINIBOINE 84
83
CROW 85
86
BLACKFEET & GROS VENTRE

CHEYENNE & ARAPAHO
NORTHERN CHEYENNE
NORTHERN ARAPAHO 112

KIOWA COMANCHE & APACHE
133
135
136
TIQUA
MESCALERO APACHE

JICARILLA APACHE 134
132 131 130
127 129
125 126 128
ZUNI
139
CHIRICAHUA APACHE 138

89
88
87
KOOTENAI
FLATHEAD
110
LEMHI
90
NEZ PERCE
92 91
93
94
100 99
101
102
103
96 95
98 97
YAKIMA
SEE INSET
106
107
104
108

SHOSHONE 111
U T E
GOSHUTE
UINTAH UTE 121
120
WESTERN SHOSHONE
119

NAVAJO 124
HOPI 123
SOUTHERN PAIUTE 122
142
143
144
145
YAVAPAI 146
148
PAPAGO 149
141
147
140

109
113
KLAMATH 114
115
NORTHERN PAIUTE 116
117
NORTHERN PAIUTE 116
118
INDIANS OF CALIFORNIA
105

INSET
150
152 153
151
154
155
156 157
160
165 166
162
159
167
158
161
163
164
169
170 171
168 172
173 174
COWLITZ 175
98
176
105

FPP

3. Indian Land Areas Judicially Established

6

1. Seneca, 1797
2. Delaware, Wyandot, Potawatomi, Ottawa, Chippewa, 1805
3. Ottawa, 1808
4. Delaware, Ottawa, Shawnee, Wyandot, 1819
5. Delaware, 1795
6. Shawnee, 1795
7. Potawatomi, Ottawa, Chippewa, 1819
8. Potawatomi, 1807
9. Potawatomi, 1821
10. Potawatomi, 1827
11. Potawatomi, 1832
12. Potawatomi, 1816
13. Potawatomi, 1795
14. Potawatomi, 1829
15. Potawatomi, 1833
16. Sault St. Marie Band (Chippewa), 1821
17. Ottawa, Chippewa, 1820
18. Saginaw, Chippewa, 1820
19. Saginaw, Chippewa, 1808
20. Grand River Band (Ottawa), 1821
21. Miami, Potawatomi, 1818
22. Miami, Potawatomi, 1827
23. Miami, 1818
24. Miami, Eel River, 1809
25. Miami, Delaware, 1818
26. Miami, Wea, 1809
27. Potawatomi, Wea, 1818
28. Potawatomi, Wea, Kickapoo, 1818
29. Wea, Kickapoo, 1810
30. Wea, 1818
31. Delaware, Piankeshaw, 1804
32. Potawatomi, Kickapoo, 1819
33. Kickapoo, 1819
34. Kaskaskia, Kickapoo, 1803
35. Piankeshaw (Peoria), 1805
36. Kaskaskia (Peoria), 1803
37. Cherokee, 1785–1835
38. Creek, 1816
39. Creek, 1832
40. Creek, 1814
41. Seminole, 1823
42. Lake Superior Bands, Mississippi Bands (Chippewa), 1843
43. Lake Superior Bands, Mississippi Bands (Chippewa), 1838
44. Lake Superior Bands (Chippewa), 1855
45. Bois Forte Band (Chippewa), 1866
46. Mississippi Bands (Chippewa), 1855
47. Lake Superior Bands, Mississippi Bands (Chippewa), 1848
48. Pillager and Lake Winnibigoshish Bands (Chippewa), 1855
49. Pillager Band (Chippewa), 1848
50. Red Lake Band (Chippewa), 1863
51. Red Lake Band, Pembina Band (Chippewa), 1863
52. Pembina Band (Chippewa), 1905
53. Potawatomi, 1833
54. Winnebago, 1829
55. Sac & Fox, 1805
56. Sac & Fox, 1832
57. Sac & Fox, 1831
58. Sac & Fox, 1842
59. Sac & Fox, 1837
60. Iowa, 1838, Sac & Fox, 1832
61. Sac & Fox, 1824
62. Iowa, 1838
63. Iowa, 1824
64. Otoe & Missouria, Iowa, Omaha, Sac & Fox, 1825
65. Omaha, 1854
66. Ponca, 1858
67. Otoe & Missouria, 1833
68. Pawnee, 1833
69. Osage, 1825
70. Osage, 1810
71. Osage, 1819
72. Quapaw, 1824
73. Caddo, 1835
74. Medawakanton Band (Sioux), 1837
75. Eastern or Mississippi Sioux, 1851
76. Yankton (Sioux), 1825
77. Sisseton and Wahpeton Bands (Sioux), 1872
78. Sisseton (Sioux), 1872
79. Teton and Yanktonai (Sioux), 1869
80. Yankton (Sioux), 1859
81. Sioux (Dahcotah) Nation, 1851
82. Arikara, Mandan, Hidatsa, 1870
83. Arikara, Mandan, Hidatsa, 1851
84. Assiniboine, 1851
85. Crow, 1868
86. Blackfeet & Gros Ventre, 1855
87. Flathead, 1855
88. Upper Pend d'Oreille, 1855
89. Kootenai, 1855
90. Nez Perce, 1859
91. Coeur d'Alene, 1887
92. Kalispel, 1887
93. Spokane, 1892
94. Palus, 1859
95. Cayuse (Umatilla), 1859
96. Walla Walla (Umatilla), 1859
97. Umatilla, 1859
98. Yakima, 1859
99. Colville, 1872
100. Lake Tribe (Colville), 1872
101. Sanpoil-Nespelem (Colville), 1872
102. Okanogan (Colville), 1872
103. Methow (Colville), 1872
104. Warm Springs, 1859
105. Clatsop, 1851
106. Tillamook, 1851
107. Tillamook (Alcea), 1855
108. Coquille, Chetco, Too-too-ney (Tillamook), 1855
109. Snake, 1879
110. Lemhi (Shoshone), 1875
111. Shoshone, 1869
112. Cheyenne & Arapaho, Northern Cheyenne, Northern Arapaho, 1865
113. Klamath, 1870
114. Modoc, 1870
115. Pitt River, 1853
116. Northern Paiute, 1853
117. Washoe, 1853
118. Indians of California, 1851
119. Western Shoshone, 1868
120. Goshute, 1875
121. Uintah Ute, 1865
122. Southern Paiute, 1880
123. Hopi, 1882
124. Navajo, 1868
125. Acoma, 1858
126. Laguna, 1858
127. Zia, Jemez, Santa Ana, 1912
128. Santo Domingo, 1905
129. San Ildefonso, 1905
130. Nambe, 1905
131. Santa Clara, 1905
132. Taos (Tiwa), 1905
133. Kiowa, Comanche, & Apache, 1865–1900
134. Jicarilla Apache, 1883
135. Mescalero Apache, 1873
136. Mescalero Apache, 1873
137. Lipan Apache, 1856
138. Chiricahua Apache, 1886
139. Chiricahua Apache, 1886
140. Western Apache, 1873
141. Tonto Apache, 1873
142. Havasupai, 1882
143. Hualapai, 1883
144. Mohave, 1853, 1865
145. Chemehuevi, 1853
146. Yavapai, 1875
147. Pima-Maricopa, 1883
148. Quechan, 1853, 1884
149. Papago, 1916
150. Nooksack, 1855
151. Lummi, 1859
152. Samish, 1859
153. Upper Skagit, 1859
154. Swinomish, 1859
155. Lower Skagit, 1859
156. Kikiallus, 1859
157. Stillaguamish, 1859
158. Makah, 1859
159. S'Klallam, 1859
160. Snohomish, 1855
161. Quileute, 1859
162. Skokomish, 1859
163. Skykomish, 1859
164. Snoqualmie, 1859
165. Suquamish, 1859
166. Duwamish, 1859
167. Quinaielt, 1859
168. Squaxin, 1855
169. Muckleshoot, 1859
170. Puyallup, 1855
171. Steilacoom, 1855
172. Nisqually, 1855
173. Lower Chehalis, 1855
174. Upper Chehalis, 1855
175. Cowlitz, 1855
176. Chinook, 1851

Indian population is a troublesome subject because statistics are incomplete or inaccurate and because there is no agreed-upon definition of who is to be counted as an Indian. Yet it is important to have some idea of the number of Indians, changes in population patterns, and the geographical distribution of Indians within the United States.

The enumeration of American Indians in the United States decennial censuses is perhaps the most satisfactory source for a general picture of Indian population in recent decades. There were earlier sporadic attempts to count the Indians, but only with the Eleventh Census of 1890 did the Bureau of the Census make an attempt to enumerate all Indians, including those on reservations. In that year, however, there was no accurate enumeration by counties, so that the first map shows population by states.

In 1910 and in 1930 the Bureau of the Census paid special attention to Indians and issued special reports, and more recent censuses have included supplementary or special reports on Indians and Alaska Natives. Each recent census has attempted to provide better enumeration and fuller information on Indians than the previous one.

While the maps based on the censuses appear to be comparable, in fact they must be used cautiously because of the varying criteria for deciding whom to count as Indian. As the Census Bureau noted in its special report in the 1930 Census, "Indian population, rates of increase or decrease are of little significance, as the size of the Indian population depends entirely upon the attention paid to the enumeration of mixed bloods, and the interpretation of the term 'Indian' in the instructions to the enumerators." There is also a problem of errors in gathering and recording data.

It should be noted that these maps show only counties and/or Standard Metropolitan Statistical Areas with approximately 100 Indians or more.

Despite the need for care in interpreting the maps, they offer much useful information. They show a continuing pattern of concentrations of Indian population, the increasing numbers of Indians in California and on the west coast in general, and the noticeable movement to urban areas. As James Paul Allen and Eugene James Turner remark about their ethnic population distribution maps in *We the People: An Atlas of America's Ethnic Diversity*, "Like most maps, these may be best used as heuristic devices to stimulate curiosity: about the places represented, about how and why the patterns evolved and changed over time, and about how they relate to other aspects of life in different places" (p. x).

Maps 11–13 repeat data on urbanization to show the increasing number of Indians in cities. They show Standard Metropolitan Statistical Areas that have 1000 or more Indians. In 1950 only three cities had 1000 or more Indians— New York City, Oklahoma City, and Tulsa—so no map was made for that year.

II

United States Census Enumeration of American Indians

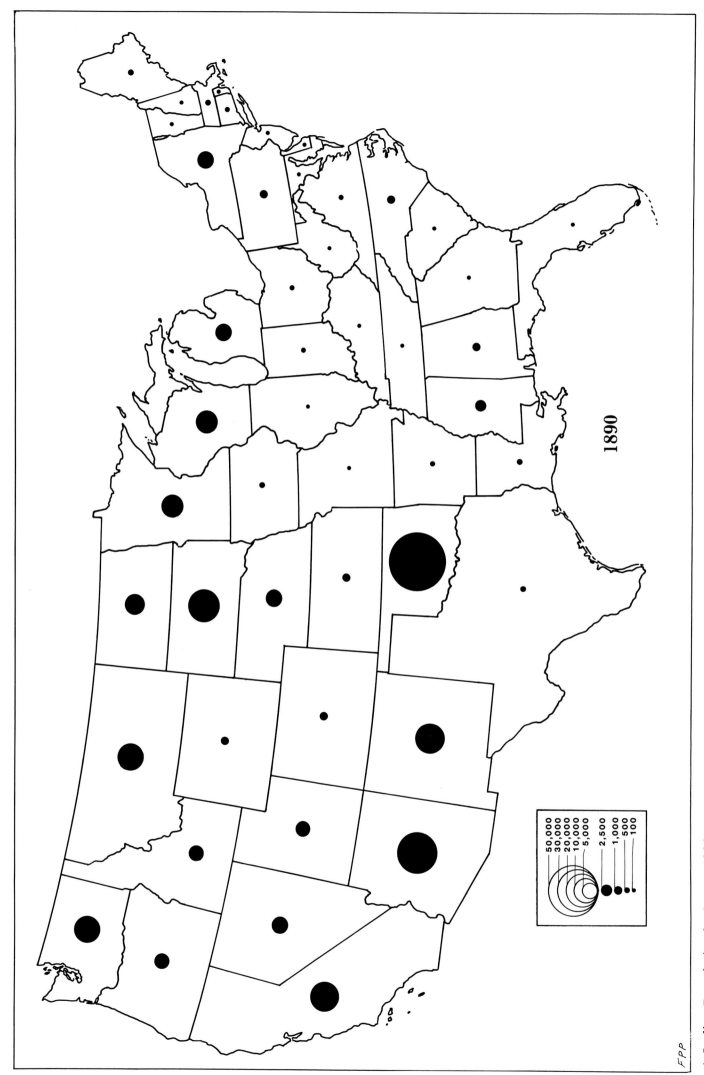

4. Indian Population by States: 1890

1890

50,000	
30,000	
20,000	
10,000	
5,000	
2,500	
1,000	
500	
100	

F.P.P.

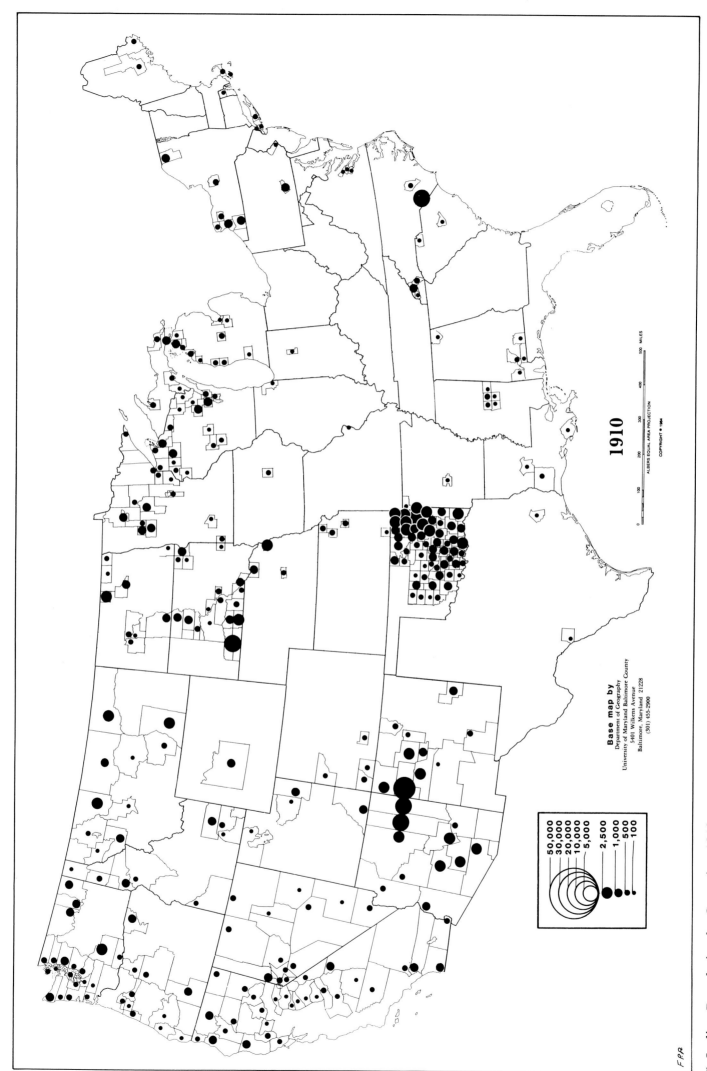

| 50,000 |
| 30,000 |
| 20,000 |
| 10,000 |
| 5,000 |
| 2,500 |
| 1,000 |
| 500 |
| 100 |

1910

ALBERS EQUAL AREA PROJECTION

COPYRIGHT © 1984

0   100   200   300   400   500   MILES

Base map by
Department of Geography
University of Maryland Baltimore County
5401 Wilkens Avenue
Baltimore, Maryland 21228
(301) 455-2900

F.P.R.

5. Indian Population by Counties: 1910

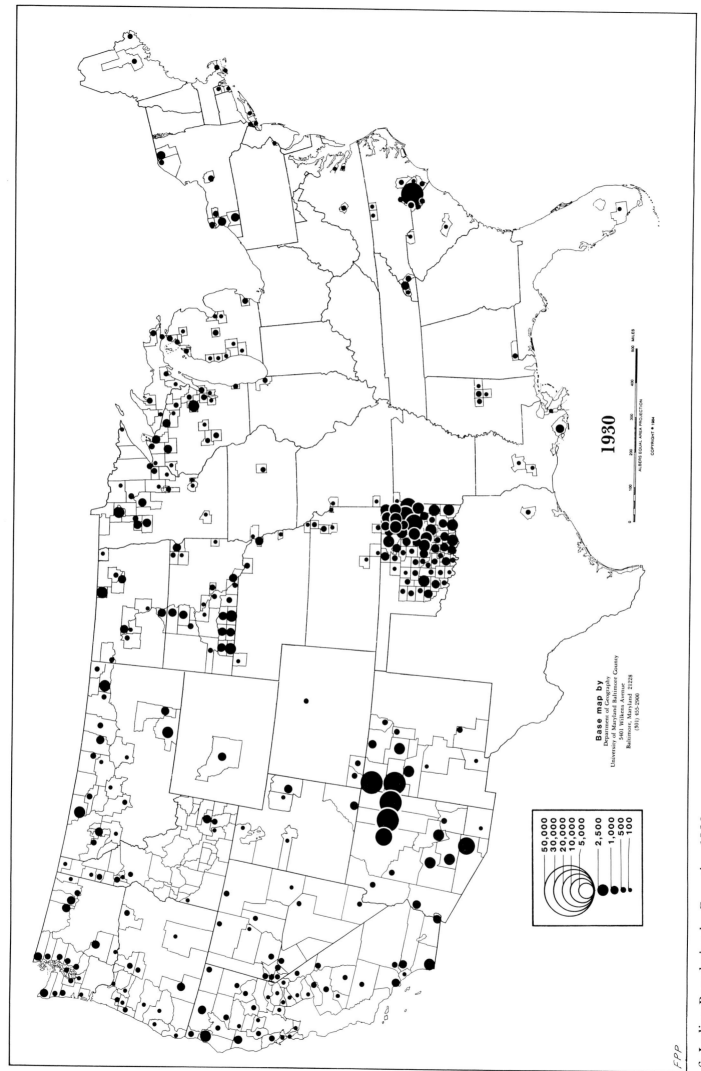

6. Indian Population by Counties: 1930

1930

ALBERS EQUAL AREA PROJECTION

COPYRIGHT © 1984

0   100   200   300   400   500
MILES

Base map by
Department of Geography
University of Maryland Baltimore County
5401 Wilkens Avenue
Baltimore, Maryland 21228
(301) 455-2900

50,000
30,000
20,000
10,000
5,000

2,500
1,000
500
100

FPP

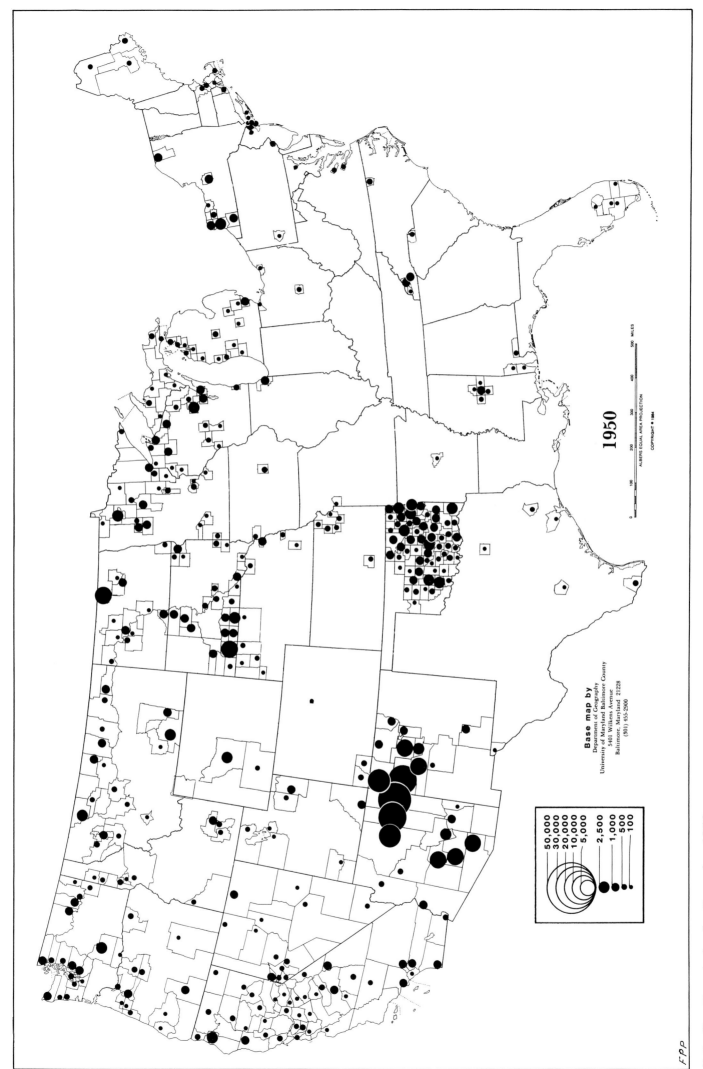

1950

ALBERS EQUAL AREA PROJECTION

COPYRIGHT © 1984

0   100   200   300   400   500
MILES

Base map by
Department of Geography
University of Maryland Baltimore County
5401 Wilkens Avenue
Baltimore, Maryland 21228
(301) 455-2900

50,000
30,000
20,000
10,000
5,000

2,500
1,000
500
100

FPP

7. Indian Population by Counties: 1950

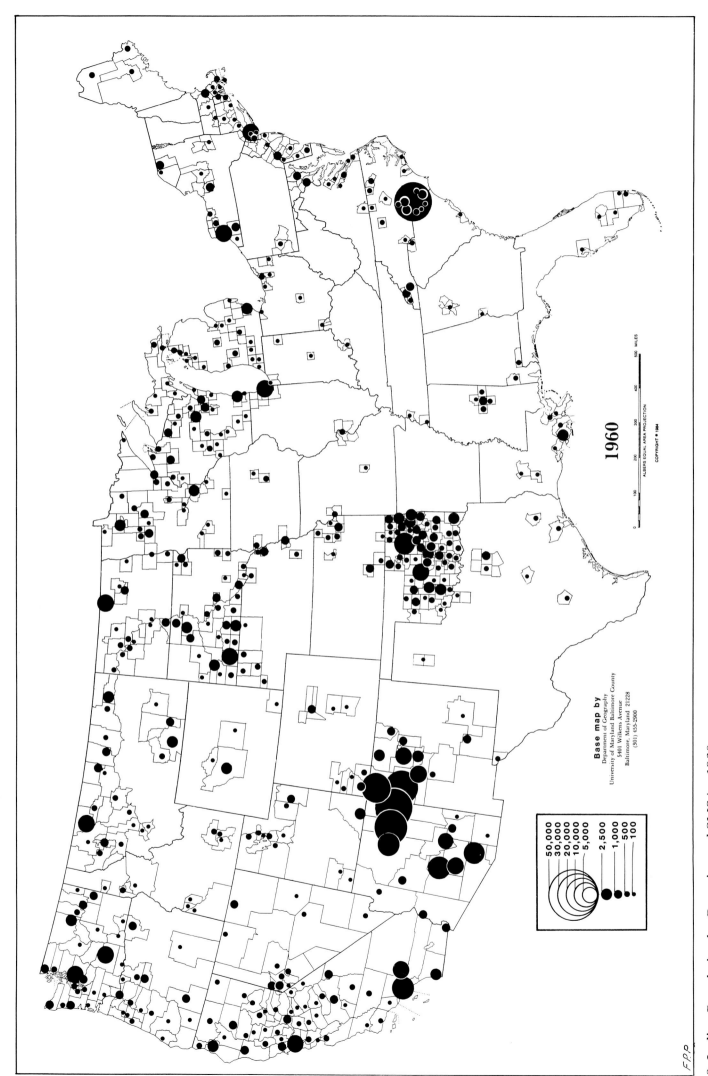

1960

ALBERS EQUAL AREA PROJECTION

COPYRIGHT © 1984

0   100   200   300   400   500 MILES

Base map by
Department of Geography
University of Maryland Baltimore County
5401 Wilkens Avenue
Baltimore, Maryland 21228
(301) 455-2900

50,000
30,000
20,000
10,000
5,000

2,500
1,000
500
100

F.P.P.

8. Indian Population by Counties and SMSAs: 1960

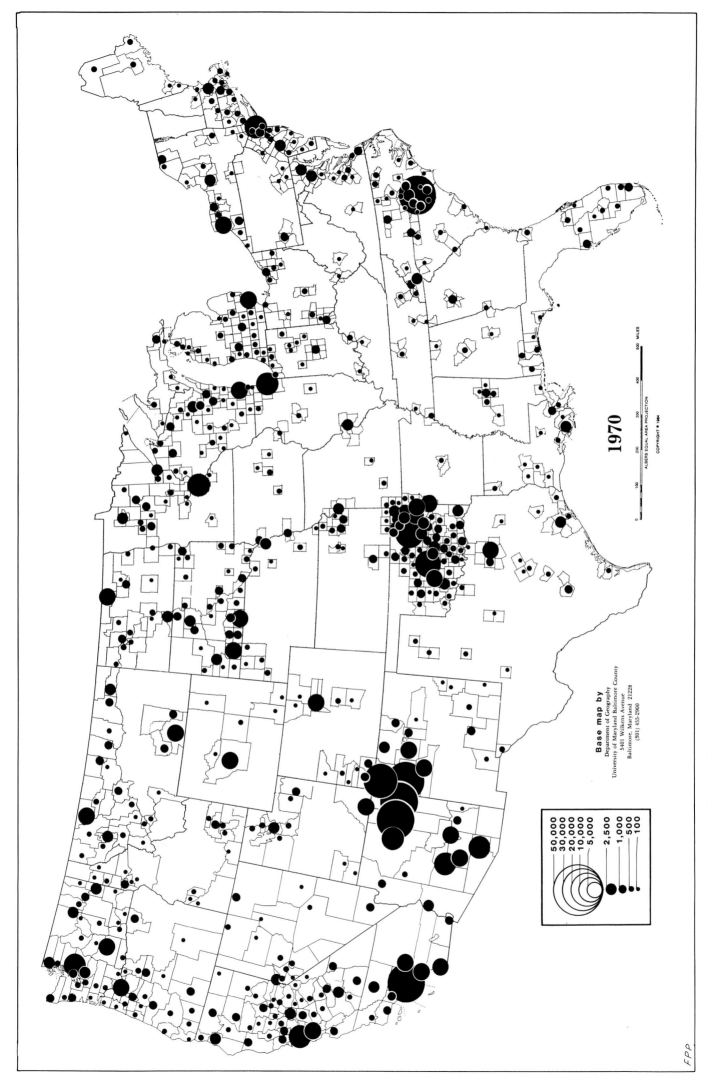

1970

ALBERS EQUAL AREA PROJECTION

COPYRIGHT © 1984

0   100   200   300   400   500 MILES

Base map by
Department of Geography
University of Maryland Baltimore County
5401 Wilkens Avenue
Baltimore, Maryland 21228
(301) 455-2900

50,000
30,000
20,000
10,000
5,000

2,500
1,000
500
100

F.P.P.

9. Indian Population by Counties and SMSAs: 1970

15

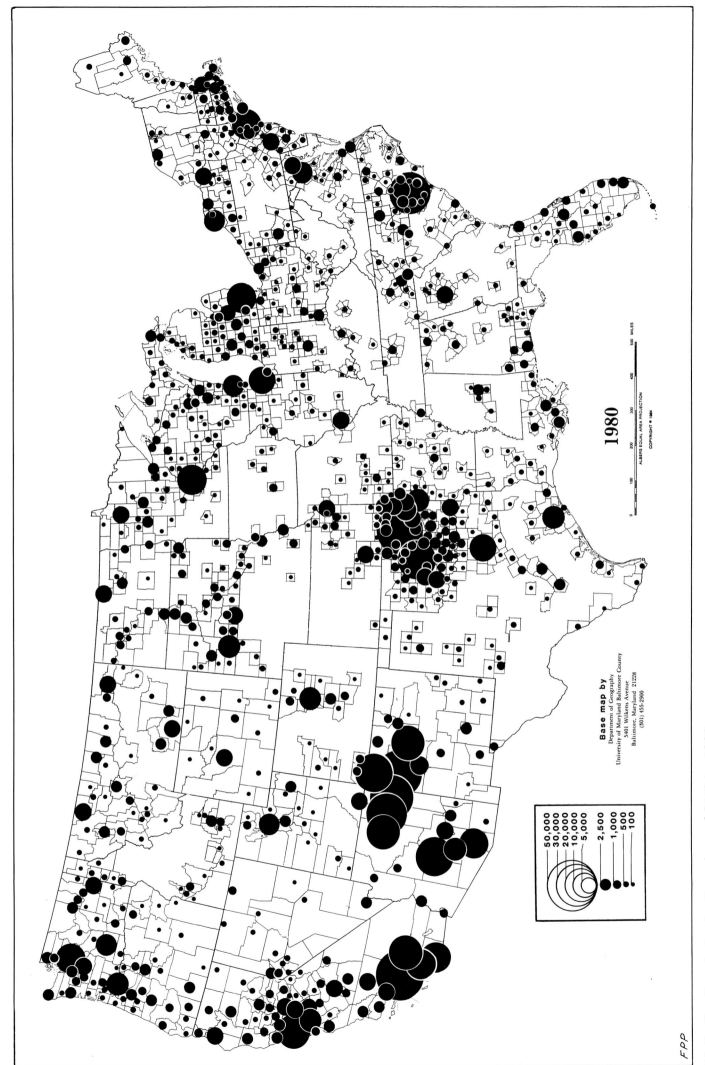

1980

ALBERS EQUAL AREA PROJECTION
COPYRIGHT © 1984

0   100   200   300   400   500   MILES

Base map by
Department of Geography
University of Maryland Baltimore County
5401 Wilkens Avenue
Baltimore, Maryland 21228
(301) 455-2900

50,000
30,000
20,000
10,000
5,000
2,500
1,000
500
100

F P P

10. Indian Population by Counties and SMSAs: 1980

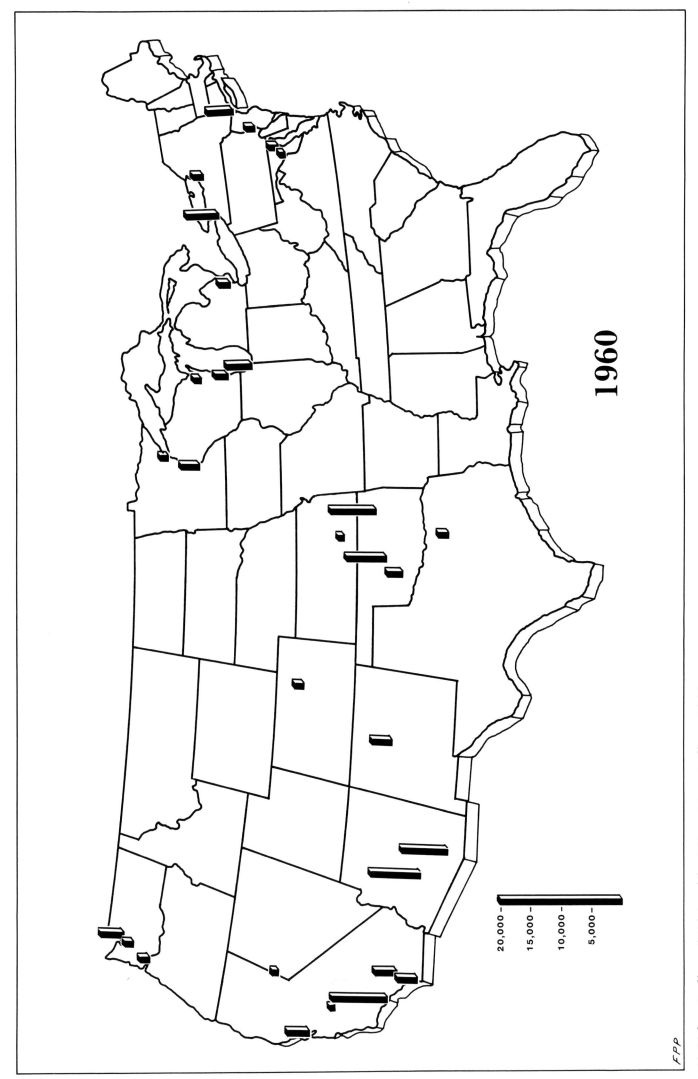

1960

11. Urban Indians, SMSAs with 1000 or More Indians: 1960

20,000 –
15,000 –
10,000 –
5,000 –

FPP

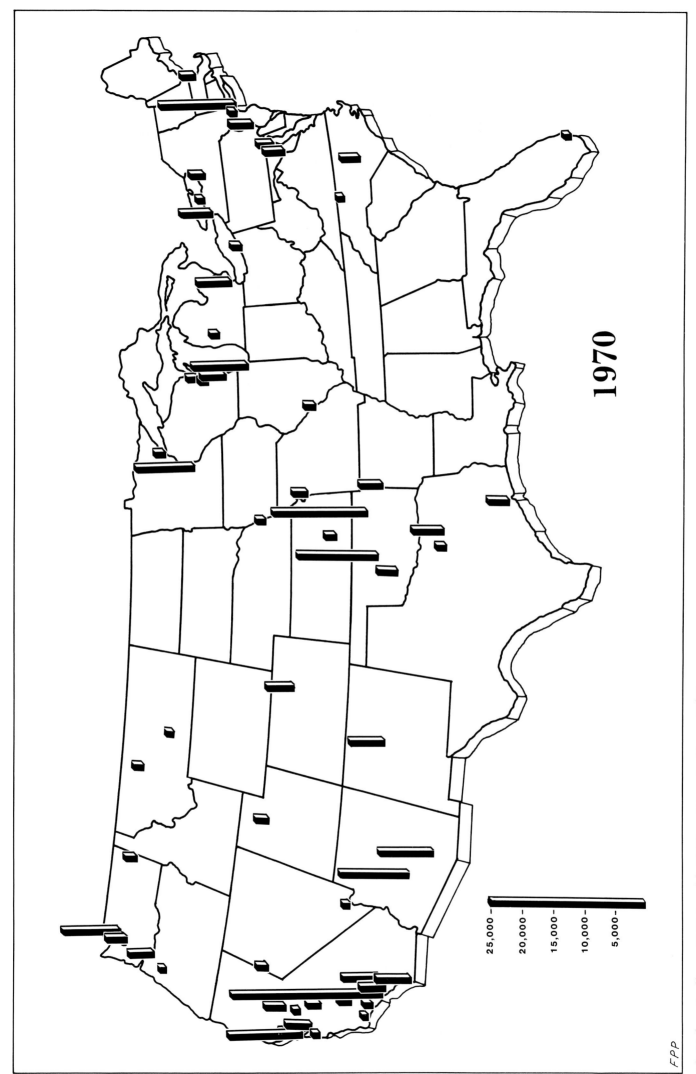

1970

25,000 —
20,000 —
15,000 —
10,000 —
5,000 —

12. Urban Indians, SMSAs with 1000 or More Indians: 1970

FPP

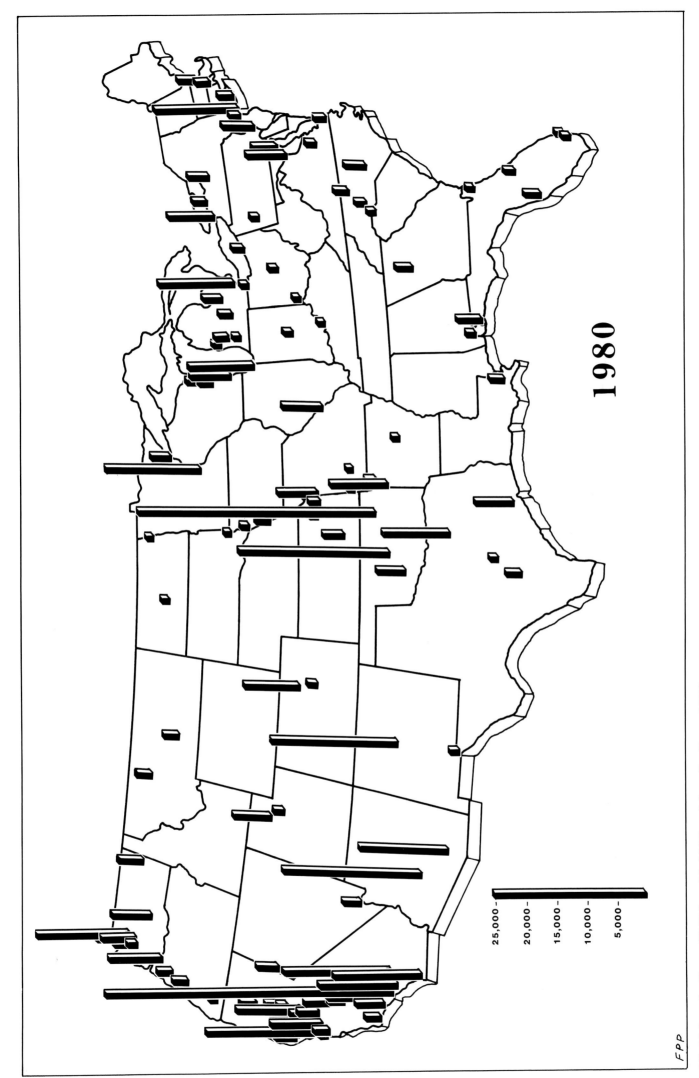

1980

| 25,000 — |
| 20,000 — |
| 15,000 — |
| 10,000 — |
| 5,000 — |

13. Urban Indians, SMSAs with 1000 or More Indians: 1980

FPP

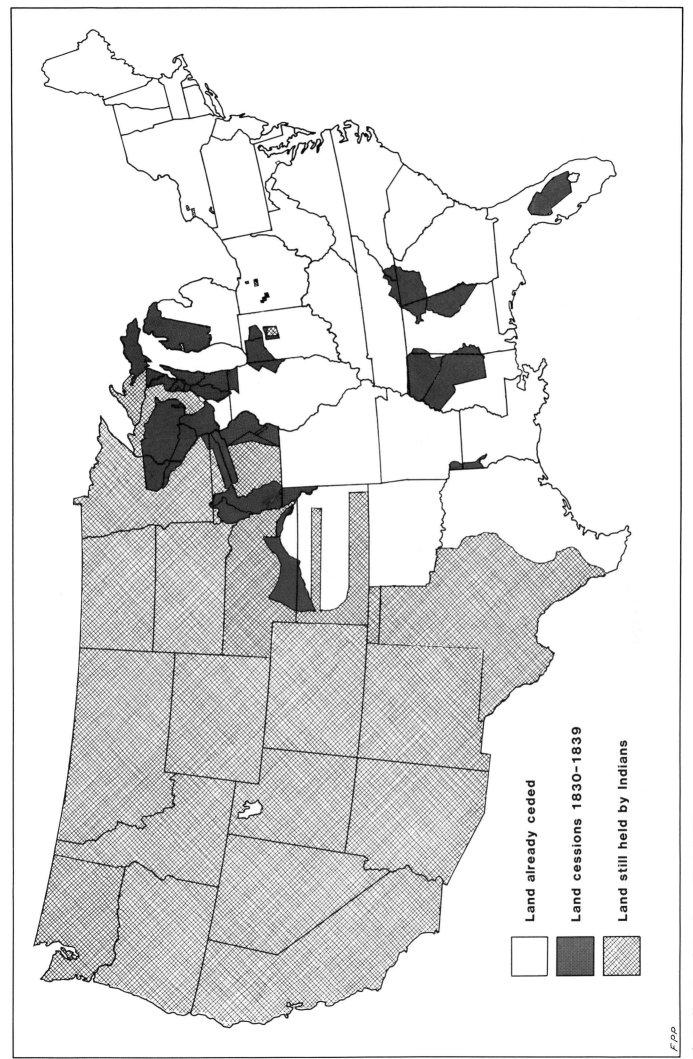

Land already ceded

Land cessions 1830–1839

Land still held by Indians

F P P

17. Indian Land Cessions: 1830–1839

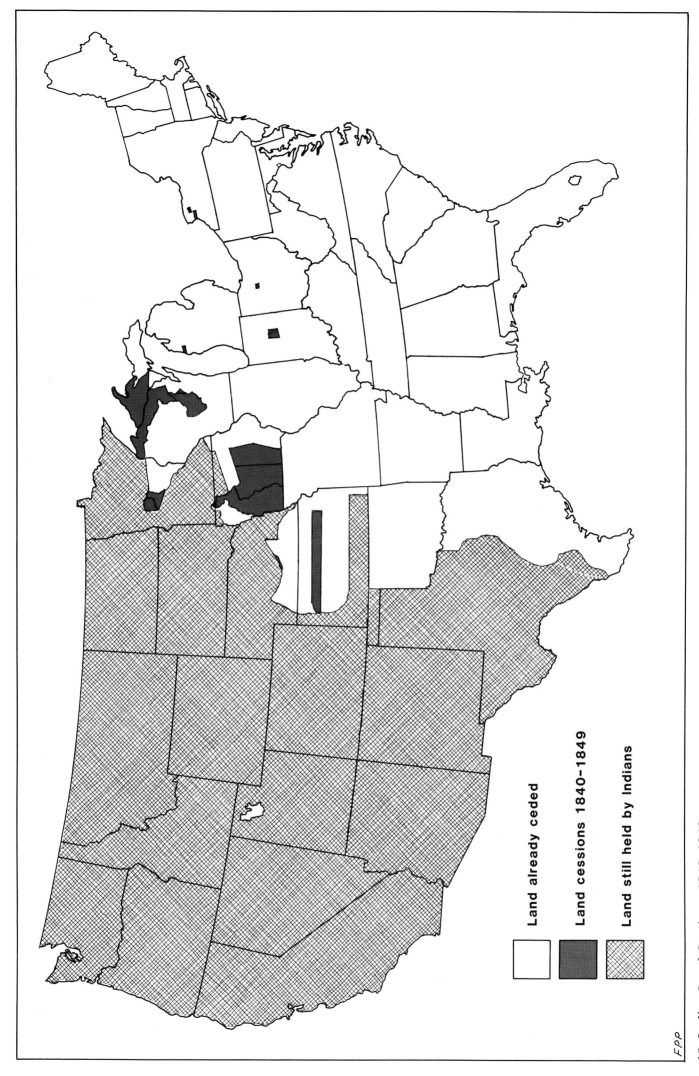

18. Indian Land Cessions: 1840–1849

Land already ceded

Land cessions 1840–1849

Land still held by Indians

FPP

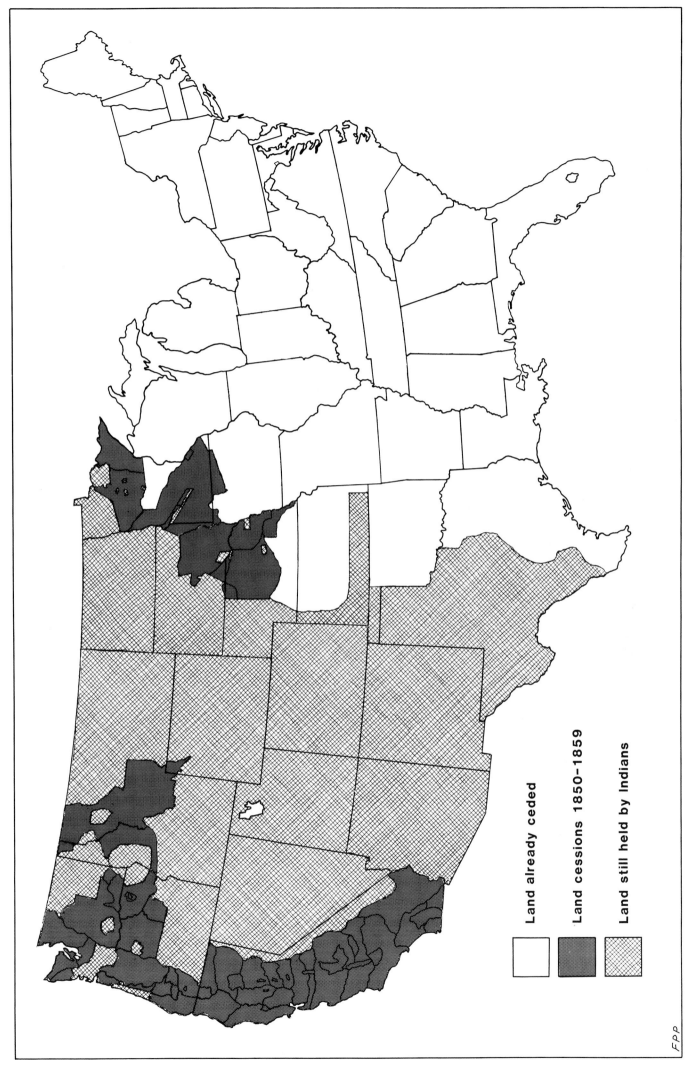

Land already ceded

Land cessions 1850–1859

Land still held by Indians

FPP

19. Indian Land Cessions: 1850–1859

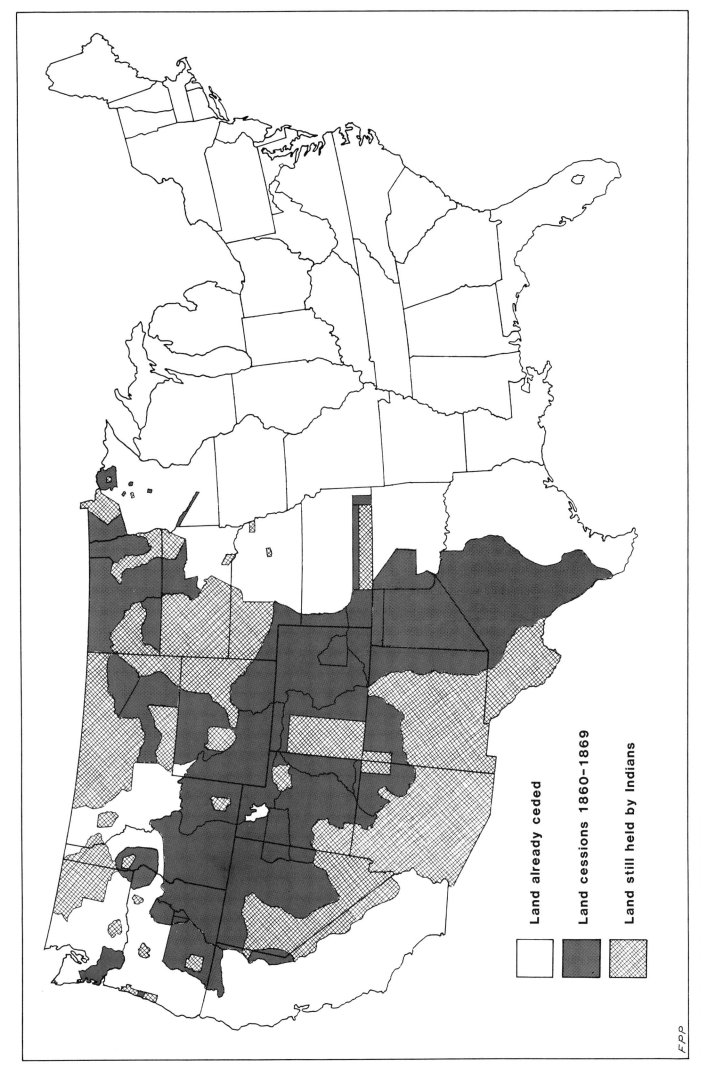

Land already ceded

Land cessions 1860–1869

Land still held by Indians

20. Indian Land Cessions: 1860–1869

FPP

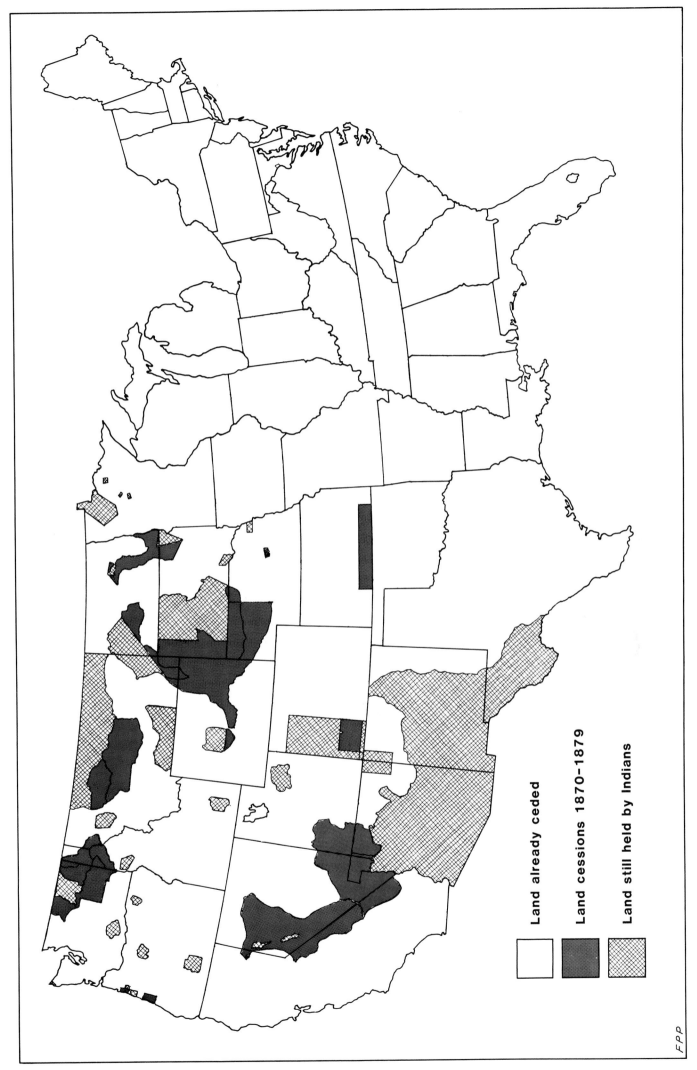

Land already ceded

Land cessions 1870–1879

Land still held by Indians

21. Indian Land Cessions: 1870–1879

F P P

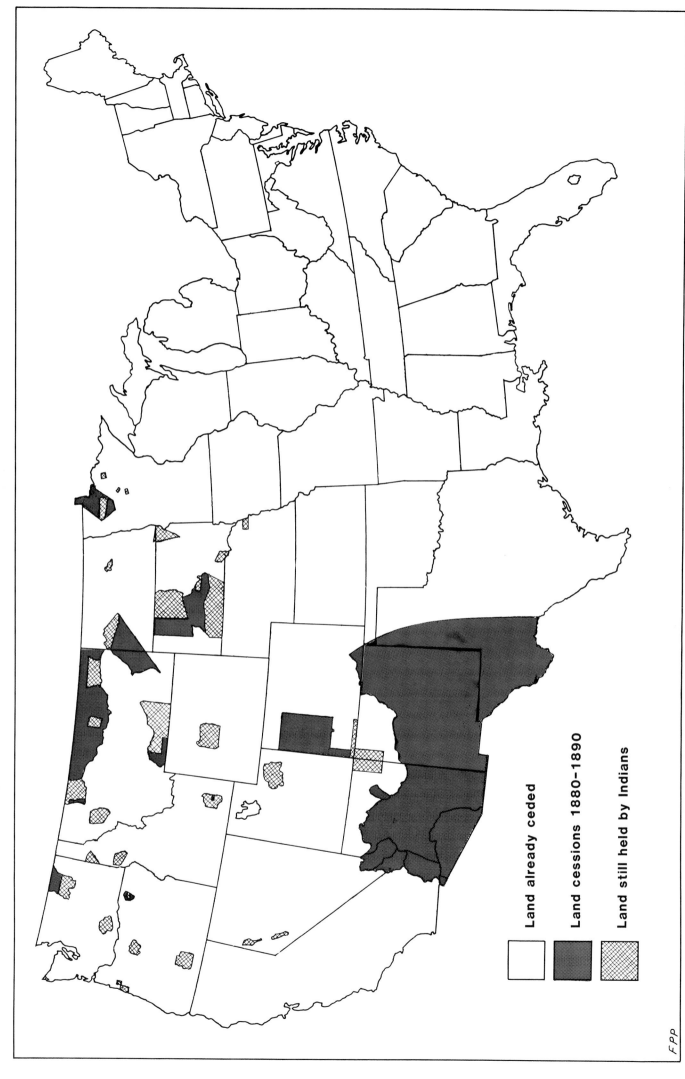

Land already ceded

Land cessions 1880–1890

Land still held by Indians

22. Indian Land Cessions: 1880–1890

FPP

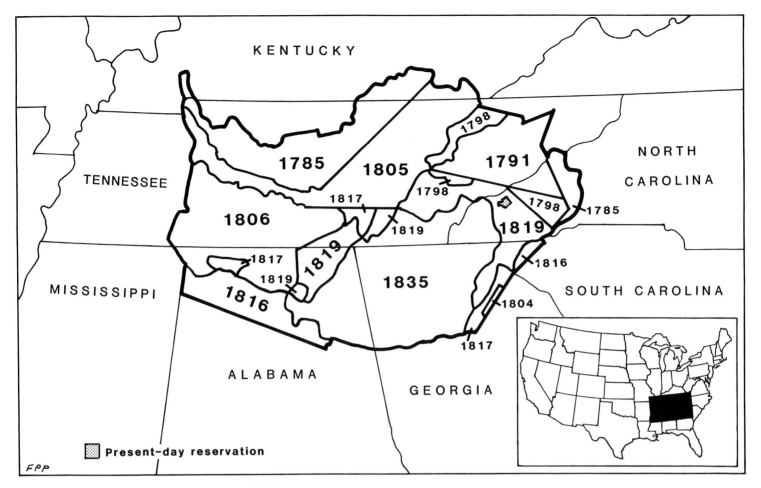

23. Cherokee Land Cessions: 1785–1835

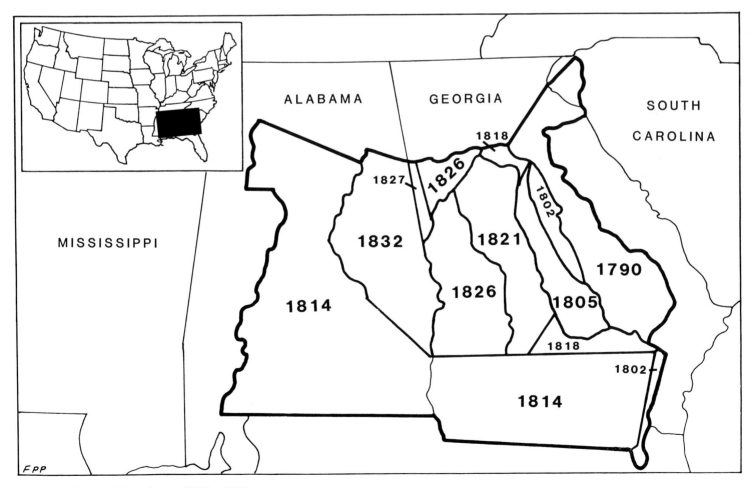

24. Creek Land Cessions: 1790–1832

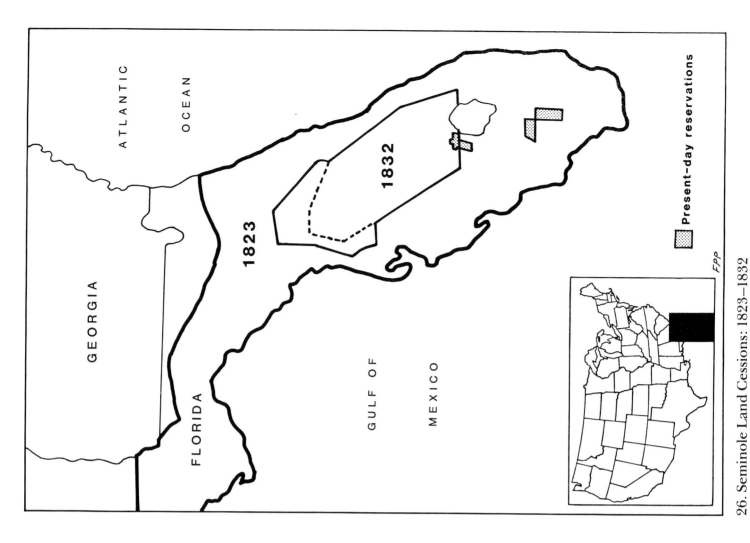

ATLANTIC OCEAN

GEORGIA

1823

1832

FLORIDA

GULF OF

MEXICO

Present-day reservations

26. Seminole Land Cessions: 1823–1832

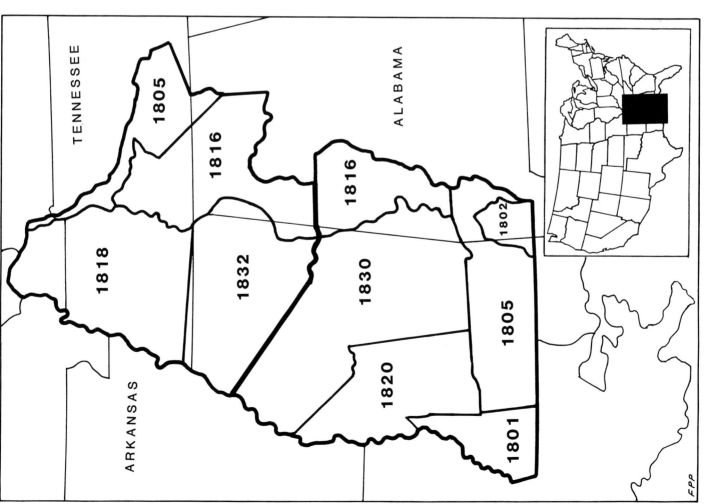

TENNESSEE

1805

1816

1818

1832

1816

ALABAMA

1830

1802

1820

1805

ARKANSAS

1801

FPP

25. Chickasaw Land Cessions: 1805–1832, and Choctaw Land Cessions: 1801–1830

32

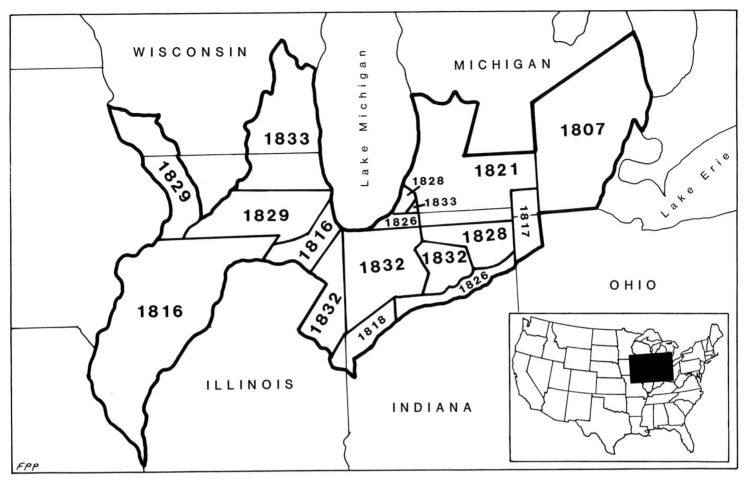

27. Potawatomi Land Cessions: 1807–1833

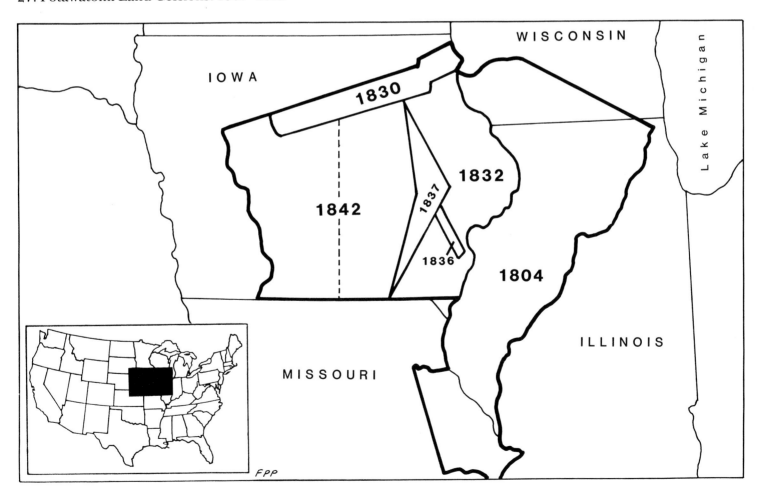

28. Sauk and Fox Land Cessions: 1804–1842

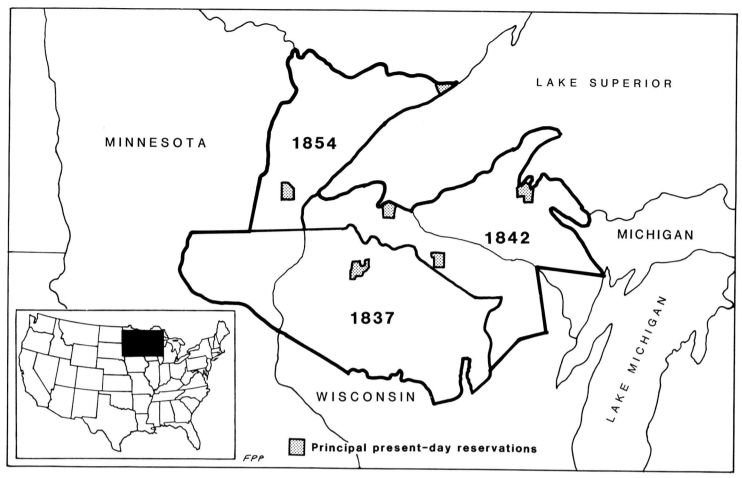

29. Lake Superior Chippewa Land Cessions: 1837–1854

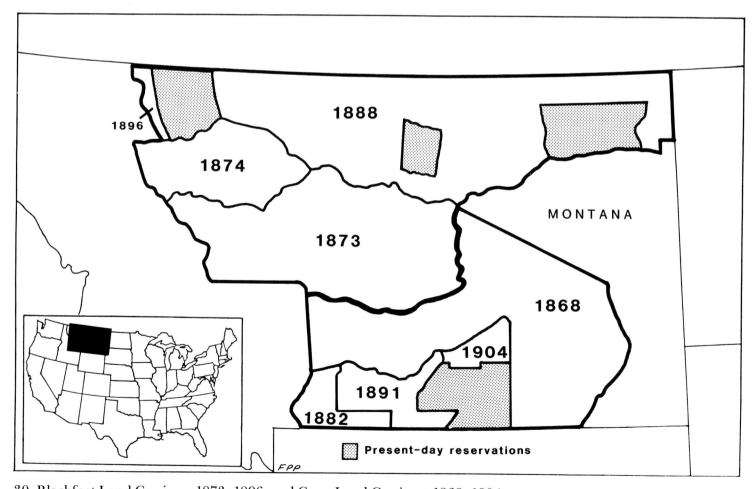

30. Blackfeet Land Cessions: 1873–1896, and Crow Land Cessions: 1868–1904

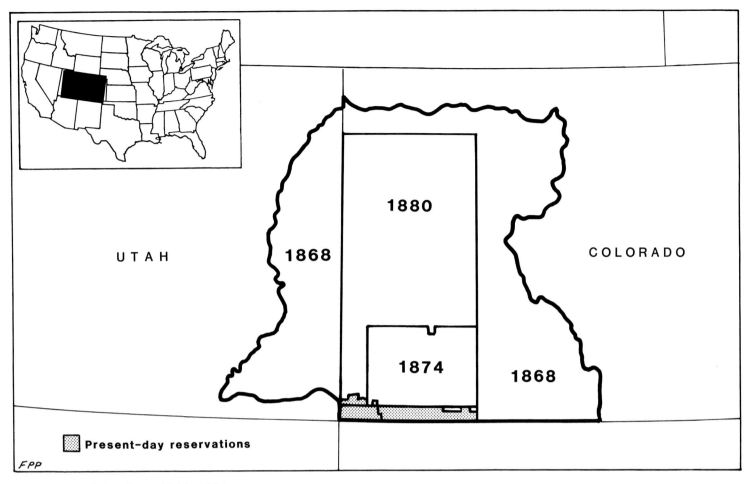

31. Ute Land Cessions: 1868–1880

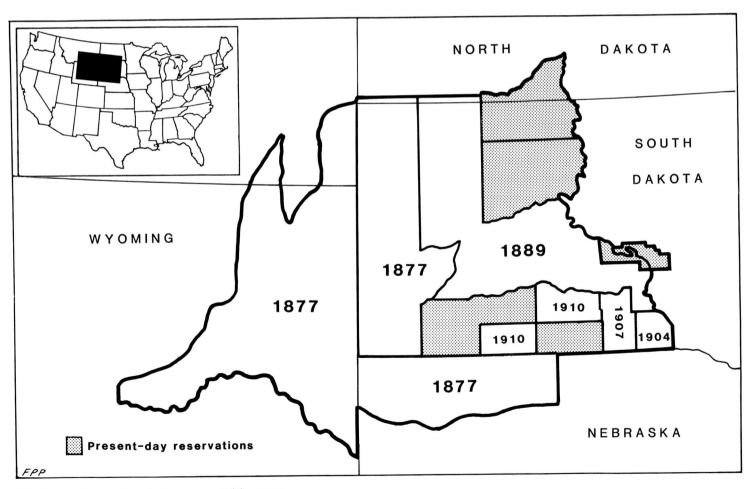

32. Teton Sioux Land Cessions: 1877–1889

Indian lands were originally distinguished from white lands by a line running from north to south. The original line, established by the Proclamation of 1763, ran down the crest of the Appalachian Mountains. Then the line was repeatedly modified by treaties of cession (often to validate illegal white settlements west of the line). At the end of the removal policy of the 1830s there was a "permanent Indian frontier" running along the western border of Arkansas and Missouri and then northeast through Iowa and Wisconsin. There were some reserves retained by Indians east of the line, but in general until the 1840s the line designated the eastern boundary of the Indian country.

The rapid expansion of the United States in the 1840s effectively ended the permanent Indian frontier. Large numbers of emigrants headed for Oregon and California, and the federal government sought to free a passageway for them by concentrating (or "colonizing") Indians to the north and the south. By numerous treaties and agreements, the Indians relinquished the great mass of their land holdings. Reservations that remained were further reduced or added to from time to time, so that the situation was nearly always in flux.

The maps in this section begin with general maps showing western Indian reservations in 1880 and 1890 and major present-day reservations as of 1987. Then there is a series of maps by geographical areas showing Indian reservations in 1987 (with 1980 census figures for both Indian and non-Indian population).

Maps showing reservations after allotment of land in severalty must be used with the understanding that not all of the land within the boundaries is owned by Indians. Allotment and subsequent disposal of reservation lands to whites resulted in a checkerboarding of the reservations that is not shown on the maps. In some cases only a small portion of the land within reservation boundaries is in tribal or individual Indian ownership. The population figures on Maps 36–45 give some indication of this proportional land ownership.

IV

Indian Reservations

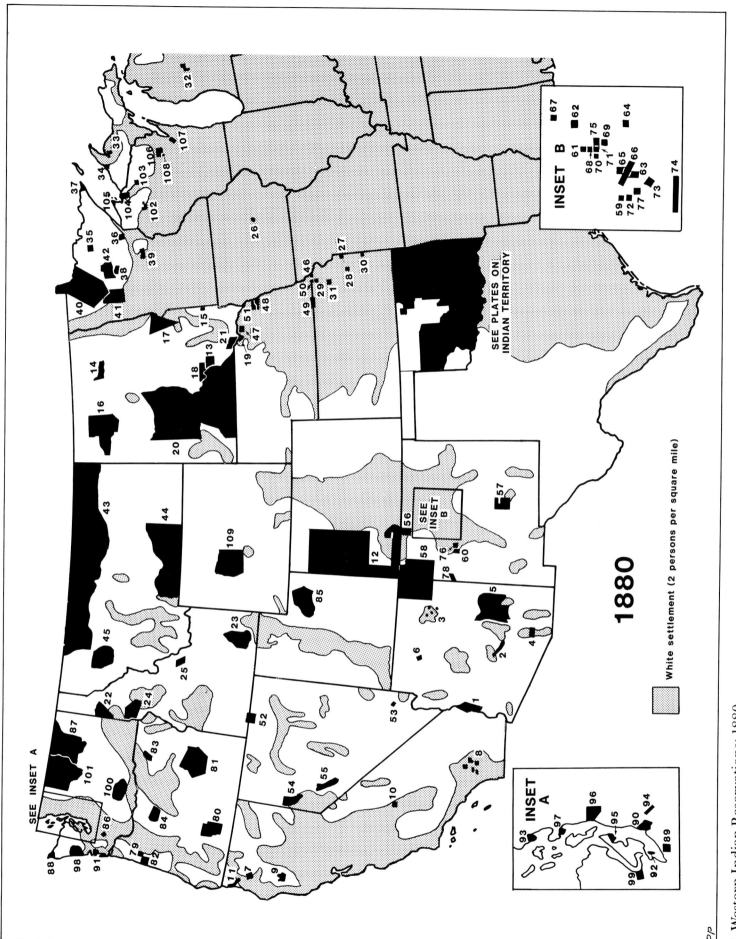

1880

INSET B

67	62
61	75 69
68 70 71 65 66 64
59 72 77 73 63
	74

INSET A

93 96 97 95 90 94 89 92 99

SEE PLATES ON INDIAN TERRITORY

SEE INSET B

SEE INSET A

White settlement (2 persons per square mile)

FPP

33. Western Indian Reservations: 1880

ARIZONA TERRITORY
1. Colorado River
2. Gila River
3. Moqui Pueblo
4. Papago
5. White Mountain
6. Suppai

CALIFORNIA
7. Hoopa Valley
8. Mission
9. Round Valley
10. Tule River
11. Klamath River

COLORADO
12. Ute

DAKOTA TERRITORY
13. Crow Creek
14. Devil's Lake
15. Flandreau
16. Fort Berthold
17. Lake Traverse
18. Old Winnebago
19. Ponca
20. Sioux
21. Yankton

IDAHO TERRITORY
22. Coeur d'Alene
23. Fort Hall
24. Lapwai
25. Lemhi

INDIAN TERRITORY
See Maps 58–60

IOWA
26. Sac and Fox

KANSAS
27. Black Bob
28. Chippewa and Munsee
29. Kickapoo
30. Miami
31. Pottawatomie

MICHIGAN
32. Isabella
33. L'Anse
34. Ontonagon

MINNESOTA
35. Bois Forte
36. Fond du Lac
37. Grand Portage
38. Leech Lake
39. Mille Lac
40. Red Lake
41. White Earth
42. Winnebagoshish

MONTANA TERRITORY
43. Blackfeet
44. Crow
45. Jocko

NEBRASKA
46. Iowa
47. Niobrara
48. Omaha
49. Otoe
50. Sac and Fox
51. Winnebago

NEVADA
52. Duck Valley
53. Moapa River
54. Pyramid Lake
55. Walker River

NEW MEXICO TERRITORY
56. Jicarilla Apache
57. Mescalero Apache
58. Navajo
Pueblos
59. Jemez
60. Acoma
61. San Juan
62. Picuris
63. San Felipe
64. Pecos
65. Cochiti
66. Santo Domingo
67. Taos
68. Santa Clara
69. Tesuque
70. San Ildefonso
71. Pojoaque
72. Zia
73. Sandia
74. Isleta
75. Nambe
76. Laguna
77. Santa Ana
78. Zuni

OREGON
79. Grand Ronde
80. Klamath
81. Malheur
82. Siletz
83. Umatilla
84. Warm Springs

UTAH TERRITORY
85. Uinta Valley

WASHINGTON TERRITORY
86. Chehalis
87. Colville
88. Makah
89. Nisqually
90. Puyallup
91. Shoalwater
92. Squaxin Island
93. Lummi
94. Muckleshoot
95. Port Madison
96. Snohomish (Tulalip)
97. Swinomish
98. Quinaielt
99. Skokomish
100. Yakama
101. Columbia

WISCONSIN
102. Lac Court Oreilles
103. Lac de Flambeau
104. La Pointe (Bad River)
105. Red Cliff
106. Menomonee
107. Oneida
108. Stockbridge

WYOMING TERRITORY
109. Wind River

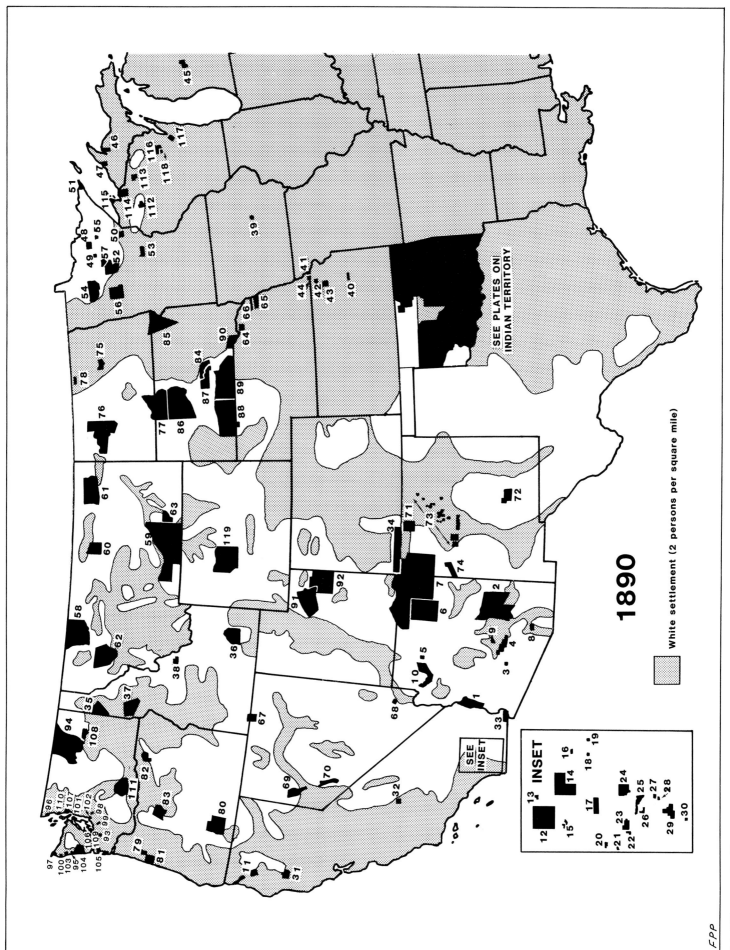

1890

White settlement (2 persons per square mile)

SEE PLATES ON INDIAN TERRITORY

34. Western Indian Reservations: 1890

FPP

40

ARIZONA TERRITORY
1. Colorado River
2. Fort Apache
   (White Mountain)
3. Gila Bend
4. Gila River
5. Suppai
6. Hopi
7. Navajo
8. Papago
9. Salt River
10. Hualpai

CALIFORNIA
11. Hoopa Valley

Mission
12. Morongo
13. Mission
14. Agua Caliente
15. San Jacinto
16. Villages
17. Coahuila
18. Torros
19. Cabizon
20. Temecula
21. Pala
22. Rincon
23. La Jolla
24. Los Coyotes
25. Santa Ysabel
26. Mesa Grande
27. Cosmit
28. Inaja
29. Capitan Grande
30. Sycuan

31. Round Valley
32. Tule River
33. Yuma

COLORADO
34. Ute

IDAHO
35. Coeur d'Alene
36. Fort Hall
37. Lapwai
38. Lemhi

INDIAN TERRITORY
See Map 60

IOWA
39. Sac and Fox

KANSAS
40. Chippewa and Munsee
41. Iowa
42. Kickapoo
43. Pottawatomie
44. Sac and Fox

MICHIGAN
45. Isabella
46. L'Anse
47. Ontonagon

MINNESOTA
48. Boise Fort
49. Deer Creek
50. Fond du Lac
51. Grand Portage
52. Leech Lac
53. Mille Lac
54. Red Lake
55. Vermillion Lake
56. White Earth
57. Winnibigoshish
    (White Oak Point)

MONTANA
58. Blackfeet
59. Crow
60. Fort Belknap
61. Fort Peck
62. Jocko
63. Northern Cheyenne

NEBRASKA
64. Niobrara
65. Omaha
66. Winnebago

NEVADA
67. Duck Valley
68. Moapa River
69. Pyramid Lake
70. Walker River

NEW MEXICO TERRITORY
71. Jicarilla Apache
72. Mescalero Apache
73. Pueblo
74. Zuni

NORTH DAKOTA
75. Devil's Lake
76. Fort Berthold
77. Standing Rock
78. Turtle Mountain

OKLAHOMA TERRITORY
See Maps 58–60

OREGON
79. Grande Ronde
80. Klamath
81. Siletz
82. Umatilla
83. Warm Springs

SOUTH DAKOTA
84. Crow Creek
85. Lake Traverse
86. Cheyenne River
87. Lower Brule
88. Pine Ridge
89. Rosebud
90. Yankton

UTAH
91. Uinta Valley
92. Uncompahgre

WASHINGTON
93. Chehalis
94. Colville
95. Hoh River
96. Lummi
97. Makah
98. Muckleshoot
99. Nisqually
100. Osette
101. Port Madison
102. Puyallup
103. Quillehute
104. Quinaielt
105. Shoalwater
106. S'Kokomish
107. Snohomish (Tulalip)
108. Spokane
109. Squaxin Island
110. Swinomish
111. Yakama

WISCONSIN
112. Lac Court Oreilles
113. Lac du Flambeau
114. La Pointe (Bad River)
115. Red Cliff
116. Menomonee
117. Oneida
118. Stockbridge

WYOMING
119. Wind River

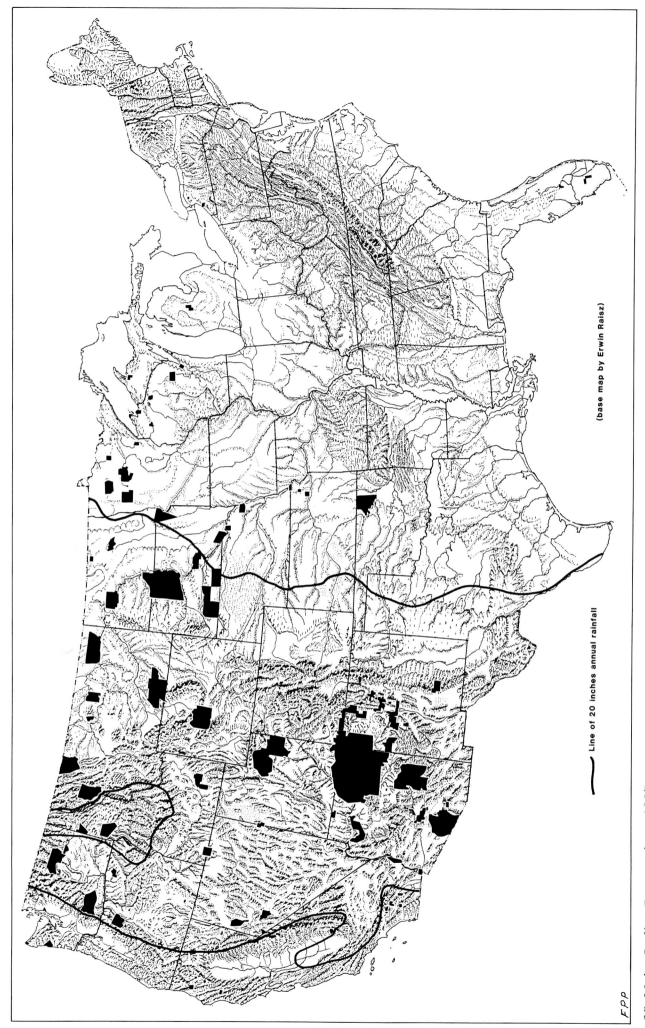

35. Major Indian Reservations: 1987

(base map by Erwin Raisz)

Line of 20 inches annual rainfall

F P P

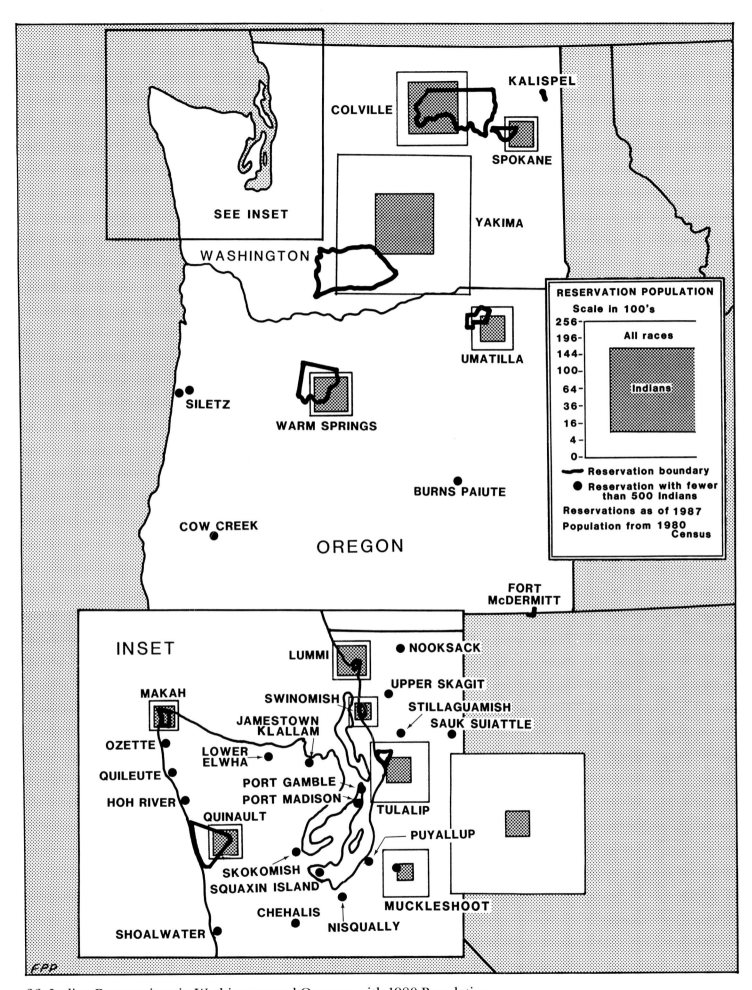

KALISPEL

COLVILLE

SPOKANE

SEE INSET

YAKIMA

WASHINGTON

UMATILLA

SILETZ

WARM SPRINGS

BURNS PAIUTE

COW CREEK

OREGON

RESERVATION POPULATION

Scale in 100's

256−
196−
144−
100−
64−
36−
16−
4−
0−

All races

Indians

⌇ Reservation boundary
● Reservation with fewer
than 500 Indians
Reservations as of 1987
Population from 1980
Census

FORT McDERMITT

INSET

LUMMI

● NOOKSACK

MAKAH

SWINOMISH

UPPER SKAGIT

JAMESTOWN KLALLAM

STILLAGUAMISH

SAUK SUIATTLE

OZETTE

LOWER ELWHA

QUILEUTE

PORT GAMBLE

PORT MADISON

HOH RIVER

TULALIP

QUINAULT

PUYALLUP

SKOKOMISH

SQUAXIN ISLAND

MUCKLESHOOT

CHEHALIS

NISQUALLY

SHOALWATER

FPP

36. Indian Reservations in Washington and Oregon, with 1980 Population

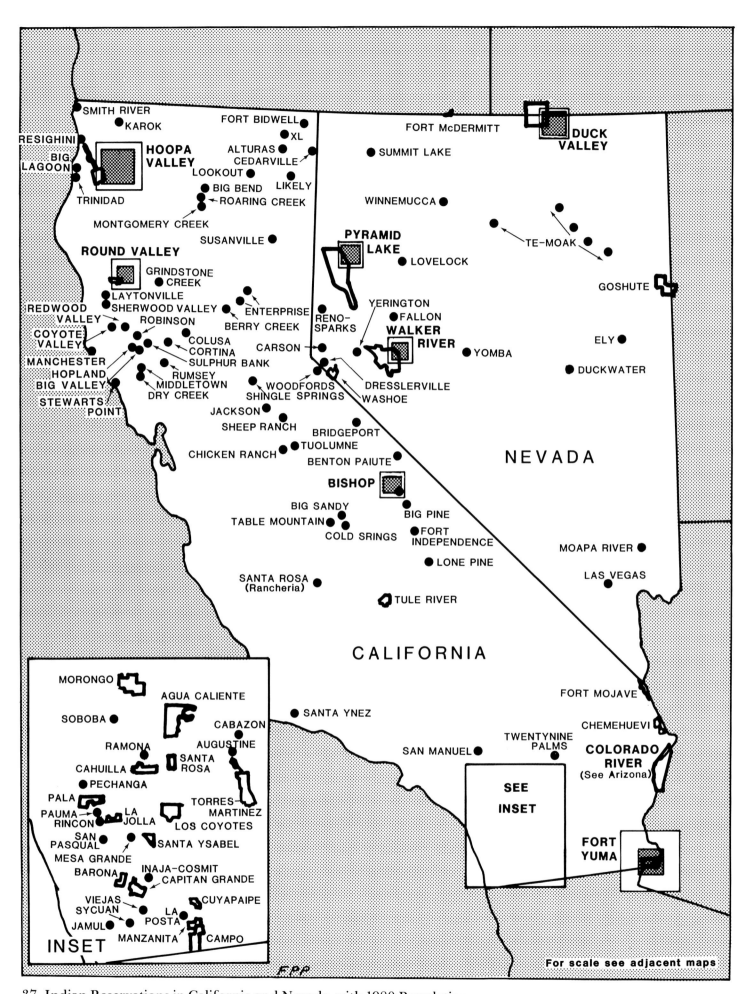

37. Indian Reservations in California and Nevada, with 1980 Population

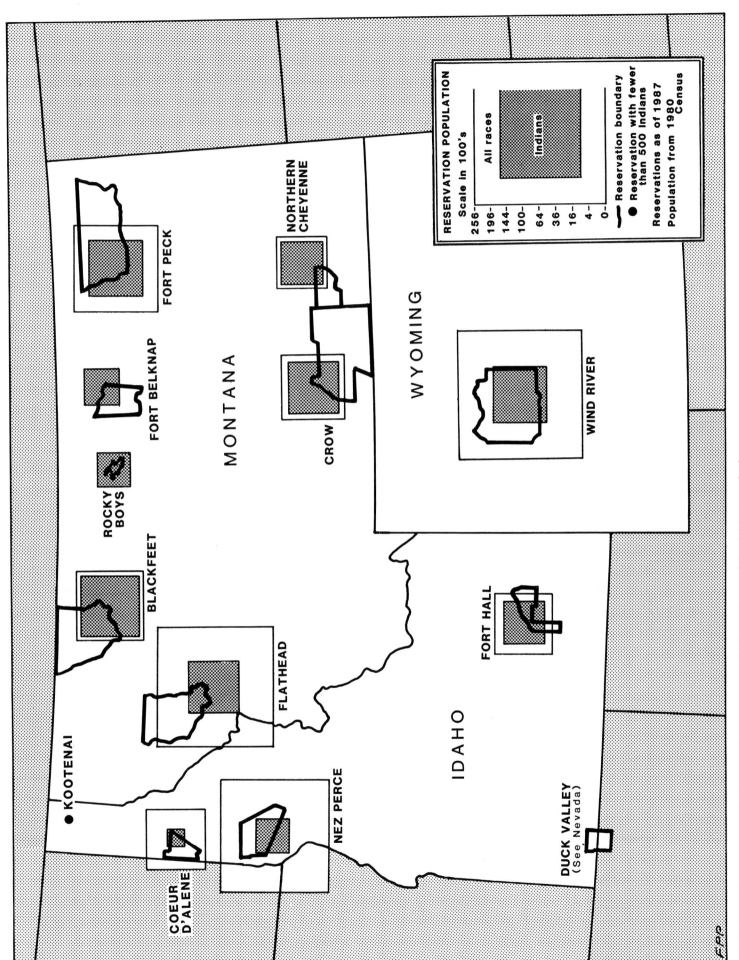

RESERVATION POPULATION
Scale in 100's

256
196
144
100
64
36
16
4
0

All races

Indians

— Reservation boundary

● Reservation with fewer than 500 Indians

Reservations as of 1987
Population from 1980 Census

FORT PECK

NORTHERN CHEYENNE

FORT BELKNAP

MONTANA

ROCKY BOYS

CROW

WYOMING

BLACKFEET

WIND RIVER

● KOOTENAI

FLATHEAD

FORT HALL

IDAHO

NEZ PERCE

COEUR D'ALENE

DUCK VALLEY
(See Nevada)

38. Indian Reservations in Idaho, Montana, and Wyoming, with 1980 Population

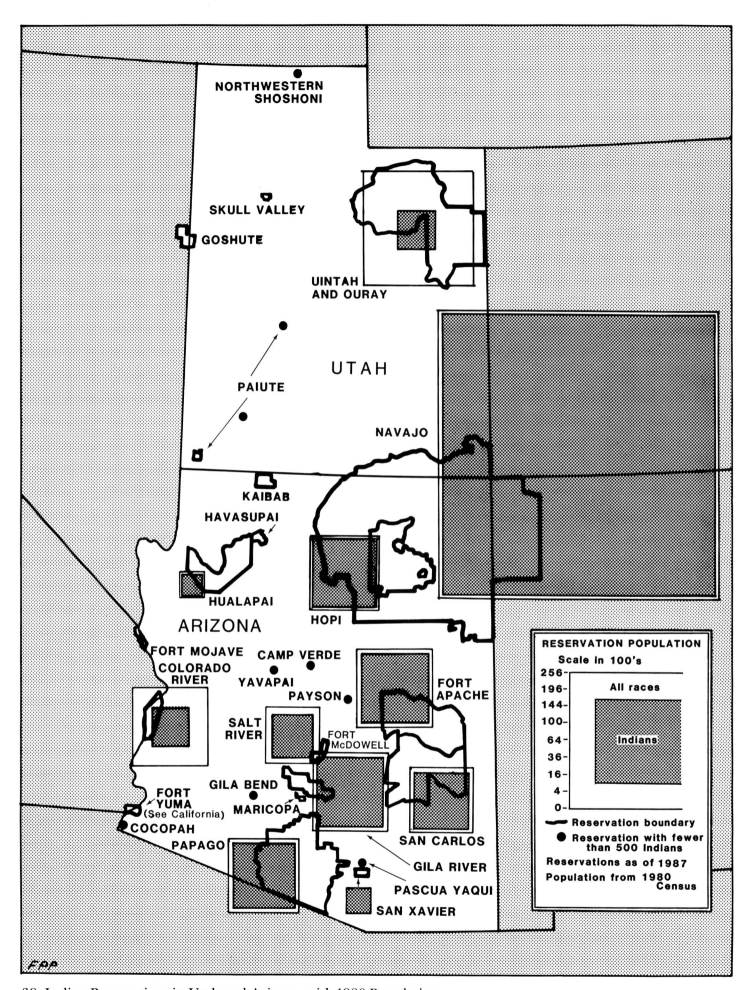

39. Indian Reservations in Utah and Arizona, with 1980 Population

46

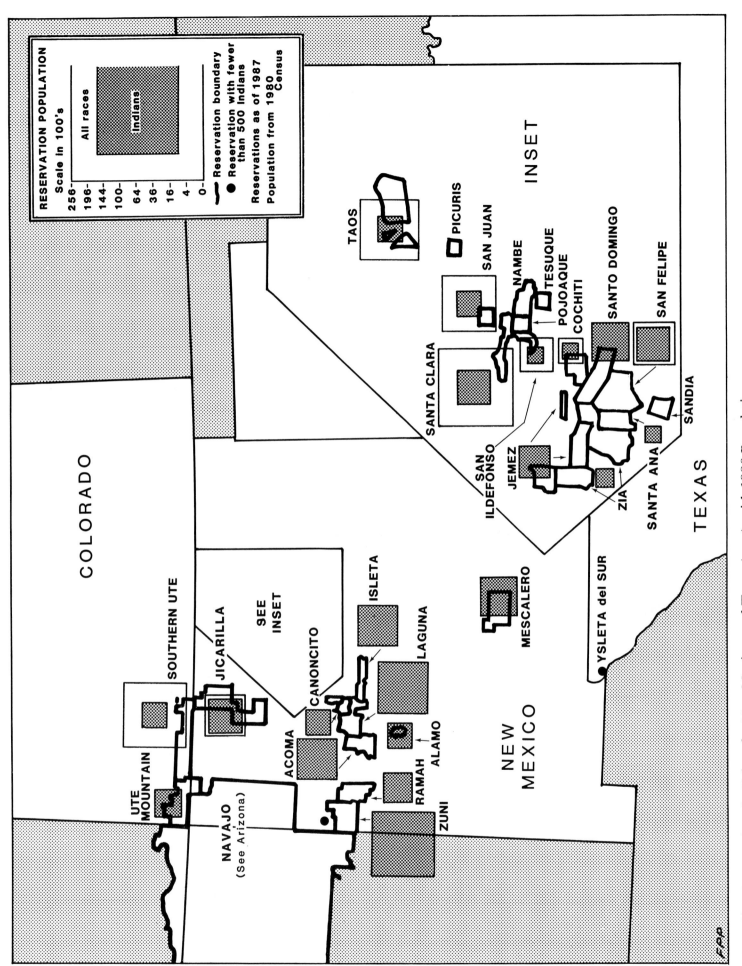

40. Indian Reservations in Colorado, New Mexico, and Texas (part), with 1980 Population

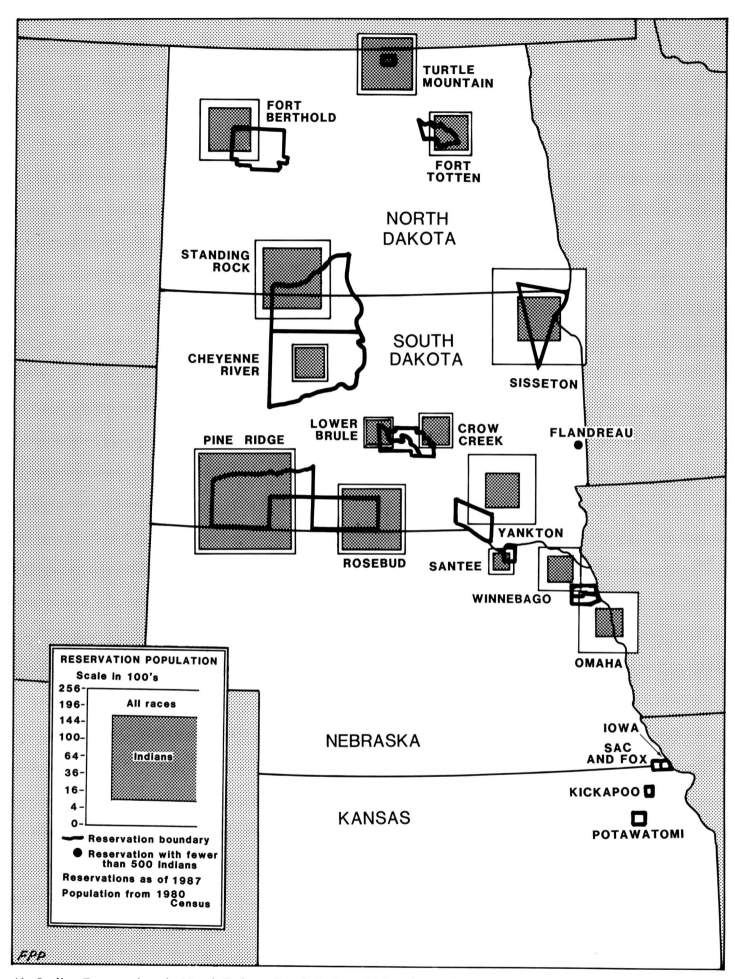

41. Indian Reservations in North Dakota, South Dakota, Nebraska, and Kansas, with 1980 Population

OSAGE

OKLAHOMA

TEXAS

LOUISIANA

TUNICA-BILOXI ●

ALABAMA-COUSHATTA ●   COUSHATTA ●

CHITIMACHA ●

● TEXAS KICKAPOO

RESERVATION POPULATION

Scale in 100's

256–
196–
144–   **All races**
100–
64–
36–   **Indians**
16–
4–
0–

━━ Reservation boundary

● Reservation with fewer
    than 500 Indians

Reservations as of 1987

Population from 1980
                Census

42. Indian Reservations in Oklahoma, Louisiana, and Texas (part), with 1980 Population

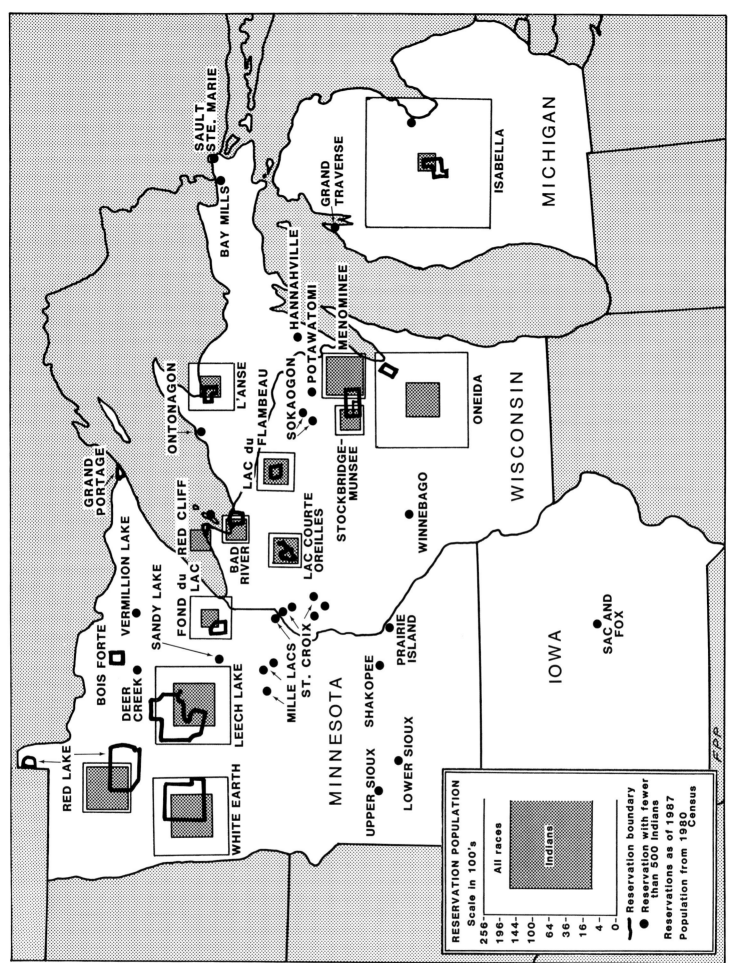

43. Indian Reservations in Minnesota, Wisconsin, Iowa, and Michigan, with 1980 Population

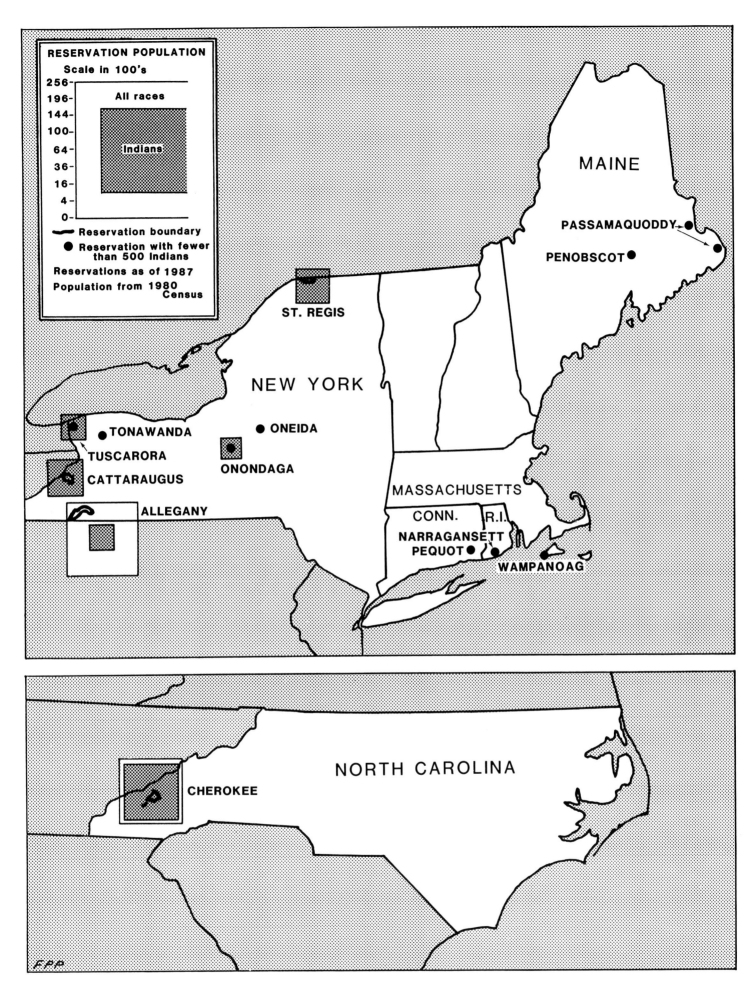

RESERVATION POPULATION
Scale in 100's

256–
196–
144–
100–
64–
36–
16–
4–
0–

All races

Indians

~ Reservation boundary
● Reservation with fewer
    than 500 Indians
Reservations as of 1987
Population from 1980
                Census

MAINE

PASSAMAQUODDY →●

PENOBSCOT ●

ST. REGIS

NEW YORK

● TONAWANDA   ● ONEIDA

TUSCARORA

                    ONONDAGA

CATTARAUGUS

ALLEGANY

MASSACHUSETTS

CONN.   R.I.

NARRAGANSETT
PEQUOT ●   ●
          WAMPANOAG

NORTH CAROLINA

CHEROKEE

FPP

44. Indian Reservations in New York, New England, and North Carolina, with 1980 Population

51

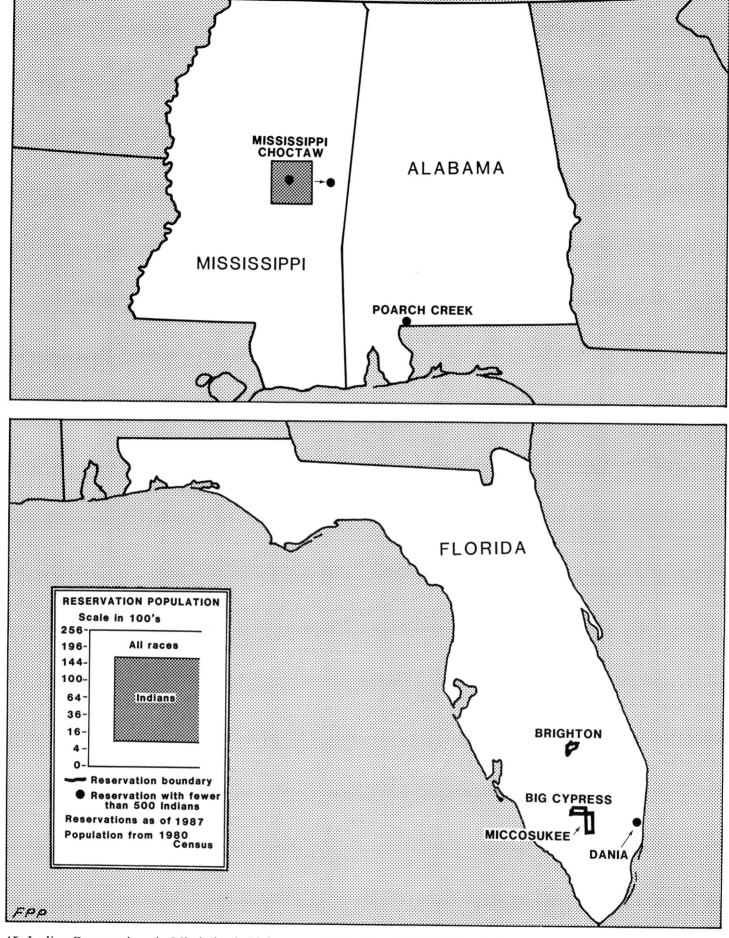

45. Indian Reservations in Mississippi, Alabama, and Florida, with 1980 Population

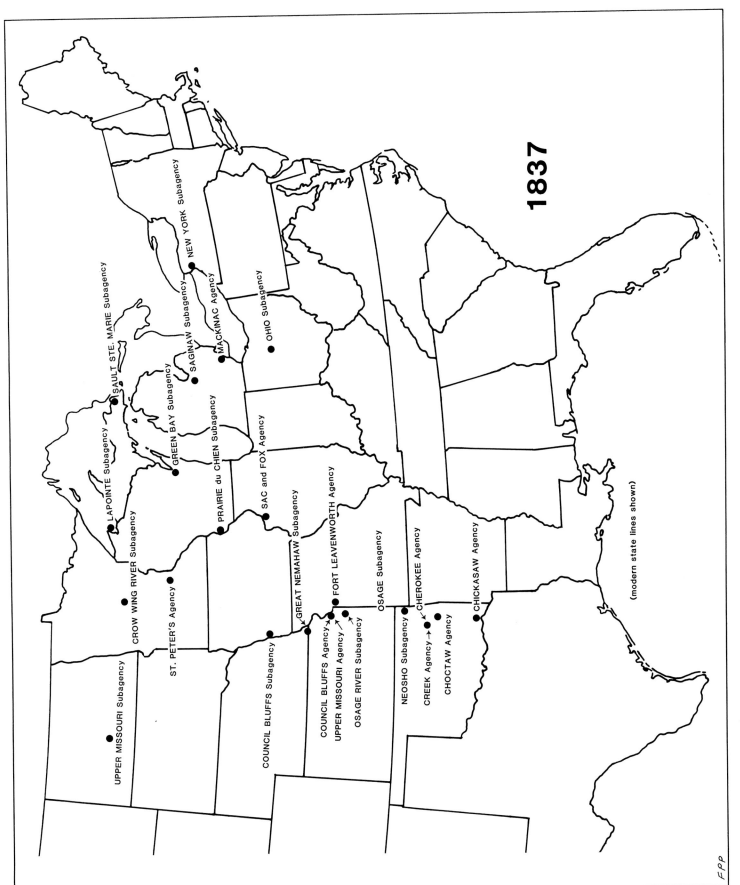

1837

SAULT STE. MARIE Subagency
NEW YORK Subagency
SAGINAW Subagency
MACKINAC Agency
OHIO Subagency
LAPOINTE Subagency
GREEN BAY Subagency
PRAIRIE du CHIEN Subagency
SAC and FOX Agency
CROW WING RIVER Subagency
GREAT NEMAHAW Subagency
FORT LEAVENWORTH Agency
OSAGE Subagency
CHEROKEE Agency
CHICKASAW Agency
ST. PETER'S Agency
COUNCIL BLUFFS Subagency
COUNCIL BLUFFS Agency
UPPER MISSOURI Agency
OSAGE RIVER Subagency
NEOSHO Subagency
CREEK Agency
CHOCTAW Agency
UPPER MISSOURI Subagency

(modern state lines shown)

F.P.P.

48. Indian Agencies: 1837

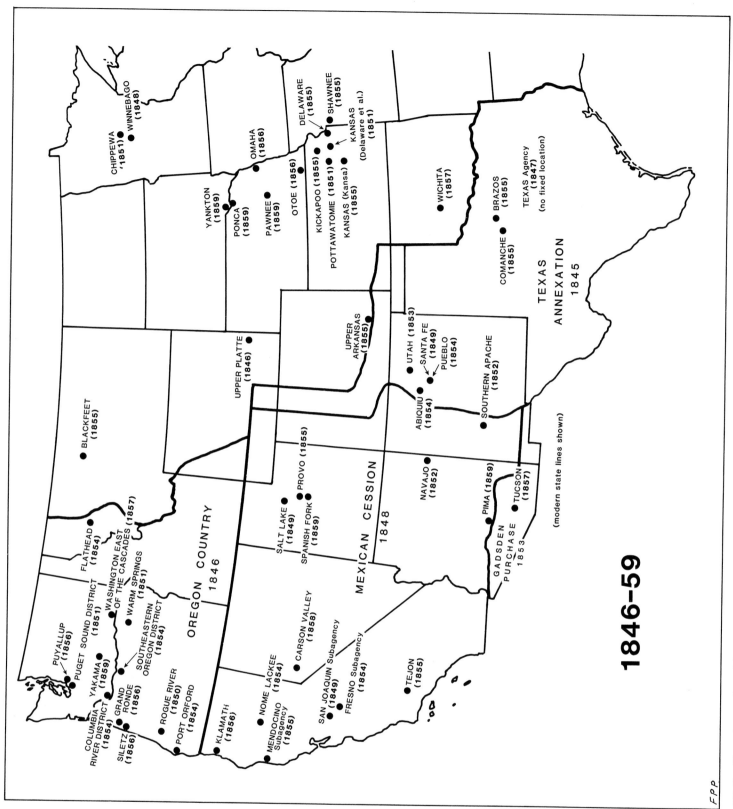

1846–59

CHIPPEWA (1851)
WINNEBAGO (1848)
OMAHA (1856)
DELAWARE (1855)
SHAWNEE (1855)
KANSAS (Delaware et al.) (1851)
YANKTON (1859)
PONCA (1859)
PAWNEE (1859)
OTOE (1856)
KICKAPOO (1855)
POTTAWATOMIE (1851)
KANSAS (Kansa) (1855)
WICHITA (1857)
BRAZOS (1855)
TEXAS Agency (1847) (no fixed location)
TEXAS ANNEXATION 1845
UPPER PLATTE (1846)
UPPER ARKANSAS (1855)
UTAH (1853)
SANTA FE (1849)
PUEBLO (1854)
ABIQUIU (1854)
SOUTHERN APACHE (1852)
BLACKFEET (1855)
NAVAJO (1852)
PIMA (1859)
TUCSON (1857)
GADSDEN PURCHASE 1853
(modern state lines shown)
MEXICAN CESSION 1848
SALT LAKE (1849)
PROVO (1855)
SPANISH FORK (1859)
FLATHEAD (1854)
WASHINGTON EAST OF THE CASCADES (1857)
WARM SPRINGS (1851)
OREGON COUNTRY 1846
SOUTHEASTERN OREGON DISTRICT (1854)
CARSON VALLEY (1858)
SAN JOAQUIN Subagency (1849)
FRESNO Subagency (1854)
TEJON (1855)
PUYALLUP (1856)
PUGET SOUND DISTRICT (1851)
YAKAMA (1859)
COLUMBIA RIVER DISTRICT (1854)
GRAND RONDE (1856)
SILETZ (1856)
ROGUE RIVER (1850)
PORT ORFORD (1854)
KLAMATH (1856)
NOME LACKEE (1854)
MENDOCINO Subagency (1855)

49. Indian Agencies: 1846–1859

FPP

58

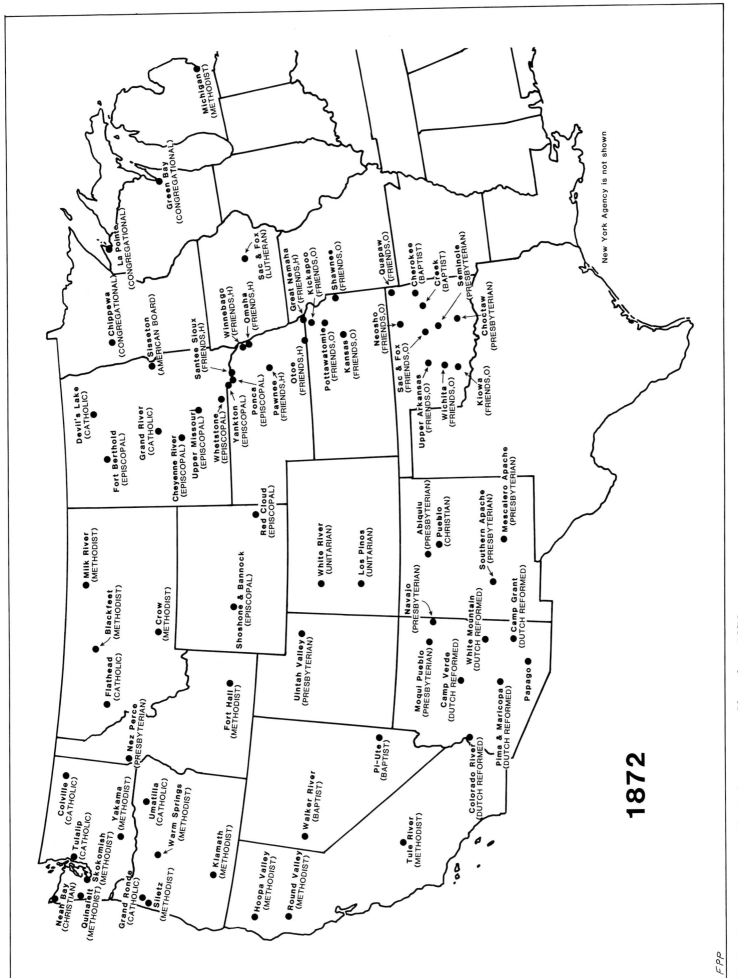

50. Indian Agencies, with Assignment to Churches: 1872

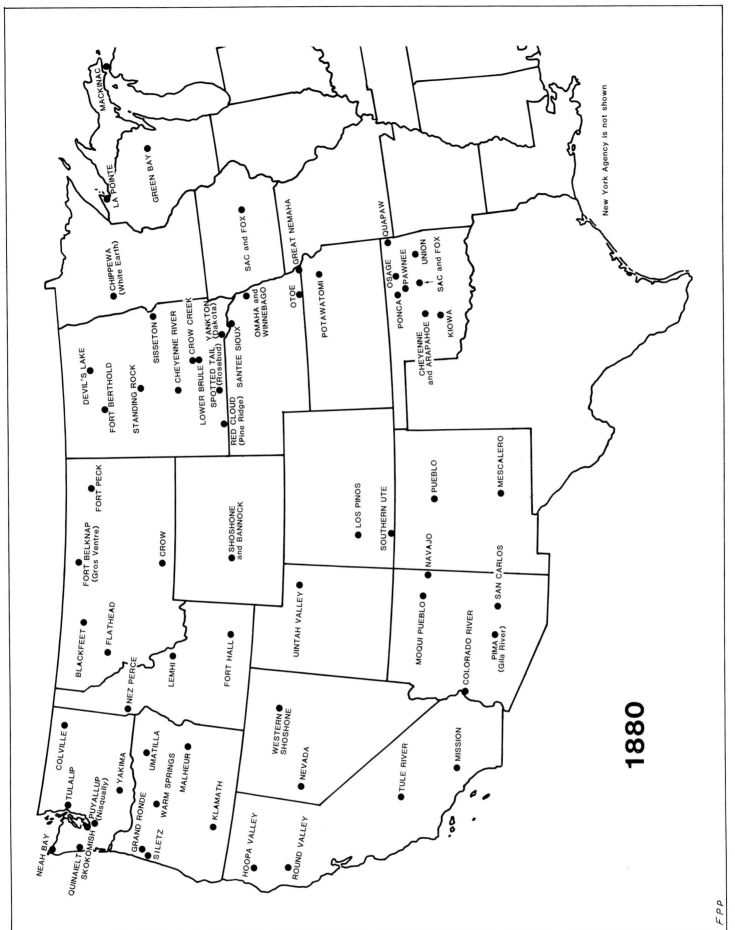

1880

New York Agency is not shown

MACKINAC
LA POINTE
GREEN BAY
CHIPPEWA (White Earth)
SISSETON
DEVIL'S LAKE
FORT BERTHOLD
STANDING ROCK
CHEYENNE RIVER
CROW CREEK
LOWER BRULE
SPOTTED TAIL (Rosebud)
YANKTON (Dakota)
SANTEE SIOUX
RED CLOUD (Pine Ridge)
SAC and FOX
OMAHA and WINNEBAGO
GREAT NEMAHA
OTOE
POTAWATOMI
QUAPAW
OSAGE
PAWNEE
UNION
SAC and FOX
PONCA
CHEYENNE and ARAPAHOE
KIOWA
FORT PECK
FORT BELKNAP (Gros Ventre)
CROW
SHOSHONE and BANNOCK
LOS PINOS
SOUTHERN UTE
PUEBLO
MESCALERO
NAVAJO
SAN CARLOS
MOQUI PUEBLO
COLORADO RIVER
PIMA (Gila River)
BLACKFEET
FLATHEAD
NEZ PERCE
LEMHI
FORT HALL
UINTAH VALLEY
WESTERN SHOSHONE
NEVADA
COLVILLE
TULALIP
PUYALLUP (Nisqually)
YAKIMA
UMATILLA
WARM SPRINGS
MALHEUR
GRAND RONDE
SILETZ
KLAMATH
NEAH BAY
QUINAIELT
SKOKOMISH
HOOPA VALLEY
ROUND VALLEY
TULE RIVER
MISSION

FPP

51. Indian Agencies: 1880

60

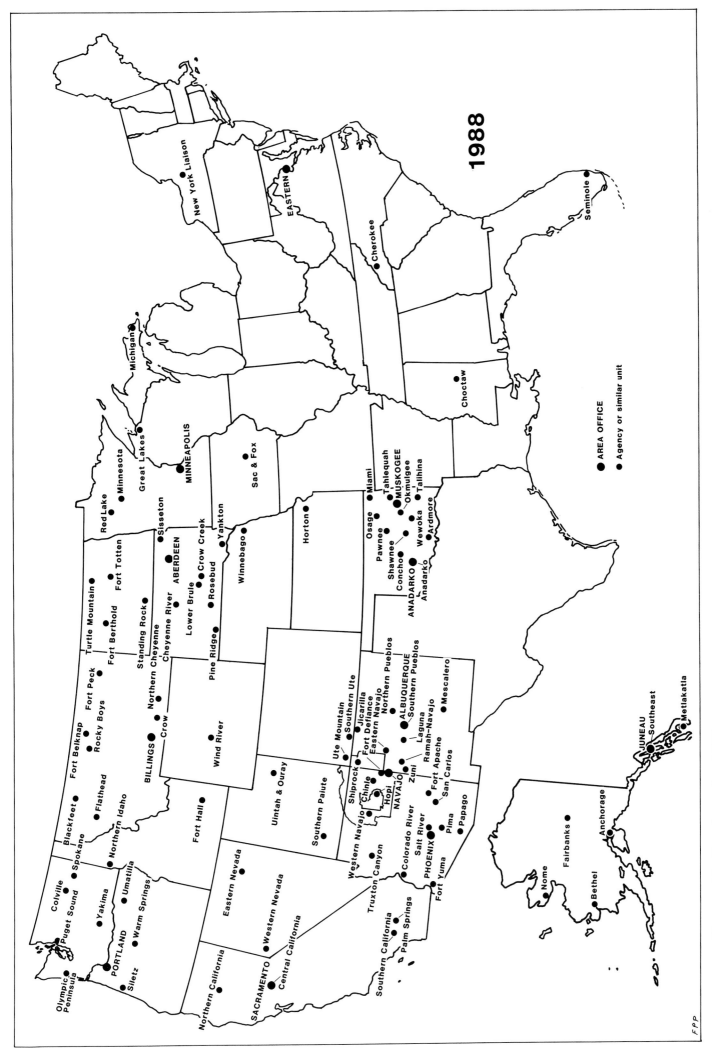

1988

New York Liaison

EASTERN

Cherokee

Seminole

Michigan

Choctaw

Great Lakes

Minnesota

MINNEAPOLIS

Red Lake

Sac & Fox

Miami

Tahlequah

MUSKOGEE

Okmulgee

Tallihina

Sisseton

Yankton

Horton

Osage

Pawnee

Shawnee

Concho

Wewoka

Ardmore

Fort Totten

Crow Creek

ABERDEEN

Lower Brule

Rosebud

Winnebago

ANADARKO

Anadarko

Turtle Mountain

Fort Berthold

Standing Rock

Cheyenne River

Northern Cheyenne

Pine Ridge

Fort Peck

Rocky Boys

BILLINGS

Crow

Wind River

Northern Pueblos

ALBUQUERQUE

Southern Pueblos

Fort Belknap

Uintah & Ouray

Ute Mountain

Southern Ute

Jicarilla

Fort Defiance

Eastern Navajo

Laguna

Ramah-Navajo

Mescalero

Blackfeet

Flathead

Northern Idaho

Fort Hall

Southern Paiute

Western Navajo

Shiprock

Chinle

Hopi

NAVAJO

Zuni

Fort Apache

San Carlos

JUNEAU

Southeast

Metlakatla

Colville

Spokane

Umatilla

Warm Springs

Eastern Nevada

Truxton Canyon

Colorado River

Salt River

Pima

Papago

Puget Sound

Yakima

PORTLAND

Siletz

Western Nevada

Central California

Palm Springs

Fort Yuma

PHOENIX

Fairbanks

Anchorage

Olympic Peninsula

Northern California

SACRAMENTO

Southern California

Nome

Bethel

● AREA OFFICE

● Agency or similar unit

FPP

52. BIA Area Offices and Indian Agencies: 1988

61

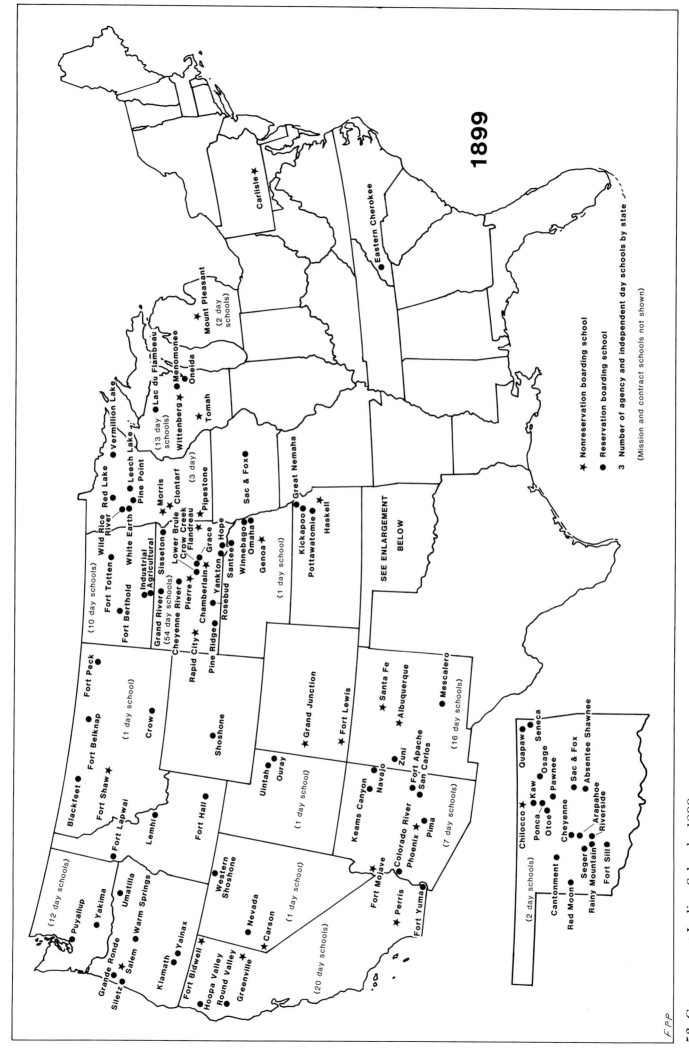

1899

★ Nonreservation boarding school
● Reservation boarding school
3 Number of agency and independent day schools by state

(Mission and contract schools not shown)

Carlisle ★

Eastern Cherokee ●

Mount Pleasant ★
(2 day schools)

Lac du Flambeau ● Vermillion Lake ●
Menomonee ●
(13 day schools) Wittenberg ★ Oneida ●
Tomah ★

Red Lake ● Leech Lake
Pine Point ●
Morris ★ Clontarf ●
Wild Rice River ● White Earth ● (3 day)
Fort Totten ★ Grace ● Pipestone ●
(10 day schools) Industrial ★ Sisseton Hope ● Sac & Fox ●
Fort Berthold ● Agricultural Lower Brule Yankton ●
Grand River ● Crow Creek Flandreau ★ Winnebago ● Great Nemaha ●
(54 day schools) Cheyenne River ● Pierre ★ Santee ★ Omaha ★
Rapid City ★ Chamberlain ● Rosebud ● Genoa ★ Kickapoo ●
Pine Ridge ● Haskell ★
Pottawatomie ●
(1 day school)

Fort Peck ●

Fort Belknap ●
Fort Shaw ★ (1 day school)
Blackfeet ● Crow ●
Fort Lapwai ★
Lemhi ● Shoshone ●
Fort Hall ●

Grand Junction ★

Fort Lewis ★
Uintah ● Santa Fe ★
Ouray ● Albuquerque ★
(1 day school) Zuni ● SEE ENLARGEMENT
Navajo ● Fort Apache ● BELOW
Keams Canyon ● San Carlos ●
(1 day school) (16 day schools)
Mescalero ●

Western
Shoshone ● Colorado River ●
Nevada ● Phoenix ●
Carson ★ Pima ●
Fort Mojave ★ (7 day schools)
(1 day school) Perris ★

(20 day schools) Fort Yuma ●

(12 day schools)
Puyallup ●
Yakima ●
Grande Ronde ● Umatilla ●
Siletz ● Salem ● Warm Springs ●
Klamath ● Yainax ●
Fort Bidwell ★
Hoopa Valley ● Round Valley ●
Greenville ★

(2 day schools)
Chilocco ★ Quapaw ●
Ponca ● Kaw ● Seneca ●
Cantonment ● Otoe ● Osage ●
Red Moon ● Cheyenne ● Pawnee ●
Seger ● Sac & Fox ●
Rainy Mountain ● Arapahoe ● Absentee Shawnee ●
Fort Sill ● Riverside ●

F.P.P.

53. Government Indian Schools: 1899

62

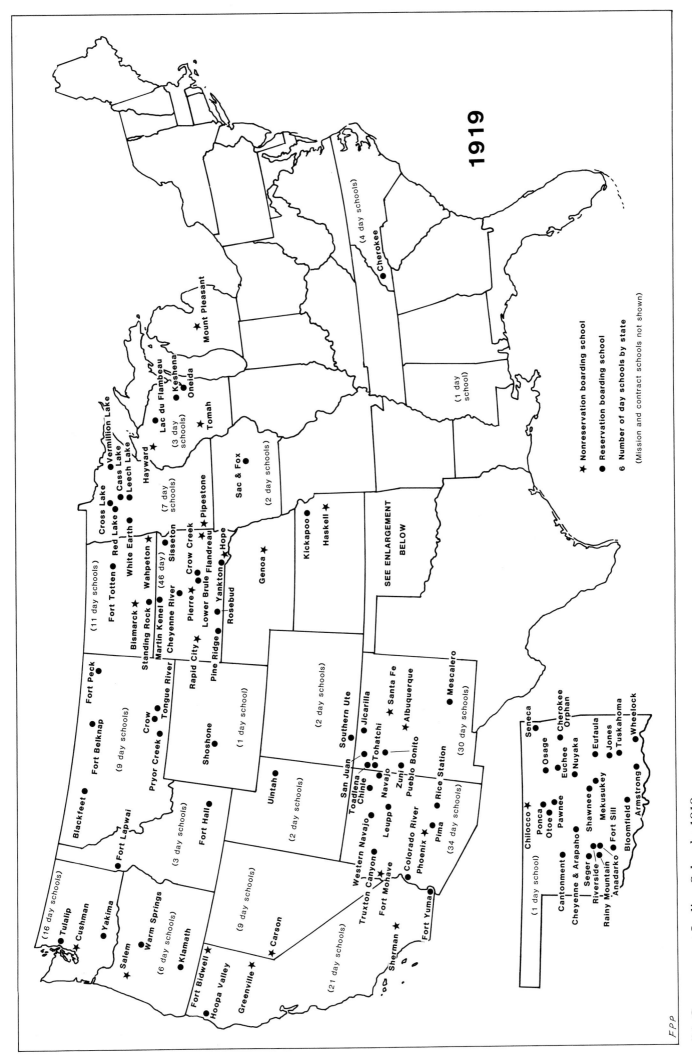

54. Government Indian Schools: 1919

1919

Nonreservation boarding school
Reservation boarding school
Number of day schools by state
(Mission and contract schools not shown)

Cherokee
(4 day schools)

(1 day school)

Mount Pleasant

Lac du Flambeau
Keshena
Oneida
Tomah
(3 day schools)

Vermillion Lake
Cross Lake
Cass Lake
Leech Lake
Red Lake
Hayward

Sac & Fox
(2 day schools)

Pipestone
(7 day schools)

White Earth
Fort Totten
(11 day schools)
Bismarck
Standing Rock
Wahpeton
Martin Kenel (46 day)
Cheyenne River
Sisseton
Crow Creek
Pierre
Lower Brule
Flandreau
Hope
Yankton
Rosebud
Pine Ridge
Rapid City

Kickapoo
Haskell

Genoa

SEE ENLARGEMENT
BELOW

Fort Peck
Fort Belknap
Blackfeet
(9 day schools)
Crow
Tongue River
Pryor Creek

Shoshone
(1 day school)

Southern Ute
(2 day schools)
Jicarilla
Santa Fe
Albuquerque
Mescalero
(30 day schools)

Fort Lapwai
Fort Hall
(3 day schools)

Uintah
(2 day schools)

San Juan
Toadlena
Chinle
Tohatchi
Navajo
Zuni
Pueblo Bonito
Rice Station
Western Navajo
Leupp
Truxton Canyon
(34 day schools)
Colorado River
Pima
Phoenix
Fort Mohave

(16 day schools)
Tulalip
Cushman
Yakima
Warm Springs
Salem
(6 day schools)
Klamath
Fort Bidwell
Hoopa Valley
Greenville
Carson
(9 day schools)
(21 day schools)
Sherman
Fort Yuma

Seneca
Osage
Cherokee Orphan
Euchee
Nuyaka
Eufaula
Jones
Tuskahoma
Wheelock
Shawnee
Mekusukey
Fort Sill
Bloomfield
Armstrong
Chilocco
Ponca
Otoe
Pawnee
Cantonment
Cheyenne & Arapaho
Seger
Riverside
Rainy Mountain
Anadarko
(1 day school)

FPP

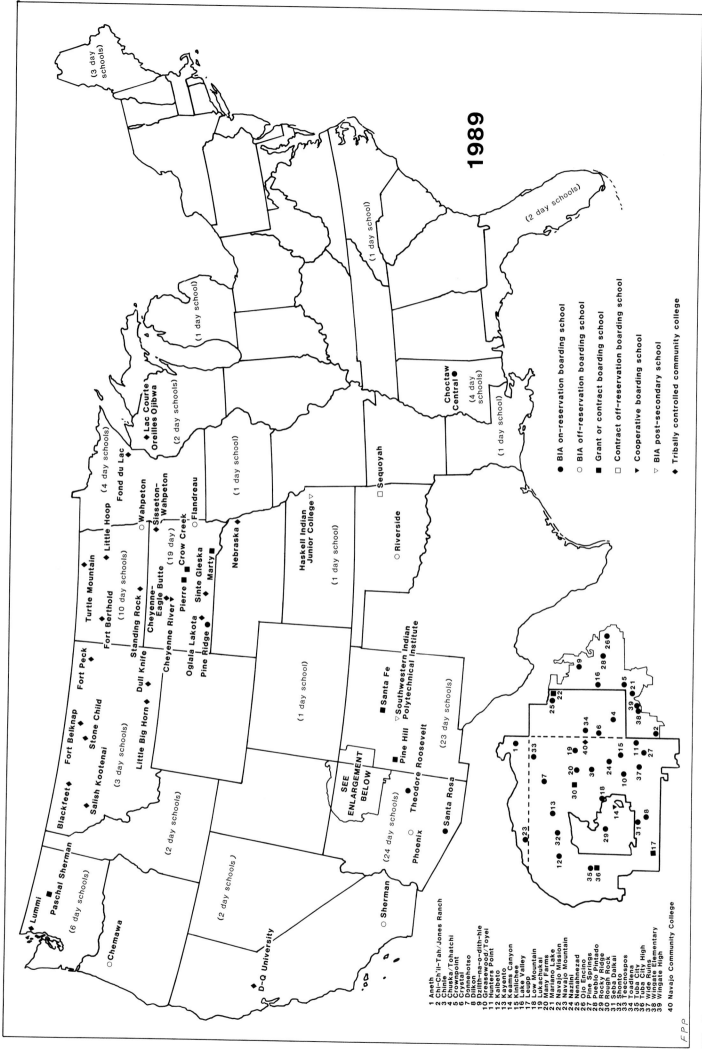

1989

BIA on-reservation boarding school ●
BIA off-reservation boarding school ○
Grant or contract boarding school ■
Contract off-reservation boarding school □
Cooperative boarding school ▼
BIA post-secondary school ▽
Tribally controlled community college ◆

(3 day schools)

(2 day schools)

(1 day school)

Choctaw Central ●

(4 day schools)

(1 day school)

Sequoyah □

(1 day school)

Lac Courte Oreilles Ojibwa ◆

(2 day schools)

Fond du Lac ◆

Little Hoop ◆
Wahpeton ○
Sisseton-Wahpeton ■
Crow Creek ◆
Flandreau ○

(4 day schools)

Turtle Mountain ◆
Fort Berthold ◆
Standing Rock ◆
Cheyenne-Eagle Butte ◆
Pierre ■
Sinte Gleska ◆
Marty ■

Nebraska ◆

(10 day schools)

(19 day)

Haskell Indian Junior College ▽

(1 day school)

Riverside ○

Fort Peck ◆
Dull Knife ◆
Cheyenne River ▼
Oglala Lakota ◆
Pine Ridge ●

Fort Belknap ◆
Stone Child ◆
Little Big Horn ◆

(1 day school)

Salish Kootenai ◆

Blackfeet ◆

(3 day schools)

Santa Fe ■
Southwestern Indian Polytechnical Institute ▽

SEE ENLARGEMENT BELOW

Pine Hill ■
Theodore Roosevelt ●

(24 day schools)

Phoenix ○
Santa Rosa ●

(23 day schools)

Lummi
Paschal Sherman ■

(6 day schools)

Chemawa ○

Sherman ○

D-Q University ◆

55. Government Indian Schools: 1989

1 Aneth
2 Chi-Ch'il-Tah/Jones Ranch
3 Chinle
4 Chuska/Tohatchi
5 Crownpoint
6 Crystal
7 Dennehotso
8 Dilkon
9 Dzilith-na-o-dith-hle
10 Greasewood/Toyei
11 Hunters Point
12 Kaibeto
13 Kayento
14 Keams Canyon
15 Kinlichee
16 Lake Valley
17 Leupp
18 Low Mountain
19 Lukachukai
20 Many Farms
21 Mariano Lake
22 Navajo Mission
23 Navajo Mountain
24 Nazlini
25 Nenahnezad
26 Ojo Encino
27 Pine Springs
28 Pueblo Pintado
29 Rocky Ridge
30 Rough Rock
31 Seba Dalkai
32 Shonto
33 Toadlena
34 Tohonospos
35 Tuba City
36 Tuba City High
37 Wide Ruins
38 Wingate Elementary
39 Wingate High
40 Navajo Community College

FPP

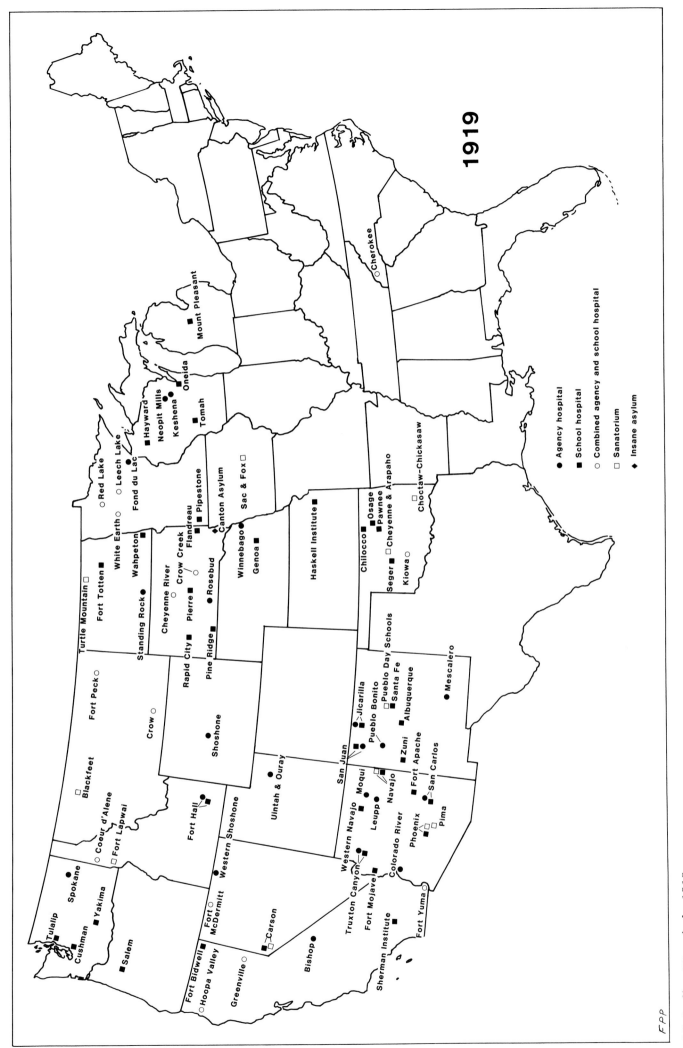

1919

Agency hospital ●
School hospital ■
Combined agency and school hospital ○
Sanatorium □
Insane asylum ◆

Cherokee ○

Mount Pleasant ■

Oneida ●
Neopit Mills
Keshena ●
Hayward ■
Tomah ■

Red Lake ○
Leech Lake ○
Fond du Lac ■
White Earth ○
Pipestone ■
Wahpeton ■
Flandreau ■
Canton Asylum ◆
Sac & Fox □
Winnebago ●
Genoa ■

Turtle Mountain □
Fort Totten ■
Standing Rock ●
Cheyenne River
Crow Creek ○
Pierre ■
Rosebud ●
Rapid City ■
Pine Ridge ■

Haskell Institute ■

Chilocco ■
Osage ■
Pawnee
Cheyenne & Arapaho □
Seger ■
Kiowa ○
Choctaw-Chickasaw □

Fort Peck ○
Crow ○
Shoshone ●

Mescalero ●

Blackfeet □
Coeur d'Alene ○
Fort Lapwai □
Fort Hall ●

Uintah & Ouray ●

San Juan
Jicarilla
Pueblo Day Schools
Pueblo Bonito ●
Santa Fe ■
Albuquerque ■
Zuni ●
Fort Apache ■
San Carlos ■

Spokane ●
Yakima ■
Western Shoshone
Fort McDermitt ○

Carson ●
Bishop ●

Western Navajo ■
Moqui ■
Leupp ■
Navajo
Phoenix
Pima ●

Tulalip ■
Cushman ■
Salem ■

Fort Bidwell ■
Hoopa Valley ○
Greenville ○

Truxton Canyon ■
Fort Mojave ■
Colorado River ■
Sherman Institute ■
Fort Yuma ●

F.P.P.

56. Indian Hospitals: 1919

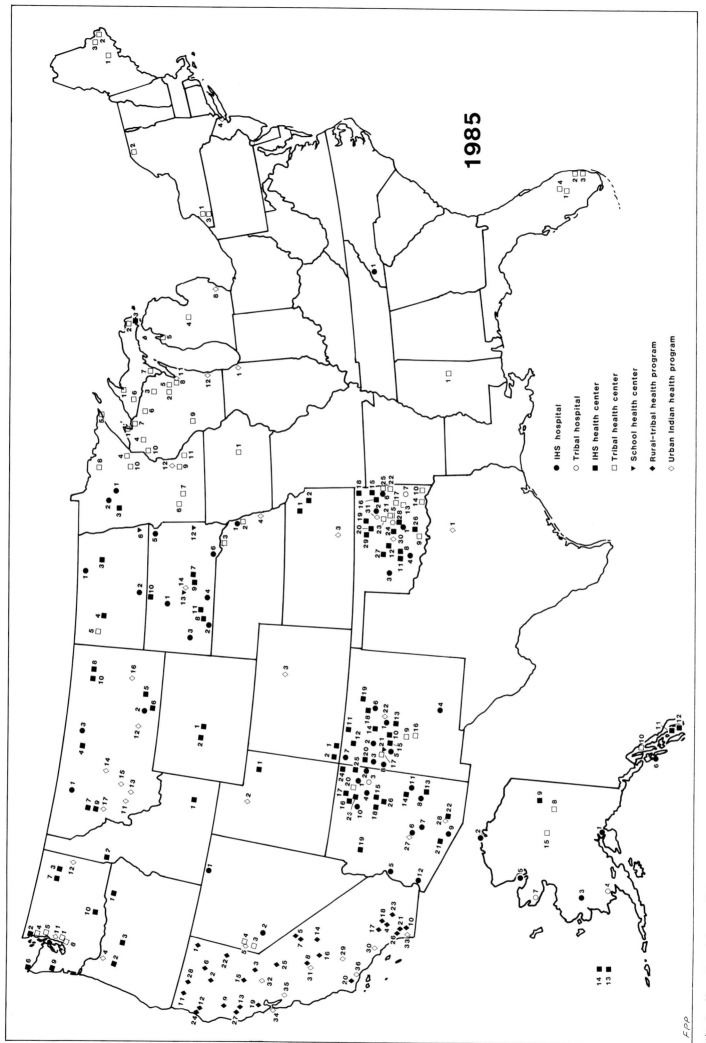

57. Indian Health Facilities: 1985

1985

- ● IHS hospital
- ○ Tribal hospital
- ■ IHS health center
- □ Tribal health center
- ▼ School health center
- ◆ Rural–tribal health program
- ◇ Urban Indian health program

FPP

66

ALASKA

Hospitals
1 Anchorage
2 Barrow
3 Bethel
*4 Dillingham
5 Kotzebue
*6 Mt Edgecumbe
*7 Nome

Health Centers
*8 Fairbanks
9 Fort Yukon
*10 Juneau
11 Ketchikan
12 Metlakatla
13 St George
14 St Paul
*15 Tanana

ARIZONA

Hospitals
1 Chinle
2 Ft. Defiance
*3 Ganado
4 Keams Canyon
5 Parker
6 Phoenix
7 Sacaton
8 San Carlos
9 Sells
10 Tuba City
11 Whiteriver
12 Yuma

Health Centers
13 Bylas
14 Cibecue
15 Dilkon
16 Inscription House
17 Kayenta
18 Leupp
19 Peach Springs
*20 Rough Rock
21 Santa Rosa
22 San Xavier
23 Second Mesa
24 Teec Nos Pos
25 Tsaile
26 Winslow

Urban Programs
27 Phoenix
28 Tucson

CALIFORNIA

Rural Tribal Health Programs
1 Alturas
2 Anderson
3 Auburn
4 Banning
5 Bishop
6 Burney
7 Camp Antelope
8 Clovis
9 Covelo
10 El Cajon
11 Happy Camp
12 Hoopa
13 Lakeport
14 Lone Pine
15 Oroville
16 Porterville
17 San Bernardino
18 San Jacinto
19 Santa Rosa
20 Santa Ynez
21 Santa Ysabel
22 Susanville
23 Torres Martinez
24 Trinidad
25 Tuolumne
26 Valley Center
27 Ukiah
28 Yreka

Urban Programs
29 Bakersfield
30 Compton
31 Fresno
32 Sacramento
33 San Diego
34 San Francisco
35 San Jose
36 Santa Barbara

COLORADO

Health Centers
1 Ignacio
2 Towaoc

Urban Programs
3 Denver

FLORIDA

Health Centers
*1 Clewiston
*2 Hollywood
*3 Miami
*4 Okeechobee

IDAHO

Health Centers
1 Ft. Hall
2 Lapwai

ILLINOIS

Urban Program
1 Chicago

IOWA

Health Center
*1 Tama

KANSAS

Health Centers
1 Holton
2 Lawrence

Urban Program
3 Wichita

MAINE

Health Centers
*1 Old Town
*2 Perry
*3 Princeton

MICHIGAN

Health Centers
*1 Baraga
*2 Brimley
3 Kincheloe
*4 Mt Pleasant
*5 Sultons Bay
*6 Watersmeet
*7 Wilson

Urban Program
8 Detroit

MINNESOTA

Hospitals
1 Cass Lake
2 Red Lake

Health Centers
3 White Earth
*4 Cloquet
*5 Grand Portage
*6 Granite Falls
*7 Morton
*8 Nett Lake
*9 Prior Lake
*10 Vineland
*11 Welch

Urban Program
12 Minneapolis

MISSISSIPPI

Hospital
*1 Philadelphia

MONTANA

Hospitals
1 Browning
2 Crow Agency
3 Harlem

Health Centers
4 Box Elder
5 Lame Deer
6 Lodge Grass
7 Polson
8 Poplar
9 St Ignatius
10 Wolf Point

Urban Programs
11 Anaconda
12 Billings
13 Butte
14 Great Falls
15 Helena
16 Miles City
17 Missoula

NEBRASKA

Hospital
1 Winnebago

Health Centers
*2 Macy
*3 Santee

Urban Program
4 Omaha

NEVADA

Hospitals
1 Owyhee
2 Schurz

Health Centers
*3 Gardnerville
*4 Reno-Sparks

Urban Program
5 Reno

NEW MEXICO

Hospitals
1 Albuquerque
2 Crownpoint
3 Gallup
4 Mescalero
5 San Fidel
6 Santa Fe
7 Shiprock
8 Zuni

Health Centers
*9 Alamo
10 Canoncita
11 Dulce
12 Huerfano
13 Isleta
14 Jemez
15 Laguna
*16 Magdalena
*17 Ramah
18 Santa Clara
19 Taos
20 Tohatchi

School Health Center
21 Ft. Wingate

Urban Program
22 Albuquerque

NEW YORK

Health Centers
*1 Cattaraugus
*2 Hogansburg
*3 Steamburg

Urban Program
4 New York

NORTH CAROLINA

Hospital
1 Cherokee

NORTH DAKOTA

Hospitals
1 Belcourt
2 Ft. Yates

Health Centers
3 Ft. Totten
4 New Town
*5 Trenton–Williston

School Health Center
6 Wahpeton

OKLAHOMA

Hospitals
1 Ada
2 Claremore
3 Clinton
4 Lawton
*5 Okemah
6 Tahlequah
*7 Talihina

Health Centers
8 Anadarko
9 Ardmore
*10 Broken Bow
11 Carnegie
12 Concho
*13 Eufaula
*14 Hugo
15 Jay
16 Locust Grove
*17 McAlester
18 Miami
19 Pawhuska
20 Pawnee
*21 Okmulgee
*22 Sallisaw
*23 Sapulpa
24 Shawnee
*25 Stilwell
26 Tishomingo
27 Watonga
28 Wewoka
29 White Eagle

Urban Programs
30 Oklahoma City
31 Tulsa

OREGON

Health Centers
1 Pendleton
2 Salem
3 Warm Springs

Urban Program
4 Portland

SOUTH DAKOTA

Hospitals
1 Eagle Butte
2 Pine Ridge
3 Rapid City
4 Rosebud
5 Sisseton
6 Wagner

Health Centers
7 Ft. Thompson
8 Kyle
9 Lower Brule
10 McLaughlin
11 Wanblee

School Health Centers
12 Flandreau
13 Pierre

Urban Program
14 Pierre

TEXAS

Urban Program
1 Dallas

UTAH

Health Center
1 Ft. Duchesne

Urban Program
2 Salt Lake City

WASHINGTON

Health Centers
*1 Auburn
2 Bellingham
3 Inchelium
*4 LaConner
*5 Marysville
6 Neah Bay
7 Nespelem
*8 Tacoma
9 Taholah
10 Toppenish

Urban Programs
11 Seattle
12 Spokane

WISCONSIN

Health Centers
*1 Bayfield
*2 Bowler
*3 Crandon
*4 Hayward
*5 Keshena
*6 Lac du Flambeau
*7 Odanah
*8 Oneida
*9 Tomah
*10 Webster

Urban Programs
11 Green Bay
12 Milwaukee

WYOMING

Health Centers
1 Arapahoe
2 Ft. Washakie

*Tribally operated facility

The removal of the Five Civilized Tribes—Cherokee, Creek, Choctaw, Chickasaw, and Seminole—to lands west of the Mississippi River in the 1830s created an Indian Territory, whose history was in many ways distinct from that of other Indian areas. Until the 1950 census, indeed, and again in 1970 Oklahoma had more Indians than any other state.

The first three maps in this section show the various stages in the land arrangements: the location of the tribes according to the initial assignment of lands; the changes made in the 1850s, when Creeks and Seminoles as well as Choctaws and Chickasaws established new distinct boundaries; and the reduction of the holdings of the Five Tribes after the Civil War and the assignment of land they gave up to other tribes.

The last two maps show population distribution in 1980, by counties and SMSAs and by Historic Indian Areas.

VI

Oklahoma (Indian Territory)

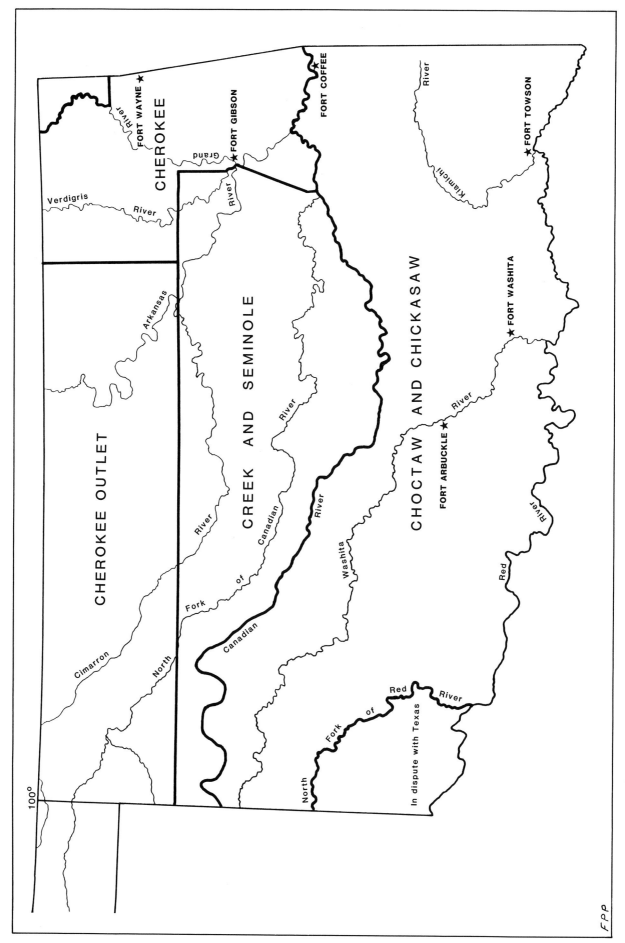

58. Indian Territory: Removal to 1855

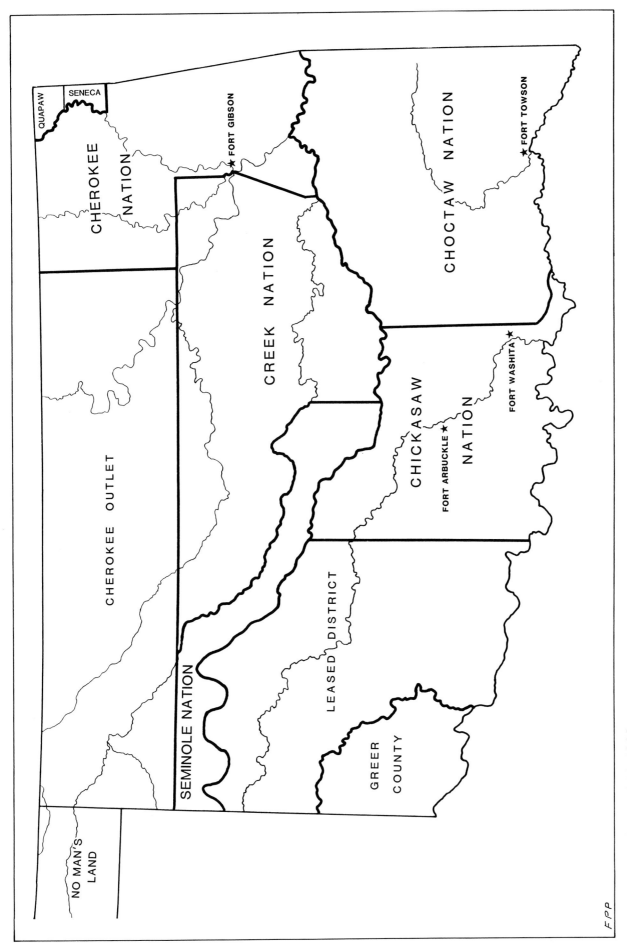

QUAPAW

SENECA

CHEROKEE NATION

FORT GIBSON

CHOCTAW NATION

FORT TOWSON

CREEK NATION

CHEROKEE OUTLET

FORT WASHITA

CHICKASAW NATION

FORT ARBUCKLE

SEMINOLE NATION

LEASED DISTRICT

GREER COUNTY

NO MAN'S LAND

F P P

59. Indian Territory: 1855–1866

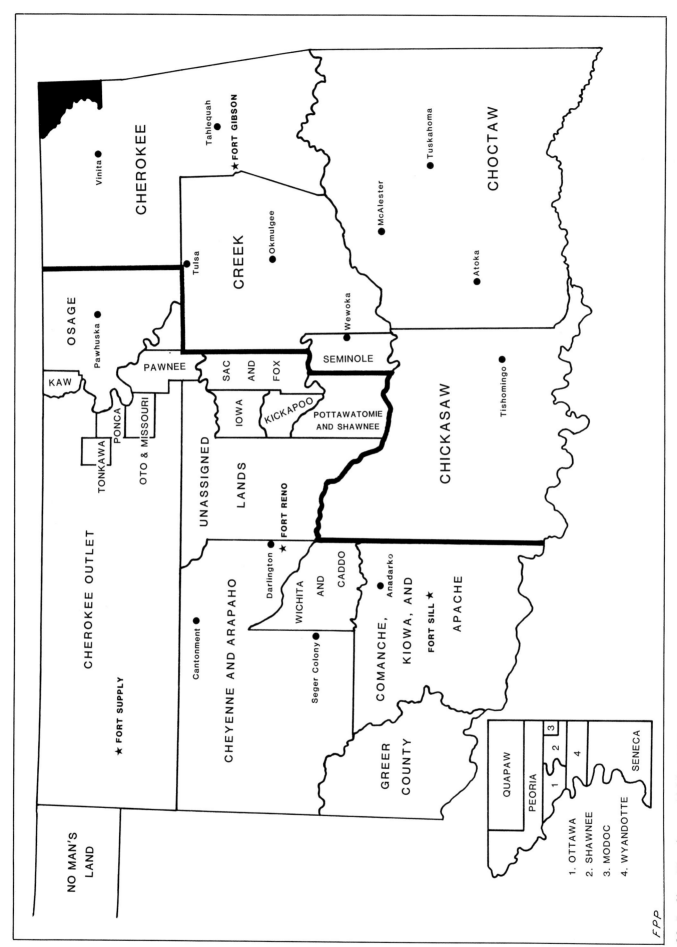

60. Indian Territory: 1866–1889

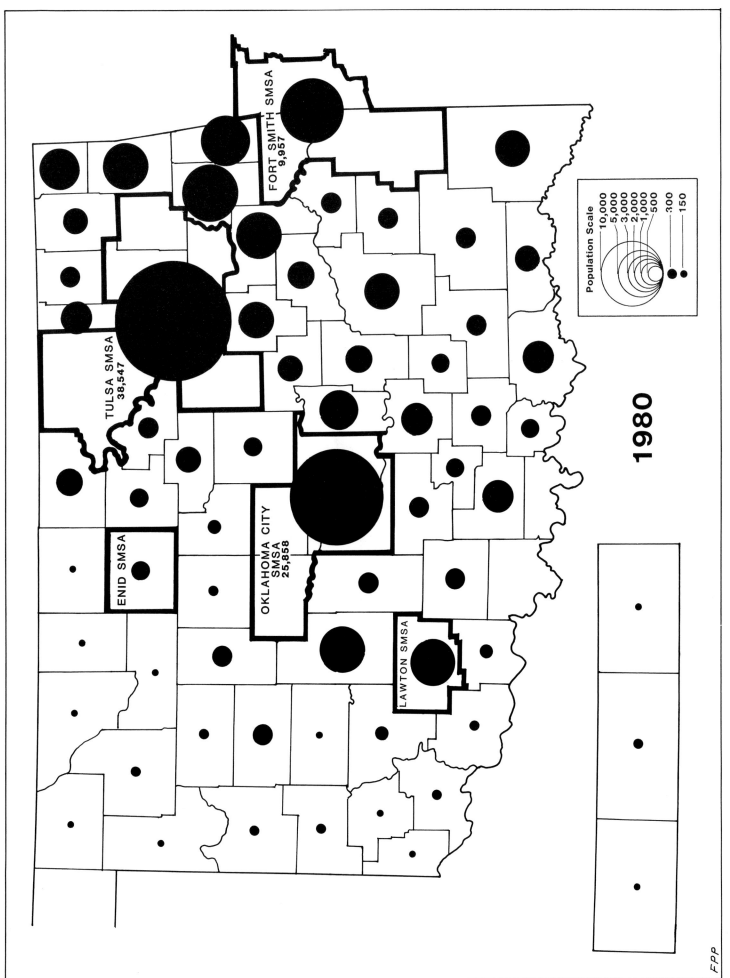

61. Oklahoma Indian Population by Counties and SMSAs: 1980

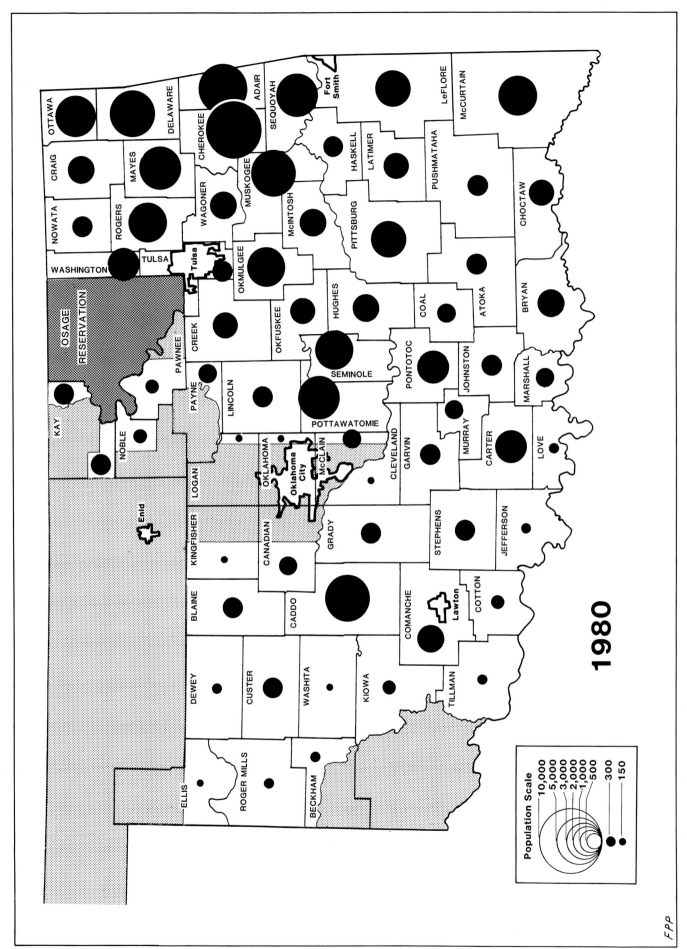

62. Oklahoma, Showing Historic Indian Areas, with Population: 1980

FPP

Alaska's native peoples did not have the same history of relations with the United States government that the Indians of the contiguous states had. There were no treaties, no reservations (except for minor exceptions), no Indian wars, and no BIA schools through most of its history. The forty-ninth state does not fit well into the patterns that embrace many of the maps in this atlas.

This section includes a map showing culture areas and general tribal areas, two maps on census enumeration of Alaska Natives (Indians, Eskimos, and Aleuts), and a map of Alaska Native villages and the regional corporations to which they belong (based on the Alaska Native Claims Settlement Act of 1971 and the 1980 census).

VII

Alaska

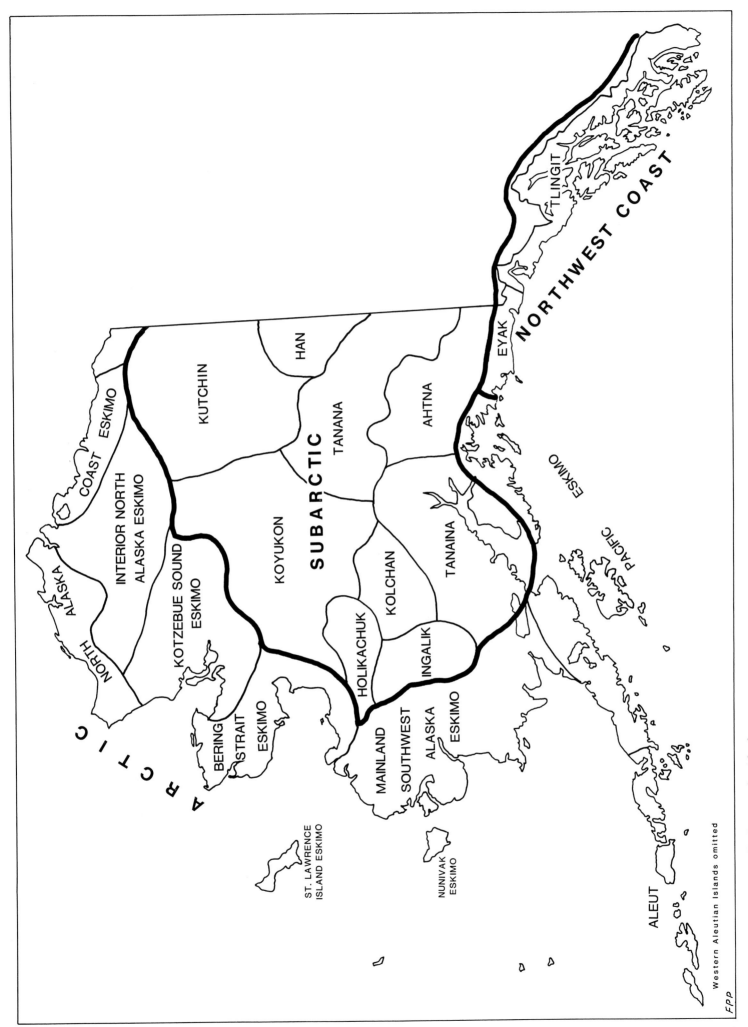

ALASKA

NORTH

ARCTIC

COAST ESKIMO

INTERIOR NORTH
ALASKA ESKIMO

KOTZEBUE SOUND
ESKIMO

BERING STRAIT ESKIMO

KUTCHIN

HAN

SUBARCTIC

TANANA

KOYUKON

AHTNA

EYAK

NORTHWEST COAST

TLINGIT

HOLIKACHUK

KOLCHAN

INGALIK

TANAINA

PACIFIC ESKIMO

MAINLAND
SOUTHWEST
ALASKA
ESKIMO

ST. LAWRENCE
ISLAND ESKIMO

NUNIVAK
ESKIMO

ALEUT

Western Aleutian Islands omitted

FPP

63. Culture Areas and Tribal Areas in Alaska

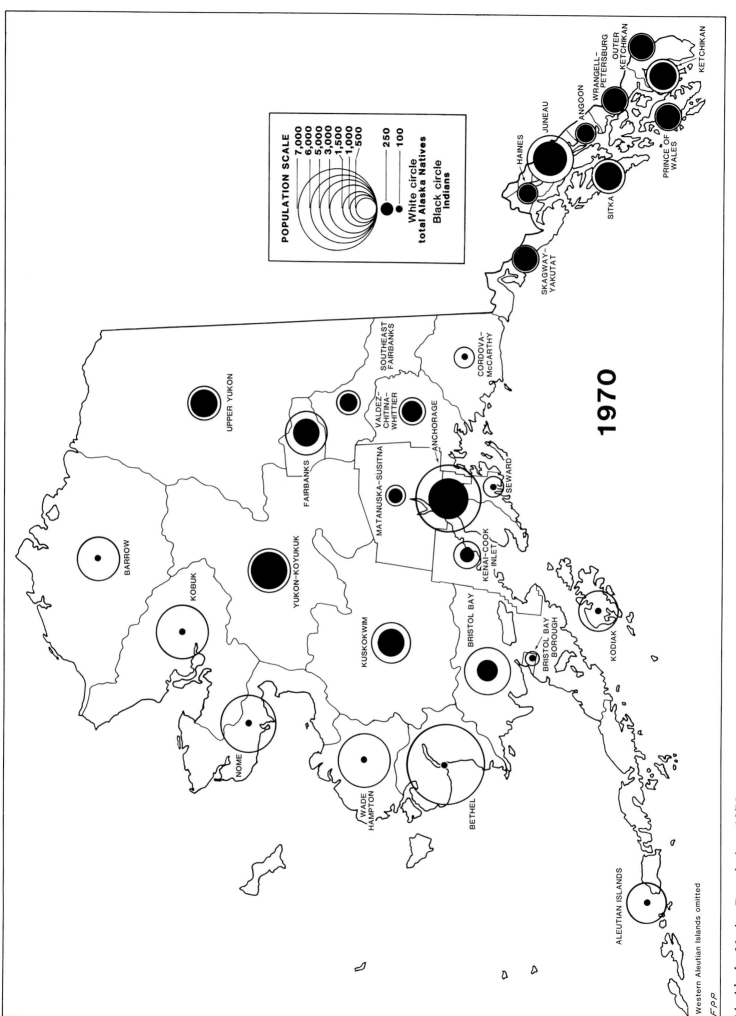

64. Alaska Native Population: 1970

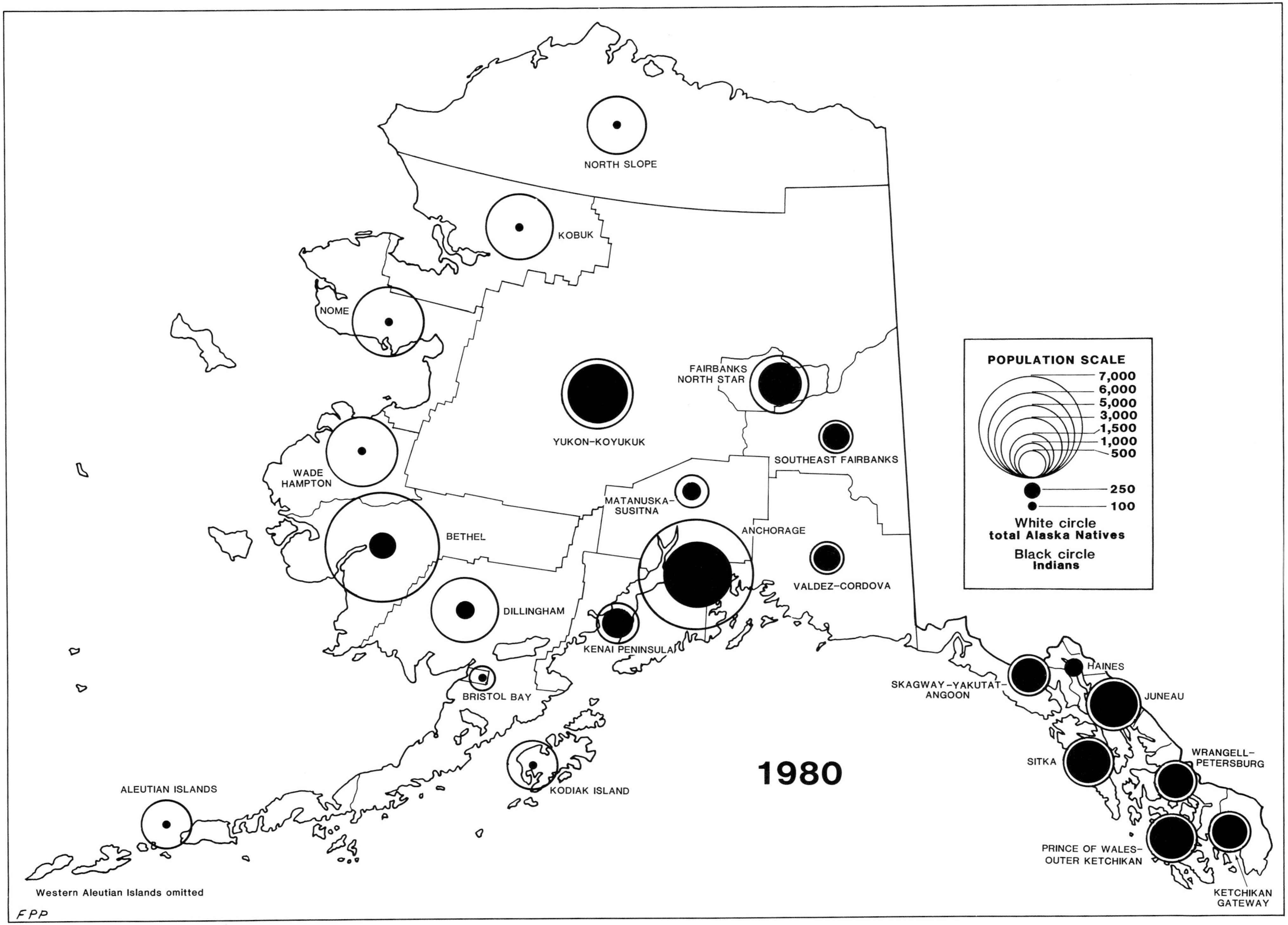

POPULATION SCALE

7,000
6,000
5,000
3,000
1,500
1,000
500

250
100

White circle
total Alaska Natives

Black circle
Indians

1980

NORTH SLOPE

KOBUK

YUKON-KOYUKUK

FAIRBANKS
NORTH STAR

SOUTHEAST FAIRBANKS

MATANUSKA–
SUSITNA

ANCHORAGE

VALDEZ–CORDOVA

KENAI PENINSULA

SKAGWAY–YAKUTAT–
ANGOON

HAINES

JUNEAU

WRANGELL–
PETERSBURG

KETCHIKAN
GATEWAY

PRINCE OF WALES–
OUTER KETCHIKAN

SITKA

NOME

WADE
HAMPTON

BETHEL

DILLINGHAM

BRISTOL BAY

KODIAK ISLAND

ALEUTIAN ISLANDS

Western Aleutian Islands omitted

F.P.P.

65. Alaska Native Population: 1980

79

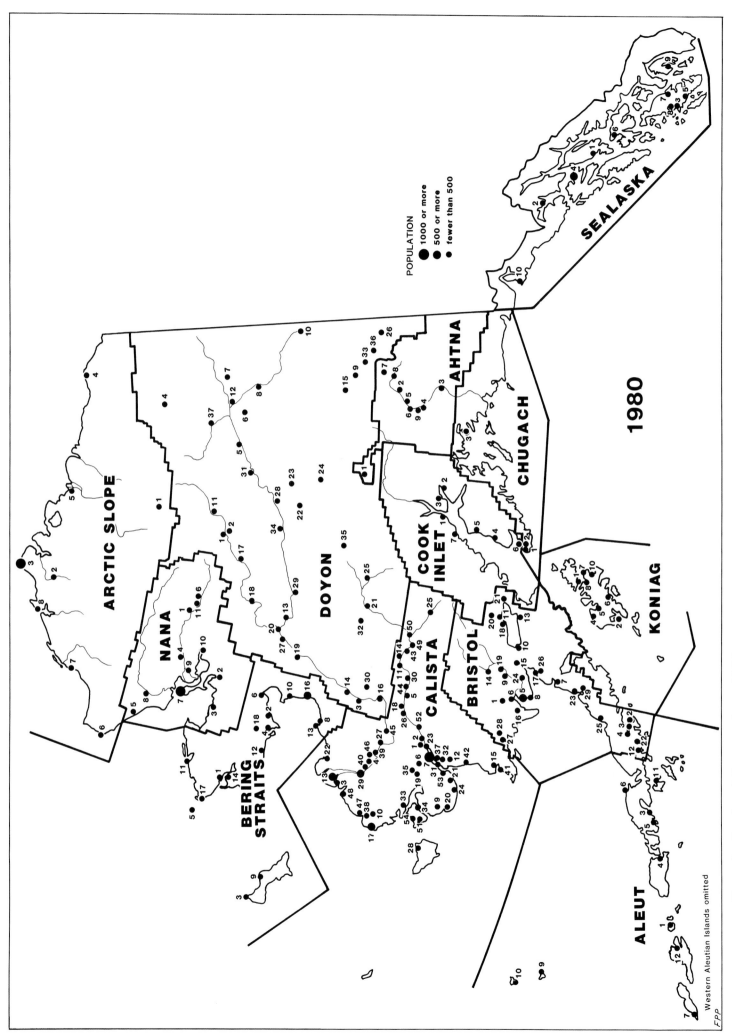

66. Alaska Native Villages by Regional Corporations: 1980

Population of Alaska Native Villages by Regional Corporations: 1980

	American Indian	Eskimo	Aleut	Total
Alaska	21,869	34,144	8,090	64,103
Native villages	8,023	24,574	4,704	39,301
Outside villages	12,904	7,559	3,381	23,844
AHTNA, INC.	268	14	2	284
1. Cantwell	28	—	—	28
2. Chistochina	27	—	—	27
3. Chitina	20	—	—	20
4. Copper Center	80	4	1	85
5. Gakona	13	—	1	14
6. Gulkana	43	—	—	43
7. Mentasta Lake	50	5	—	55
8. Slana	3	5	—	8
9. Tazlina	4	—	—	4
ALEUT CORPORATION	58	25	1,806	1,889
1. Akutan	1	—	65	66
2. Atka**	—	2	88	90
3. Belkofsky	—	—	10	10
4. False Pass	5	—	55	60
5. King Cove	3	—	364	367
6. Nelson Lagoon	—	3	52	55
7. Nikolski	—	—	48	48
8. Pauloff Harbor*	—	—	—	—
9. St. George	4	2	147	153
10. St. Paul	23	10	450	483
11. Sand Point	10	2	345	357
12. Unalaska	17	1	182	200
13. Unga*	—	—	—	—
ARCTIC SLOPE REGIONAL CORPORATION	21	3,184	3	3,208
1. Anaktuvuk Pass	—	191	—	191
2. Atkasook	—	99	—	99
3. Barrow	17	1,700	3	1,720
4. Kaktovik	3	145	—	148
5. Nuiqsut	—	181	—	181
6. Point Hope	1	433	—	434
7. Point Lay	—	63	—	63
8. Wainwright	—	372	—	372
BERING STRAITS NATIVE CORPORATION	11	3,669	5	3,685
1. Brevig Mission	—	138	—	138
2. Elim	—	203	—	203
3. Gambell	1	424	—	425
4. Golovin	—	85	—	85
5. Inalik	—	136	—	136
6. Koyuk	—	180	—	180
7. Mary's Igloo*	—	—	—	—
8. St. Michael	1	226	—	227
9. Savoonga	1	462	—	463
10. Shaktoolik	—	159	—	159
11. Shishmaref	1	368	—	369
12. Solomon	—	4	—	4
13. Stebbins	—	316	—	316
14. Teller	3	193	—	196
15. Ukivok*	—	—	—	—
16. Unalakleet	5	537	4	546
17. Wales	—	122	—	122
18. White Mountain	—	116	—	116
BRISTOL BAY NATIVE CORPORATION	271	2,049	1,460	3,780
1. Aleknagik	2	136	—	138
2. Chignik	3	5	87	95
3. Chignik Lagoon	—	2	39	41
4. Chignik Lake	2	—	121	123
5. Clark's Point	2	50	18	70
6. Dillingham	26	443	422	891
7. Egegik	1	3	53	57
8. Ekuk	—	—	6	6
9. Ekwok	—	70	1	71
10. Igiugig	—	16	9	25
11. Iliamna	19	7	12	38
12. Ivanof Bay	1	—	36	37
13. Kokhanok	9	8	63	80
14. Koliganek	2	110	—	112
15. Levelock	1	19	49	69
16. Manokotak	—	272	1	273
17. Naknek	6	25	130	161
18. Newhalen	1	13	68	82
19. New Stuyahok	—	306	5	311
20. Nondalton	161	—	—	161
21. Pedro Bay	28	2	1	31
22. Perryville	3	—	100	103
23. Pilot Point	—	1	56	57
24. Portage Creek	—	44	—	44
25. Port Heiden	—	1	58	59
26. South Naknek	2	7	115	124
27. Togiak	2	440	1	443
28. Twin Hills	—	67	—	67
29. Ugashik	—	2	9	11
CALISTA CORPORATION	270	13,222	35	13,527
1. Akiachak	—	398	—	398
2. Akiak	—	191	—	191
3. Alakanuk	—	491	—	491
4. Andreafsky	—	93	—	93
5. Aniak	11	207	—	218
6. Atmautluak	—	206	—	206
7. Bethel	114	2,281	22	2,417
8. Bill Moore's*	—	—	—	—
9. Chefornak	2	219	—	221
10. Chevak	—	445	—	445
11. Crooked Creek	5	86	—	91
12. Eek	—	220	—	220
13. Emmonak	1	516	—	517
14. Georgetown	1	1	—	2
15. Goodnews Bay	1	160	—	161
16. Hamilton*	—	—	—	—
17. Hooper Bay	4	592	2	598
18. Kalskag	4	104	—	108
19. Kasigluk	—	325	—	325
20. Kipnuk	—	358	—	358
21. Kongiganak	—	231	—	231
22. Kotlik	—	280	—	280
23. Kwethluk	1	440	—	441
24. Kwigillingok	—	343	—	343
25. Lime Village	37	2	—	39
26. Lower Kalskag	3	234	—	237
27. Marshall	—	246	—	246
28. Mekoryuk	—	153	—	153
29. Mountain Village	—	538	1	539
30. Napaimute	—	4	—	4
31. Napakiak	1	253	—	254
32. Napaskiak	—	238	1	239
33. Newtok	—	124	—	124
34. Nightmute	—	116	—	116
35. Nunapitchuk	—	295	—	295
36. Ohogamiut*	—	—	—	—
37. Oscarville	—	50	6	56
38. Paimiut	—	1	—	1
39. Pilot Station	1	305	—	306
40. Pikas Point	—	44	—	44
41. Platinum	—	44	—	44
42. Quinhagak	—	402	—	402
43. Red Devil	9	9	—	18
44. Russian Mission KU	—	9	—	9
45. Russian Mission YU	—	93	—	93
46. St. Mary's	3	156	—	159
47. Scammon Bay	—	243	—	243
48. Sheldon's Point	—	98	—	98
49. Sleetmute	48	45	2	95
50. Stony River	23	33	—	56
51. Toksook Bay	—	312	—	312
52. Tuluksak	1	227	—	228
53. Tuntutuliak	1	208	—	209
54. Tununak	—	283	—	283
CHUGACH NATIVES, INC.	5	—	287	292
1. English Bay	1	—	97	98
2. Port Graham	4	—	137	141
3. Tatitlek	—	—	53	53
COOK INLET REGION, INC.	317	42	130	489
1. Alexander	1	—	1	2
2. Eklutna	34	8	—	42
3. Knik	5	—	—	5
4. Ninilchik	15	4	39	58
5. Salamatof	19	16	8	43
6. Seldovia	30	11	76	117
7. Tyonek	214	2	6	222
DOYON, LIMITED	4,166	299	10	4,475
1. Alatna	7	22	—	29
2. Allakaket	118	11	—	129
3. Anvik	90	1	—	91
4. Arctic Village	98	—	—	98
5. Beaver	35	29	1	65
6. Birch Creek	31	—	—	31
7. Chalkyitsik	96	—	—	96
8. Circle	60	—	—	60
9. Dot Lake	29	9	—	38
10. Eagle	56	—	1	57
11. Evansville	6	21	—	27
12. Fort Yukon	440	2	—	442
13. Galena	206	9	—	215
14. Grayling	126	3	—	129
15. Healy Lake	29	—	—	29
16. Holy Cross	191	30	—	221
17. Hughes	71	—	—	71
18. Huslia	177	1	—	178
19. Kaltag	234	2	—	236
20. Koyukuk	90	1	—	91
21. McGrath	94	64	7	165
22. Manley Hot Springs	5	7	—	12
23. Minto	141	—	—	141
24. Nenana	188	26	—	214
25. Nikolai	80	2	—	82
26. Northway	102	—	—	102
27. Nulato	327	2	—	329
28. Rampart	38	9	—	47
29. Ruby	169	2	—	171
30. Shageluk	120	—	—	120
31. Stevens Village	59	2	—	61
32. Takotna	13	11	1	25
33. Tanacross	101	—	—	101
34. Tanana	275	32	—	307
35. Telida	32	—	—	32
36. Tetlin	103	1	—	104
37. Venetie	129	—	—	129
KONIAG, INC.	8	6	945	959
1. Afognak	—	—	3	3
2. Akhiok	—	—	101	101
3. Kaguyak*	—	—	—	—
4. Karluk	—	—	96	96
5. Larsen Bay	5	—	115	120
6. Old Harbor	—	4	311	315
7. Ouzinkie	1	1	161	163
8. Port Lions	2	1	155	158
9. Uyak*	—	—	—	—
10. Woody Island	—	—	3	3
NANA REGIONAL NATIVE CORPORATION	32	4,023	3	4,058
1. Ambler	—	155	—	155
2. Buckland	—	161	—	161
3. Deering	1	137	—	138
4. Kiana	—	325	—	325
5. Kivalina	—	237	—	237
6. Kobuk	—	59	—	59
7. Kotzebue	22	1,549	3	1,574
8. Noatak	2	257	—	259
9. Noorvik	4	463	—	467
10. Selawik	2	502	—	504
11. Shungnak	1	178	—	179
SEALASKA CORPORATION	2,596	41	18	2,655
1. Angoon	406	6	—	412
2. Chilkat	113	—	—	113
3. Craig	160	—	10	170
4. Hoonah	535	6	2	543
5. Hydaburg	244	7	2	253
6. Kake	466	1	—	467
7. Kasaan	9	5	—	14
8. Klawock	206	2	2	210
9. Saxman	190	4	—	194
10. Yakutat	267	10	2	279

* Omitted from map: no resident population.   ** Omitted from map: in western Aleutian Islands.

The United States army through the nineteenth century was frequently an Indian-fighting army. It was deployed across the continent to protect both white settlers and Indians as the two cultures came into contact and conflict. Most of the military installations (aside from coastal fortifications) owed their existence to the presence of Indian tribes on the frontier.

The first maps in this section (Maps 67–73), in seven regional divisions, show approximately 475 military posts for the period 1789–1895—forts, camps, cantonments, and barracks. For each post the dates of its existence are shown, although no terminal date is given for those that lasted beyond 1895. All the posts shown on the maps were regular army installations, established and garrisoned by federal troops. Omitted are trading posts or block-houses erected by local citizens and strictly wartime establishments of the War of 1812, the Mexican War, and the Civil War, as well as temporary encampments and minor subposts. The posts are located on a topographical map so that the geographical setting of each post can be seen.

The second series of maps (Maps 74–86) shows the distribution of regular army troops at selected dates, dates that illustrate important situations or changes on the military frontiers of the United States. The relative size of the garrison at each post is indicated by the size of the black dot marking the post, according to the scale on each map.

VIII

The Army and the Indian Frontier

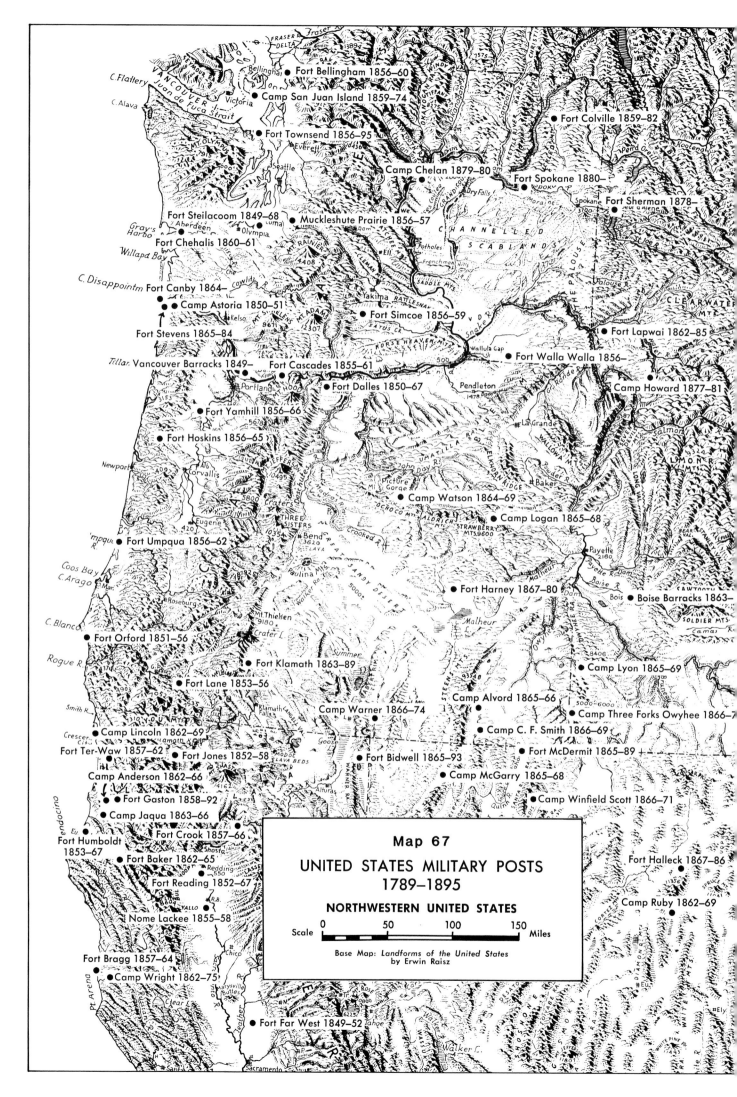

Map 67

UNITED STATES MILITARY POSTS
1789–1895

NORTHWESTERN UNITED STATES

Scale 0   50   100   150 Miles

Base Map: *Landforms of the United States*
by Erwin Raisz

Fort Bellingham 1856–60
Camp San Juan Island 1859–74
Fort Colville 1859–82
Fort Townsend 1856–95
Camp Chelan 1879–80
Fort Spokane 1880–
Fort Sherman 1878–
Fort Steilacoom 1849–68
Muckleshute Prairie 1856–57
Fort Chehalis 1860–61
Fort Canby 1864–
Camp Astoria 1850–51
Fort Simcoe 1856–59
Fort Lapwai 1862–85
Fort Stevens 1865–84
Vancouver Barracks 1849–
Fort Cascades 1855–61
Fort Walla Walla 1856–
Fort Dalles 1850–67
Camp Howard 1877–81
Fort Yamhill 1856–66
Fort Hoskins 1856–65
Camp Watson 1864–69
Camp Logan 1865–68
Fort Umpqua 1856–62
Fort Harney 1867–80
Boise Barracks 1863–
Fort Orford 1851–56
Camp Lyon 1865–69
Fort Klamath 1863–89
Fort Lane 1853–56
Camp Alvord 1865–66
Camp Warner 1866–74
Camp Three Forks Owyhee 1866–7
Camp Lincoln 1862–69
Camp C. F. Smith 1866–69
Fort Ter-Waw 1857–62
Fort Jones 1852–58
Fort Bidwell 1865–93
Fort McDermit 1865–89
Camp Anderson 1862–66
Camp McGarry 1865–68
Fort Gaston 1858–92
Camp Winfield Scott 1866–71
Camp Jaqua 1863–66
Fort Humboldt 1853–67
Fort Crook 1857–66
Fort Baker 1862–65
Fort Halleck 1867–86
Fort Reading 1852–67
Nome Lackee 1855–58
Camp Ruby 1862–69
Fort Bragg 1857–64
Camp Wright 1862–75
Fort Far West 1849–52

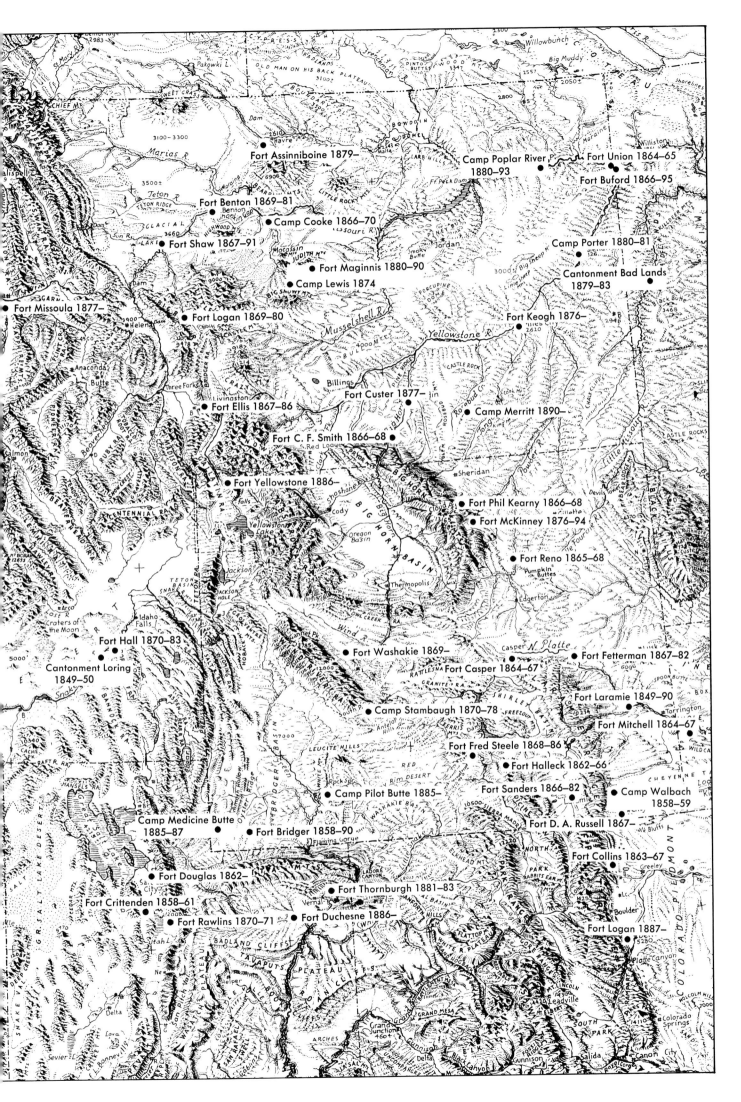

Fort Assinniboine 1879–

Camp Poplar River 1880–93

Fort Union 1864–65

Fort Buford 1866–95

Fort Benton 1869–81

Camp Cooke 1866–70

Camp Porter 1880–81

Fort Shaw 1867–91

Fort Maginnis 1880–90

Cantonment Bad Lands 1879–83

Camp Lewis 1874

Fort Missoula 1877–

Fort Logan 1869–80

Fort Keogh 1876–

Fort Ellis 1867–86

Fort Custer 1877–

Camp Merritt 1890–

Fort C. F. Smith 1866–68

Fort Yellowstone 1886–

Fort Phil Kearny 1866–68

Fort McKinney 1876–94

Fort Reno 1865–68

Fort Hall 1870–83

Fort Washakie 1869–

Fort Fetterman 1867–82

Cantonment Loring 1849–50

Fort Casper 1864–67

Fort Laramie 1849–90

Camp Stambaugh 1870–78

Fort Mitchell 1864–67

Fort Fred Steele 1868–86

Fort Halleck 1862–66

Camp Pilot Butte 1885–

Fort Sanders 1866–82

Camp Walbach 1858–59

Camp Medicine Butte 1885–87

Fort Bridger 1858–90

Fort D. A. Russell 1867–

Fort Douglas 1862–

Fort Collins 1863–67

Fort Thornburgh 1881–83

Fort Crittenden 1858–61

Fort Rawlins 1870–71

Fort Duchesne 1886–

Fort Logan 1887–

85

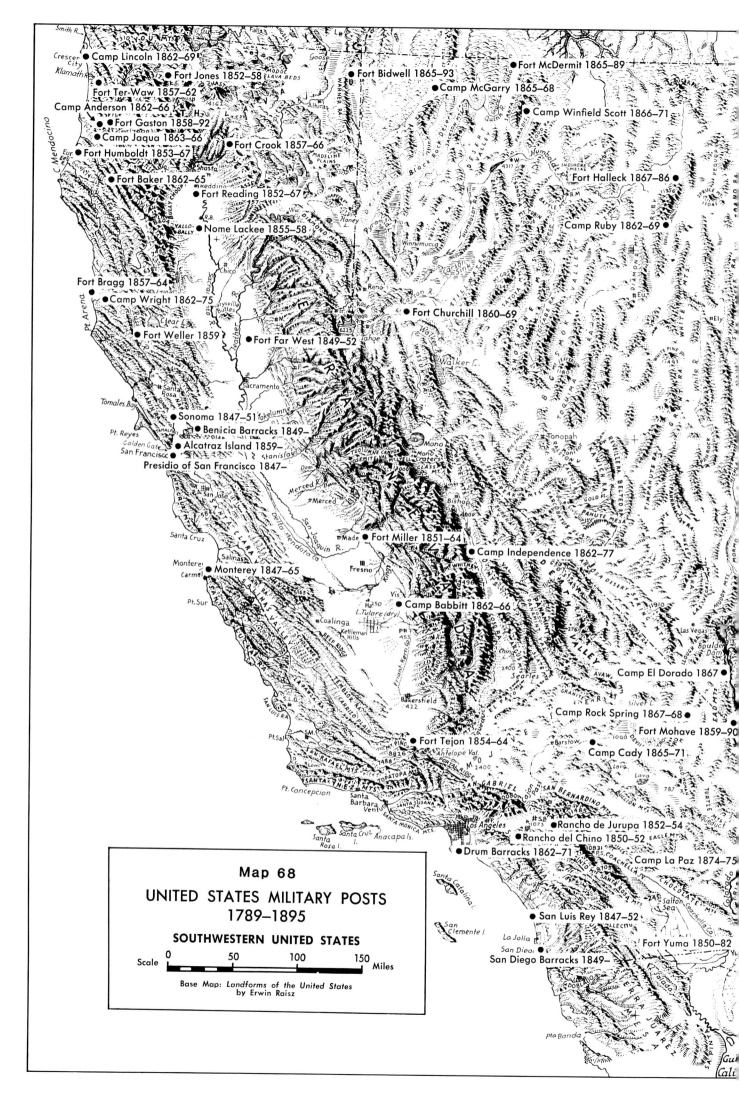

Smith R.
Crescer City ● Camp Lincoln 1862–69
Klamath
● Fort Jones 1852–58
Fort Ter-Waw 1857–62
Camp Anderson 1862–66 ●
● Fort Gaston 1858–92
● Camp Jaqua 1863–66
● Fort Humboldt 1853–67
C. Mendocino
● Fort Baker 1862–65"
● Fort Reading 1852–67
● Fort Crook 1857–66

● Fort Bidwell 1865–93
● Camp McGarry 1865–68

● Fort McDermit 1865–89

● Camp Winfield Scott 1866–71

● Fort Halleck 1867–86 ●

● Nome Lackee 1855–58

Fort Bragg 1857–64 ●
● Camp Wright 1862–75
Pt. Arena
● Fort Weller 1859
● Fort Far West 1849–52

● Camp Ruby 1862–69

● Fort Churchill 1860–69

Tomales Bay

Pt. Reyes
Golden Gate
San Francisco
● Sonoma 1847–51
● Benicia Barracks 1849–
● Alcatraz Island 1859–
Presidio of San Francisco 1847–

Santa Cruz
Monterey
Carmel
● Monterey 1847–65

● Fort Miller 1851–64
● Camp Independence 1862–77

Fresno
● Camp Babbitt 1862–66

Pt. Sur
#Coalinga
L.Tulare (dry)

Bakersfield

● Camp El Dorado 1867 ●

● Camp Rock Spring 1867–68 ●
● Fort Mohave 1859–90
● Fort Tejon 1854–64
● Camp Cady 1865–71

Pt. Concepcion
Santa Barbara
Ventu

Santa Cruz I. Anacapa Is.
Santa Rosa I.
Los Angeles
● Rancho de Jurupa 1852–54 ●
● Rancho del Chino 1850–52
● Drum Barracks 1862–71 ●
● Camp La Paz 1874–75

Santa Catalina I.

San Clemente I.

La Jolla
San Diego
San Diego Barracks 1849–
● San Luis Rey 1847–52

● Fort Yuma 1850–82

Map 68

UNITED STATES MILITARY POSTS
1789–1895

SOUTHWESTERN UNITED STATES

Scale 0   50   100   150 Miles

Base Map: Landforms of the United States
by Erwin Raisz

Pta Banda

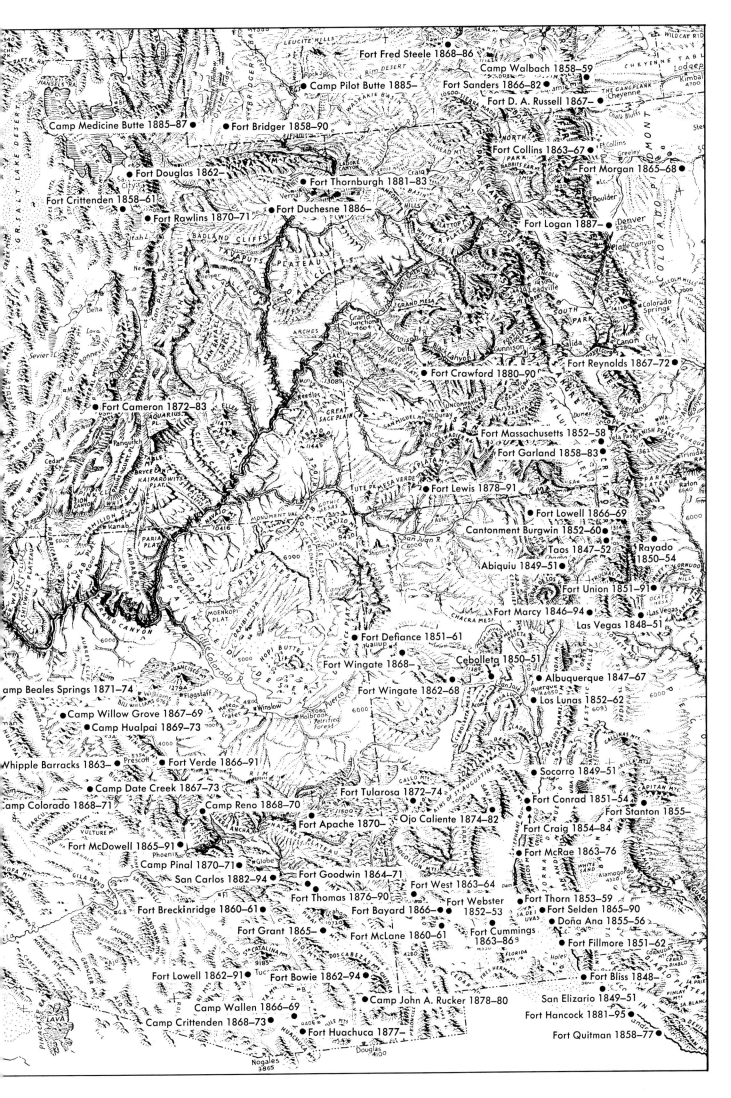

Fort Fred Steele 1868–86
Camp Walbach 1858–59
Camp Pilot Butte 1885–
Fort Sanders 1866–82
Fort D. A. Russell 1867–
Camp Medicine Butte 1885–87
Fort Bridger 1858–90
Fort Collins 1863–67
Fort Morgan 1865–68
Fort Douglas 1862–
Fort Thornburgh 1881–83
Fort Crittenden 1858–61
Fort Duchesne 1886–
Fort Rawlins 1870–71
Fort Logan 1887–
Denver
Fort Cameron 1872–83
Fort Crawford 1880–90
Fort Reynolds 1867–72
Fort Massachusetts 1852–58
Fort Garland 1858–83
Fort Lewis 1878–91
Fort Lowell 1866–69
Cantonment Burgwin 1852–60
Taos 1847–52
Rayado 1850–54
Abiquiu 1849–51
Fort Union 1851–91
Fort Marcy 1846–94
Las Vegas 1848–51
Fort Defiance 1851–61
Fort Wingate 1868–
Cebolleta 1850–51
Albuquerque 1847–67
Camp Beales Springs 1871–74
Fort Wingate 1862–68
Los Lunas 1852–62
Camp Willow Grove 1867–69
Camp Hualpai 1869–73
Whipple Barracks 1863–
Fort Verde 1866–91
Socorro 1849–51
Camp Date Creek 1867–73
Fort Tularosa 1872–74
Fort Conrad 1851–54
Camp Colorado 1868–71
Camp Reno 1868–70
Ojo Caliente 1874–82
Fort Stanton 1855–
Fort Apache 1870–
Fort Craig 1854–84
Fort McDowell 1865–91
Fort McRae 1863–76
Camp Pinal 1870–71
San Carlos 1882–94
Fort Goodwin 1864–71
Fort West 1863–64
Fort Thomas 1876–90
Fort Webster
Fort Thorn 1853–59
Fort Breckinridge 1860–61
Fort Bayard 1866–
1852–53
Fort Selden 1865–90
Fort Grant 1865–
Fort McLane 1860–61
Doña Ana 1855–56
Fort Cummings
Fort Lowell 1862–91
1863–86
Fort Fillmore 1851–62
Fort Bowie 1862–94
Fort Bliss 1848–
Camp Wallen 1866–69
Camp John A. Rucker 1878–80
San Elizario 1849–51
Camp Crittenden 1868–73
Fort Hancock 1881–95
Fort Huachuca 1877–
Fort Quitman 1858–77

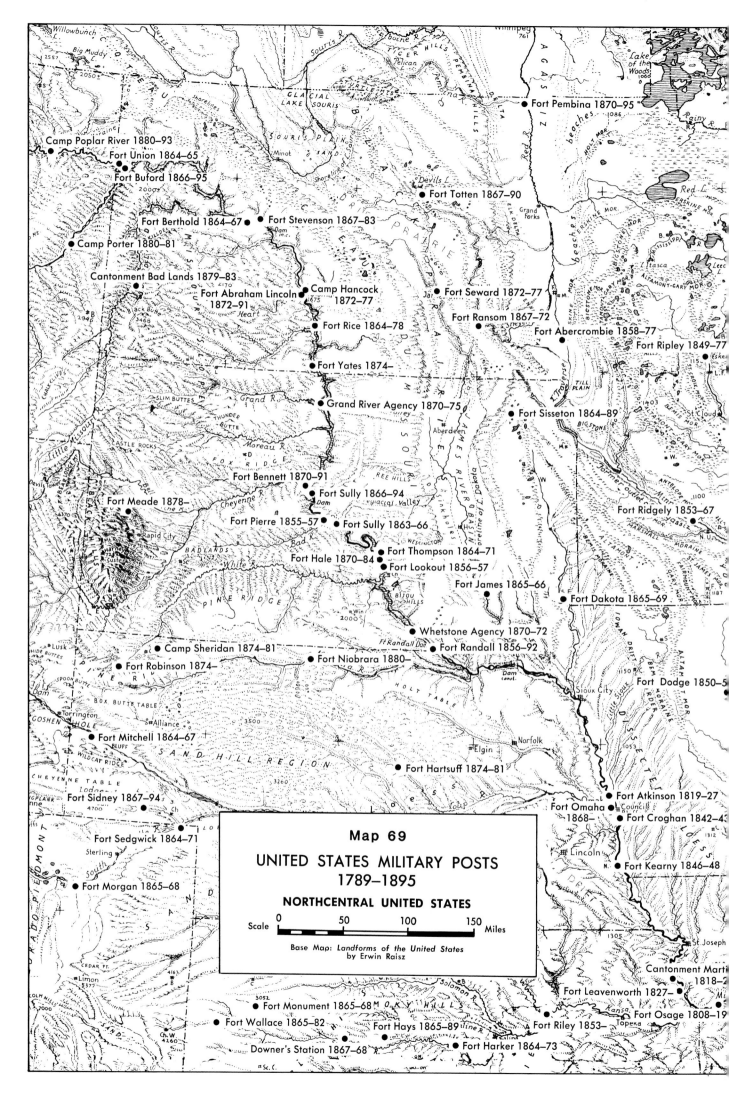

Camp Poplar River 1880–93
Fort Union 1864–65
Fort Buford 1866–95

Fort Berthold 1864–67
Fort Stevenson 1867–83

Camp Porter 1880–81

Cantonment Bad Lands 1879–83

Fort Abraham Lincoln 1872–91
Camp Hancock 1872–77

Fort Rice 1864–78

Fort Yates 1874–

Grand River Agency 1870–75

Fort Pembina 1870–95

Fort Totten 1867–90

Fort Seward 1872–77
Fort Ransom 1867–72
Fort Abercrombie 1858–77
Fort Ripley 1849–77

Fort Sisseton 1864–89

Fort Bennett 1870–91
Fort Sully 1866–94

Fort Meade 1878–

Fort Pierre 1855–57   Fort Sully 1863–66

Fort Ridgely 1853–67

Fort Thompson 1864–71
Fort Hale 1870–84
Fort Lookout 1856–57

Fort James 1865–66

Fort Dakota 1865–69

Whetstone Agency 1870–72

Camp Sheridan 1874–81
Fort Robinson 1874–

Fort Niobrara 1880–

Fort Randall 1856–92

Fort Dodge 1850–5

Fort Mitchell 1864–67

Fort Hartsuff 1874–81

Fort Atkinson 1819–27
Fort Omaha 1868–   Fort Croghan 1842–4

Fort Sidney 1867–94

Fort Sedgwick 1864–71

Fort Kearny 1846–48

Fort Morgan 1865–68

Cantonment Mart
1818–

Fort Leavenworth 1827–

Fort Osage 1808–1

Fort Monument 1865–68
Fort Wallace 1865–82
Downer's Station 1867–68
Fort Hays 1865–89
Fort Riley 1853–
Fort Harker 1864–73

Map 69

UNITED STATES MILITARY POSTS
1789–1895

NORTHCENTRAL UNITED STATES

Scale 0   50   100   150
Miles

Base Map: *Landforms of the United States*
by Erwin Raisz

88

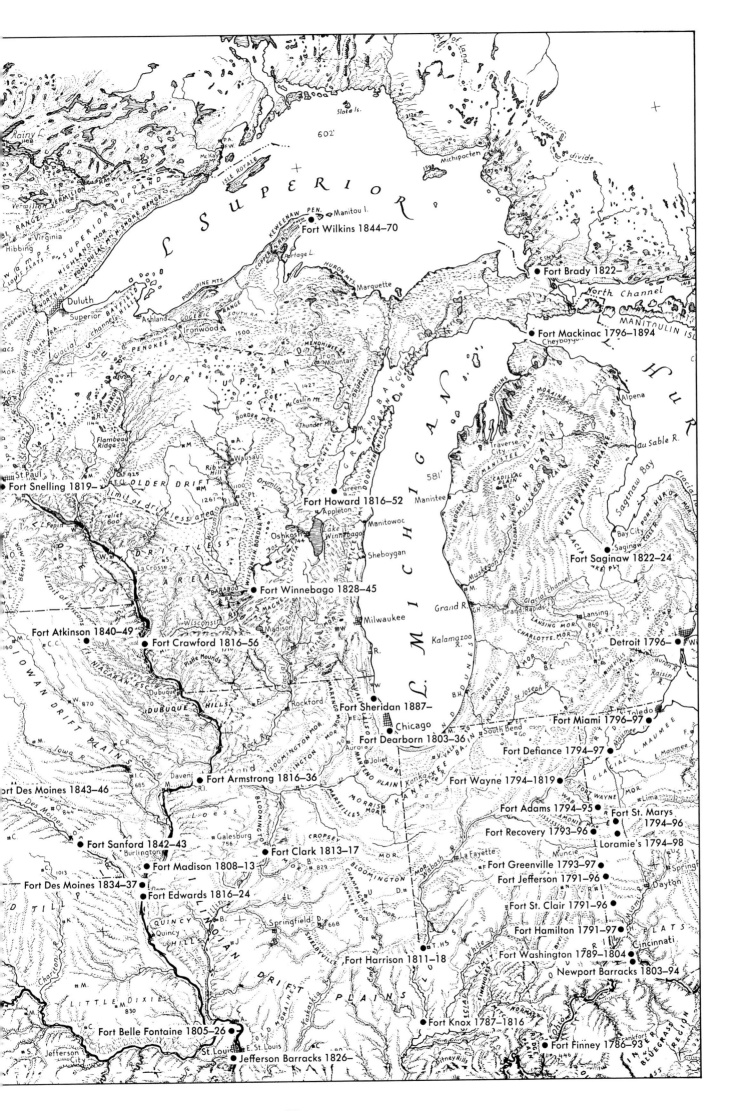

Fort Wilkins 1844–70

Fort Brady 1822–

Fort Mackinac 1796–1894

Fort Saginaw 1822–24

Fort Howard 1816–52

Detroit 1796–

Fort Snelling 1819–

Fort Winnebago 1828–45

Fort Atkinson 1840–49

Fort Crawford 1816–56

Fort Sheridan 1887–

Chicago

Fort Miami 1796–97

Fort Dearborn 1803–36

Fort Defiance 1794–97

Fort Wayne 1794–1819

Fort Armstrong 1816–36

Fort Adams 1794–95

Fort St. Marys 1794–96

Fort Des Moines 1843–46

Fort Recovery 1793–96

Loramie's 1794–98

Fort Sanford 1842–43

Fort Clark 1813–17

Fort Greenville 1793–97

Fort Madison 1808–13

Fort Jefferson 1791–96

Fort Des Moines 1834–37

Fort St. Clair 1791–96

Fort Edwards 1816–24

Fort Hamilton 1791–97

Fort Washington 1789–1804

Cincinnati

Fort Harrison 1811–18

Newport Barracks 1803–94

Fort Knox 1787–1816

Fort Belle Fontaine 1805–26

Fort Finney 1786–93

Jefferson Barracks 1826–

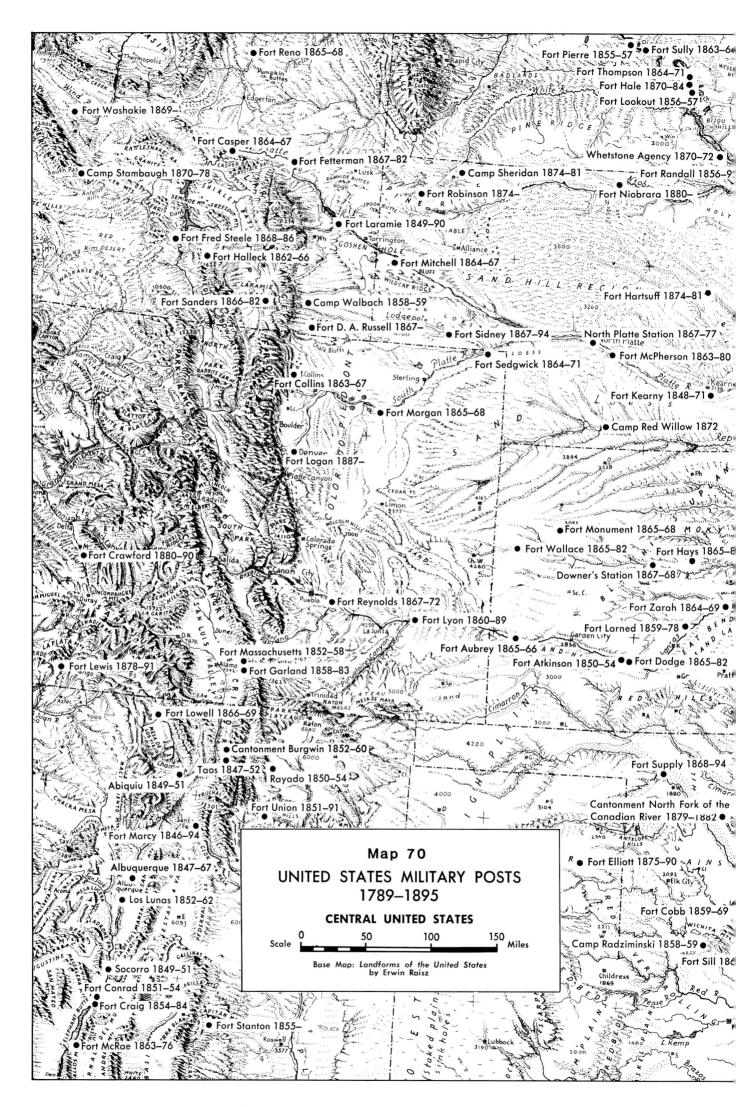

Map 70

UNITED STATES MILITARY POSTS
1789–1895

CENTRAL UNITED STATES

Scale 0   50   100   150 Miles

Base Map: *Landforms of the United States*
by Erwin Raisz

Fort Reno 1865–68
Fort Pierre 1855–57   Fort Sully 1863–6
Fort Thompson 1864–71
Fort Hale 1870–84
Fort Lookout 1856–57
Fort Washakie 1869–
Fort Casper 1864–67
Whetstone Agency 1870–72
Fort Fetterman 1867–82
Camp Stambaugh 1870–78   Camp Sheridan 1874–81   Fort Randall 1856–9
Fort Robinson 1874–   Fort Niobrara 1880–
Fort Laramie 1849–90
Fort Fred Steele 1868–86
Fort Mitchell 1864–67
Fort Halleck 1862–66   Fort Hartsuff 1874–81
Fort Sanders 1866–82   Camp Walbach 1858–59
Fort D. A. Russell 1867–   Fort Sidney 1867–94   North Platte Station 1867–77
Fort McPherson 1863–80
Fort Collins 1863–67   Fort Sedgwick 1864–71
Fort Kearny 1848–71
Fort Morgan 1865–68
Camp Red Willow 1872
Denver
Fort Logan 1887–
Fort Monument 1865–68
Fort Wallace 1865–82   Fort Hays 1865–8
Fort Crawford 1880–90   Downer's Station 1867–68
Fort Reynolds 1867–72   Fort Zarah 1864–69
Fort Lyon 1860–89   Fort Larned 1859–78
Fort Lewis 1878–91   Fort Aubrey 1865–66
Fort Massachusetts 1852–58   Fort Atkinson 1850–54   Fort Dodge 1865–82
Fort Garland 1858–83
Fort Lowell 1866–69
Cantonment Burgwin 1852–60
Fort Supply 1868–94
Taos 1847–52
Abiquiu 1849–51   Rayado 1850–54
Cantonment North Fork of the
Canadian River 1879–1882
Fort Union 1851–91
Fort Marcy 1846–94
Fort Elliott 1875–90
Albuquerque 1847–67
Los Lunas 1852–62
Fort Cobb 1859–69
Camp Radziminski 1858–59
Fort Sill 186
Socorro 1849–51
Fort Conrad 1851–54
Childress 1869
Fort Craig 1854–84
Fort Stanton 1855–
Fort McRae 1863–76
Lubbock   L. Kemp

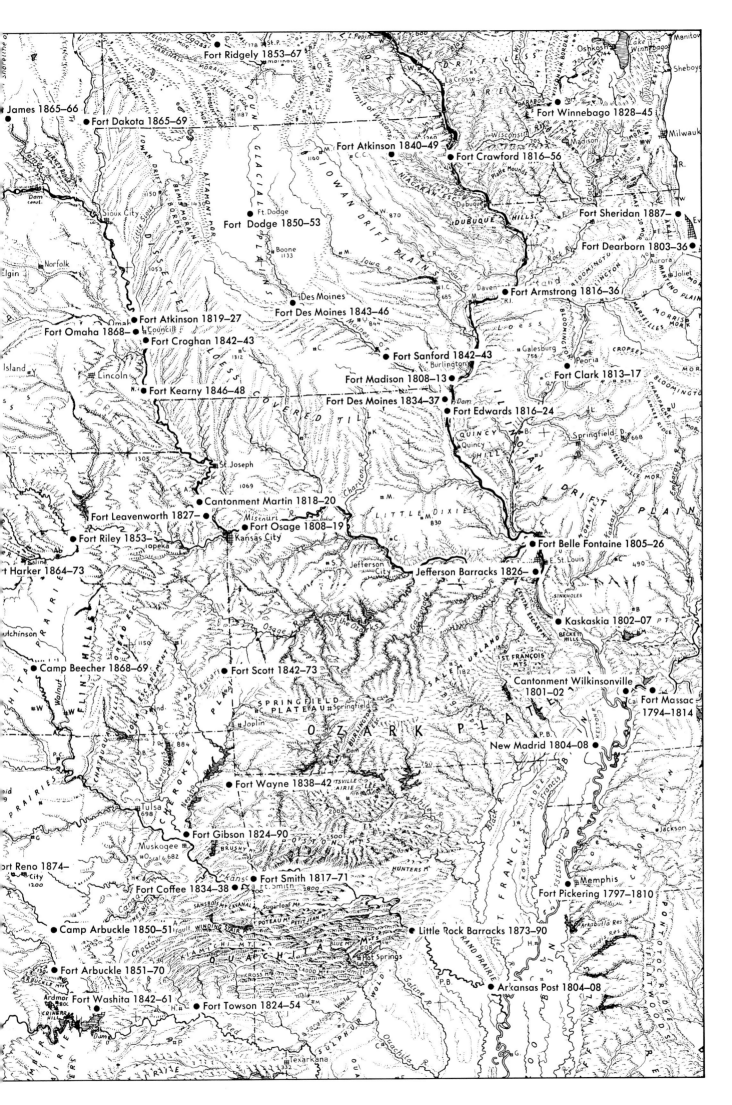

James 1865–66
Fort Dakota 1865–69
Fort Ridgely 1853–67
Fort Winnebago 1828–45
Fort Atkinson 1840–49
Fort Crawford 1816–56
Fort Sheridan 1887–
Fort Dearborn 1803–36
Fort Dodge 1850–53
Fort Armstrong 1816–36
Fort Atkinson 1819–27
Fort Des Moines 1843–46
Fort Omaha 1868–
Fort Croghan 1842–43
Fort Sanford 1842–43
Fort Clark 1813–17
Fort Madison 1808–13
Fort Kearny 1846–48
Fort Des Moines 1834–37
Fort Edwards 1816–24
Cantonment Martin 1818–20
Fort Leavenworth 1827–
Fort Osage 1808–19
Fort Riley 1853–
Fort Belle Fontaine 1805–26
Jefferson Barracks 1826–
t Harker 1864–73
Kaskaskia 1802–07
Camp Beecher 1868–69
Fort Scott 1842–73
Cantonment Wilkinsonville 1801–02
Fort Massac 1794–1814
New Madrid 1804–08
Fort Wayne 1838–42
Fort Gibson 1824–90
ort Reno 1874–
Fort Smith 1817–71
Fort Coffee 1834–38
Memphis
Fort Pickering 1797–1810
Camp Arbuckle 1850–51
Little Rock Barracks 1873–90
Fort Arbuckle 1851–70
Fort Washita 1842–61
Fort Towson 1824–54
Arkansas Post 1804–08

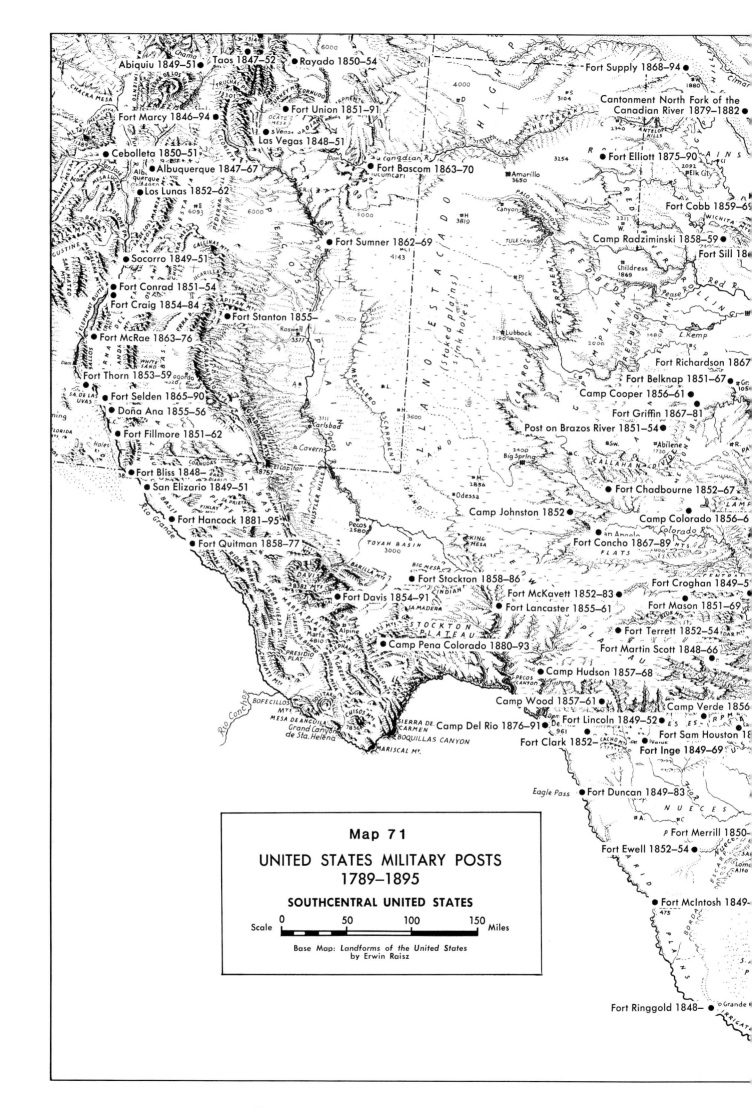

Abiquiu 1849–51 ● Taos 1847–52 ● Rayado 1850–54 ● ● Fort Supply 1868–94 ●

Cantonment North Fork of the
Canadian River 1879–1882 ●

Fort Marcy 1846–94 ● ● Fort Union 1851–91

● Fort Elliott 1875–90 ●

Las Vegas 1848–51

● Cebolleta 1850–51

● Fort Bascom 1863–70

● Albuquerque 1847–67

Fort Cobb 1859–6

● Los Lunas 1852–62

Camp Radziminski 1858–59 ●

Fort Sill 18●

● Fort Sumner 1862–69

● Socorro 1849–51

● Fort Conrad 1851–54

● Fort Craig 1854–84

● Fort Stanton 1855–

● Fort McRae 1863–76

Fort Richardson 1867

● Fort Thorn 1853–59

Fort Belknap 1851–67 ●

Camp Cooper 1856–61 ●

● Fort Selden 1865–90

Fort Griffin 1867–81

● Doña Ana 1855–56

Post on Brazos River 1851–54●

● Fort Fillmore 1851–62

● Fort Bliss 1848–

● San Elizario 1849–51

Fort Chadbourne 1852–67 ●

● Fort Hancock 1881–95

Camp Johnston 1852 ●

Camp Colorado 1856–6

● Fort Quitman 1858–77

Fort Concho 1867–89 ●

Fort Stockton 1858–86 ●

Fort Croghan 1849–5

Fort McKavett 1852–83 ●

● Fort Davis 1854–91

Fort Mason 1851–69

Fort Lancaster 1855–61 ●

Fort Terrett 1852–54●

Fort Martin Scott 1848–66

● Camp Pena Colorado 1880–93

● Camp Hudson 1857–68

Camp Wood 1857–61●

Camp Verde 1856

Camp Del Rio 1876–91 ● ● Fort Lincoln 1849–52 ●

Fort Sam Houston 18

Fort Clark 1852– ●

Fort Inge 1849–69 ●

Eagle Pass ● Fort Duncan 1849–83

N U E C E S

P Fort Merrill 1850–

Fort Ewell 1852–54 ●

● Fort McIntosh 1849–

Fort Ringgold 1848–

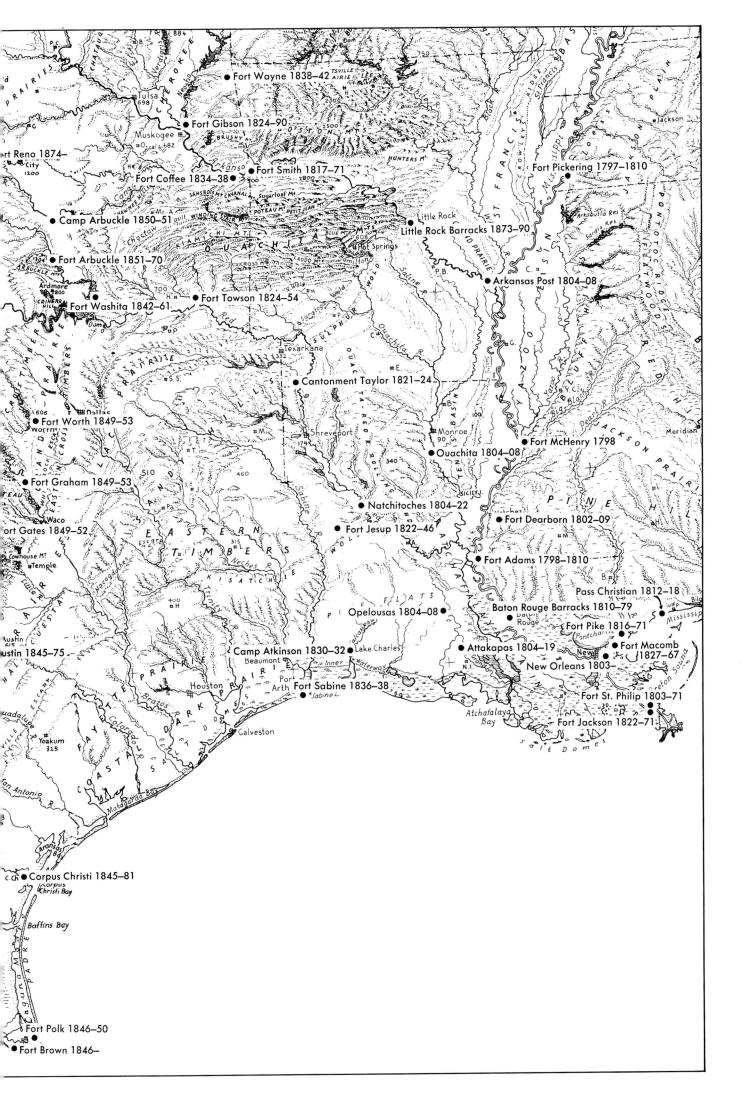

Fort Wayne 1838–42

Fort Gibson 1824–90

Fort Pickering 1797–1810

Fort Smith 1817–71

Fort Coffee 1834–38

Camp Arbuckle 1850–51

Little Rock Barracks 1873–90

Fort Reno 1874–

Fort Arbuckle 1851–70

Arkansas Post 1804–08

Fort Washita 1842–61

Fort Towson 1824–54

Cantonment Taylor 1821–24

Fort Worth 1849–53

Fort McHenry 1798

Ouachita 1804–08

Fort Graham 1849–53

Natchitoches 1804–22

Fort Dearborn 1802–09

ort Gates 1849–52

Fort Jesup 1822–46

Fort Adams 1798–1810

Pass Christian 1812–18

Opelousas 1804–08

Baton Rouge Barracks 1810–79

Fort Pike 1816–71

Camp Atkinson 1830–32

Attakapas 1804–19

Fort Macomb 1827–67

ustin 1845–75

New Orleans 1803–

Fort Sabine 1836–38

Fort St. Philip 1803–71

Fort Jackson 1822–71

Corpus Christi 1845–81

Fort Polk 1846–50

Fort Brown 1846–

93

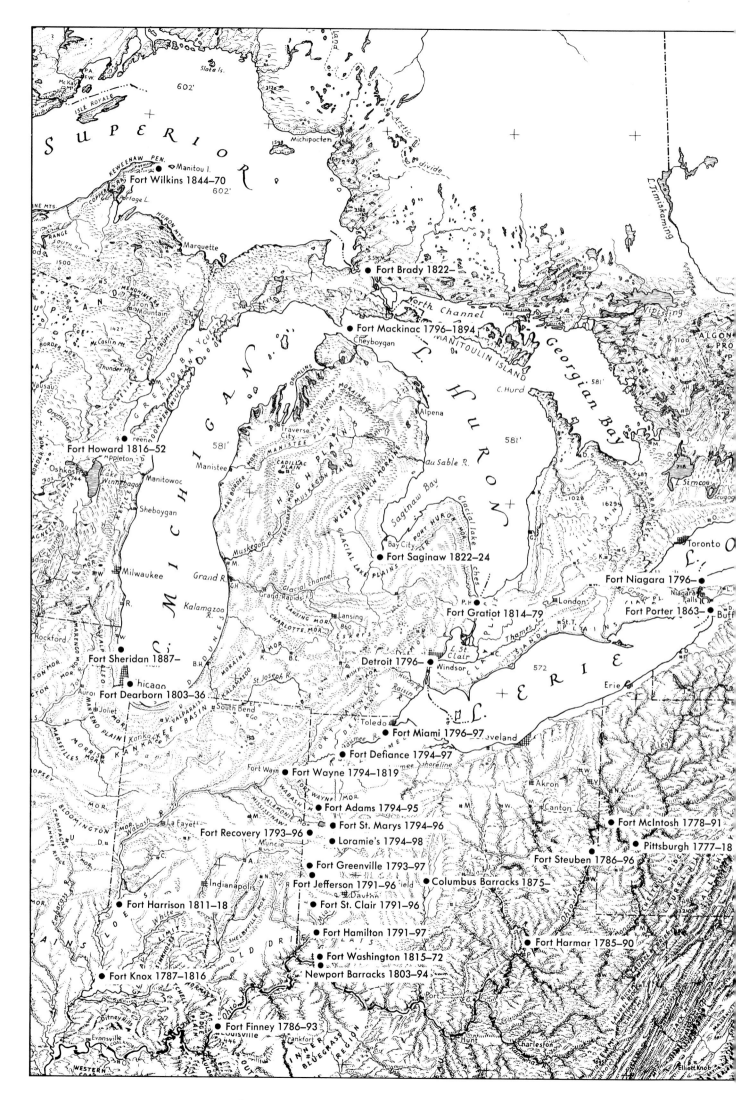

Fort Wilkins 1844–70

Fort Brady 1822–

Fort Mackinac 1796–1894

Fort Howard 1816–52

reeno

Fort Saginaw 1822–24

Fort Niagara 1796–

Fort Gratiot 1814–79

Fort Porter 1863–

Fort Sheridan 1887–

hicaao

Detroit 1796–

Fort Dearborn 1803–36

Fort Miami 1796–97

Fort Defiance 1794–97

Fort Wayne 1794–1819

Fort Adams 1794–95

Fort McIntosh 1778–91

Fort St. Marys 1794–96

Pittsburgh 1777–18

Fort Recovery 1793–96

Loramie's 1794–98

Fort Steuben 1786–96

Fort Greenville 1793–97

Columbus Barracks 1875–

Fort Jefferson 1791–96

Fort Harrison 1811–18

Fort St. Clair 1791–96

Fort Hamilton 1791–97

Fort Harmar 1785–90

Fort Washington 1815–72

Fort Knox 1787–1816

Newport Barracks 1803–94

Fort Finney 1786–93

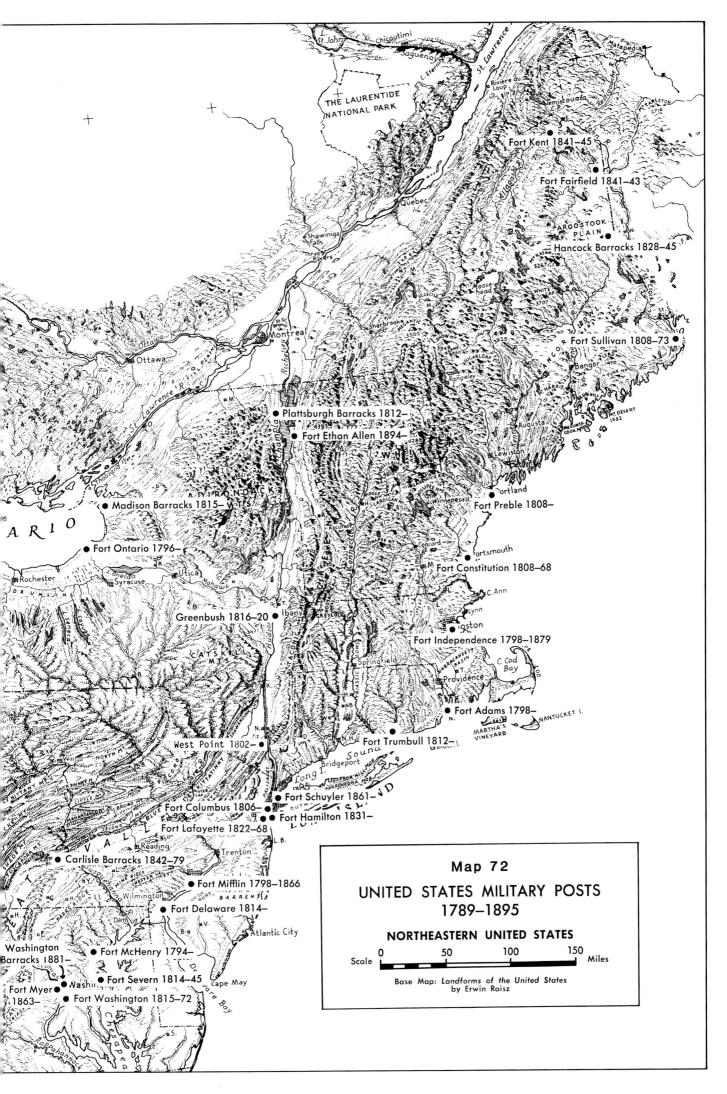

THE LAURENTIDE NATIONAL PARK

Fort Kent 1841–45

Fort Fairfield 1841–43

AROOSTOOK PLAIN

Hancock Barracks 1828–45

Fort Sullivan 1808–73

Plattsburgh Barracks 1812–

Fort Ethan Allen 1894–

Madison Barracks 1815–

Fort Preble 1808–

Fort Ontario 1796–

Fort Constitution 1808–68

Greenbush 1816–20

Fort Independence 1798–1879

Fort Adams 1798–

West Point 1802–

Fort Trumbull 1812–

Fort Schuyler 1861–

Fort Columbus 1806–

Fort Hamilton 1831–

Fort Lafayette 1822–68

Carlisle Barracks 1842–79

Fort Mifflin 1798–1866

Fort Delaware 1814–

Washington Barracks 1881–

Fort McHenry 1794–

Fort Myer 1863–

Fort Severn 1814–45

Fort Washington 1815–72

Map 72

UNITED STATES MILITARY POSTS
1789–1895

NORTHEASTERN UNITED STATES

Scale 0   50   100   150 Miles

Base Map: *Landforms of the United States*
by Erwin Raisz

95

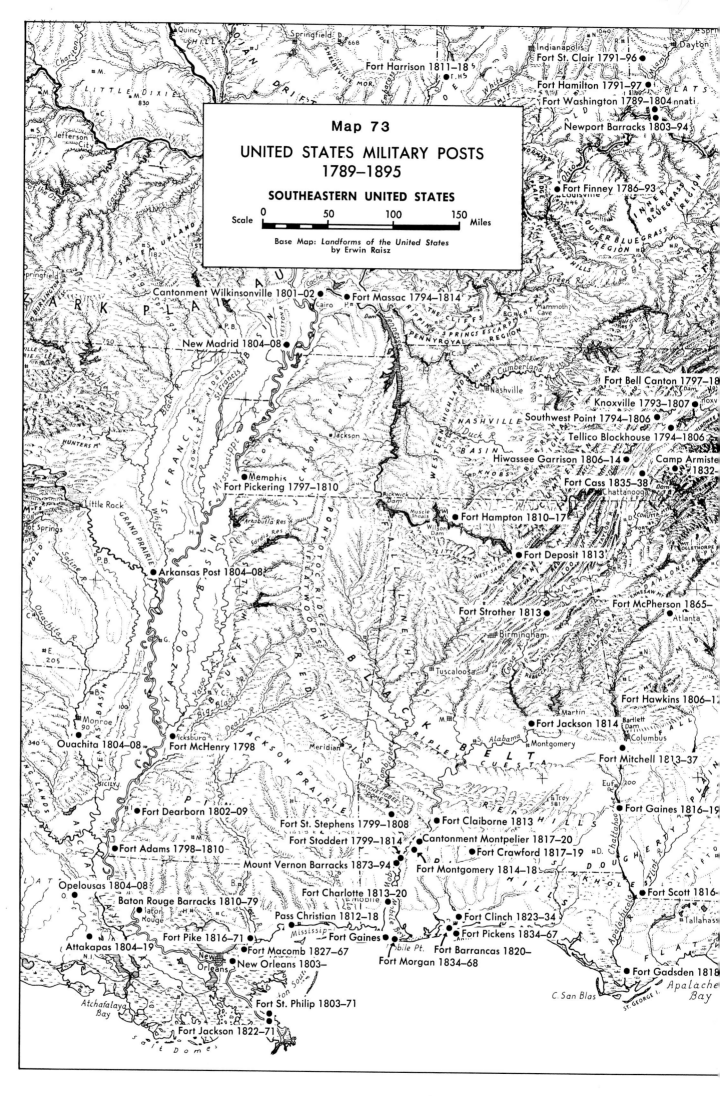

Map 73

UNITED STATES MILITARY POSTS
1789–1895

SOUTHEASTERN UNITED STATES

Scale |0   50   100   150| Miles

Base Map: *Landforms of the United States*
by Erwin Raisz

Fort St. Clair 1791–96
Fort Hamilton 1791–97
Fort Washington 1789–1804 nnati
Newport Barracks 1803–94
Fort Finney 1786–93

Fort Harrison 1811–18

Cantonment Wilkinsonville 1801–02   Fort Massac 1794–1814

New Madrid 1804–08

Fort Bell Canton 1797–18
Knoxville 1793–1807
Southwest Point 1794–1806
Tellico Blockhouse 1794–1806
Hiwassee Garrison 1806–14   Camp Armiste
Fort Cass 1835–38   1832–

Memphis
Fort Pickering 1797–1810

Fort Hampton 1810–17

Little Rock

Fort Deposit 1813

Arkansas Post 1804–08

Fort McPherson 1865
Fort Strother 1813

Fort Hawkins 1806–1

Ouachita 1804–08
Fort McHenry 1798

Fort Jackson 1814

Fort Mitchell 1813–37

Fort Dearborn 1802–09
Fort St. Stephens 1799–1808   Fort Claiborne 1813
Fort Stoddert 1799–1814   Cantonment Montpelier 1817–20
Fort Adams 1798–1810   Fort Crawford 1817–19
Mount Vernon Barracks 1873–94   Fort Montgomery 1814–18
Opelousas 1804–08   Fort Charlotte 1813–20   Fort Gaines 1816–1
Baton Rouge Barracks 1810–79   Fort Scott 1816–
Pass Christian 1812–18   Fort Clinch 1823–34
Fort Pike 1816–71   Fort Pickens 1834–67
Attakapas 1804–19   Fort Gaines   Fort Barrancas 1820–
Fort Macomb 1827–67   Fort Morgan 1834–68
New Orleans 1803–   Fort Gadsden 1818
Fort St. Philip 1803–71

Fort Jackson 1822–71

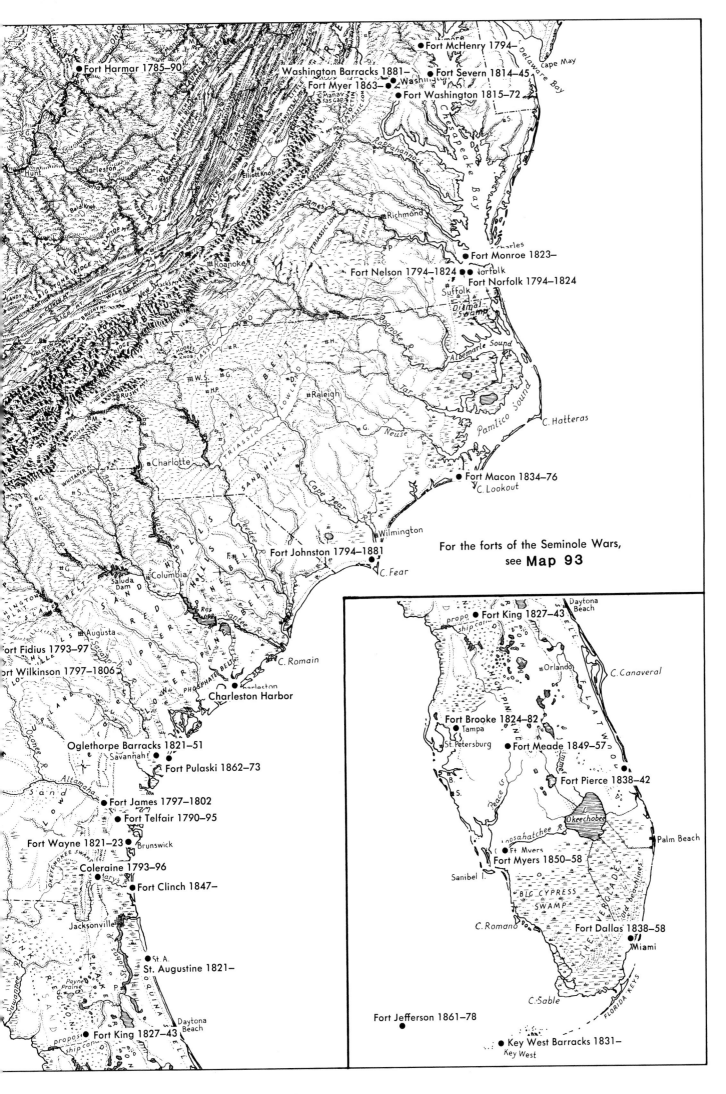

Fort Harmar 1785–90

Fort McHenry 1794–

Washington Barracks 1881–
Fort Myer 1863–
Fort Severn 1814–45
Fort Washington 1815–72

Fort Monroe 1823–

Fort Nelson 1794–1824
Fort Norfolk 1794–1824

Fort Macon 1834–76
C. Lookout

For the forts of the Seminole Wars,
see **Map 93**

Fort Johnston 1794–1881
C. Fear

ort Fidius 1793–97
ort Wilkinson 1797–1806

Charleston Harbor

Oglethorpe Barracks 1821–51
Savannah

Fort Pulaski 1862–73

Fort James 1797–1802

Fort Telfair 1790–95

Fort Wayne 1821–23
Brunswick

Coleraine 1793–96

Fort Clinch 1847–

Jacksonville

St. A.
St. Augustine 1821–

Daytona Beach

Fort King 1827–43

Fort King 1827–43
Daytona Beach

Fort Brooke 1824–82
Tampa
St. Petersburg

Fort Meade 1849–57

Fort Pierce 1838–42

Okeechobee

Palm Beach

Ft Myers
Fort Myers 1850–58

Sanibel I.

BIG CYPRESS SWAMP

C. Romano

Fort Dallas 1838–58
Miami

C. Sable

Fort Jefferson 1861–78

Key West Barracks 1831–
Key West

97

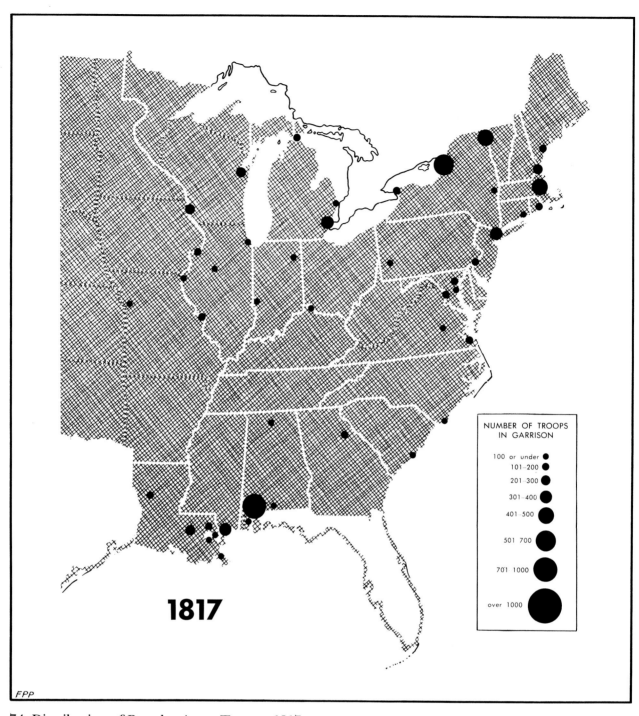

NUMBER OF TROOPS
IN GARRISON

100 or under
101–200
201–300
301–400
401–500
501–700
701–1000
over 1000

1817

FPP

74. Distribution of Regular Army Troops: 1817

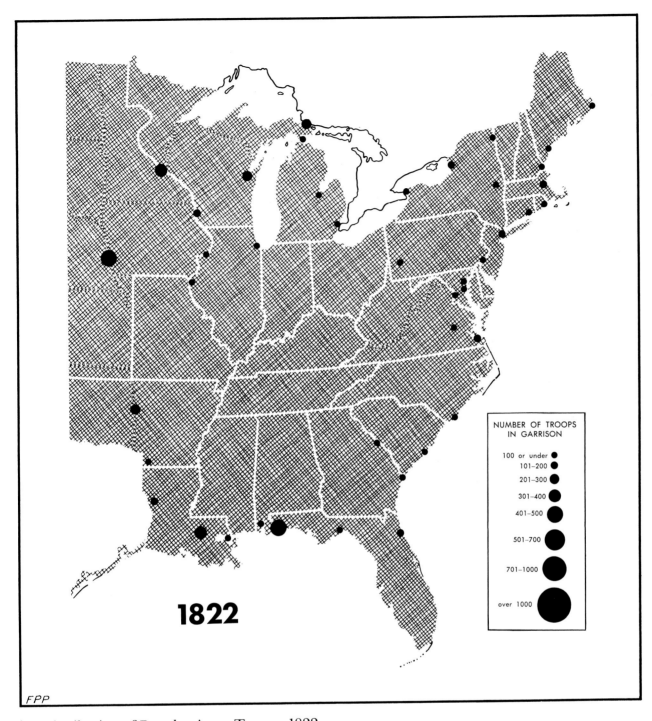

1822

NUMBER OF TROOPS
IN GARRISON

100 or under
101–200
201–300
301–400
401–500
501–700
701–1000
over 1000

FPP

75. Distribution of Regular Army Troops: 1822

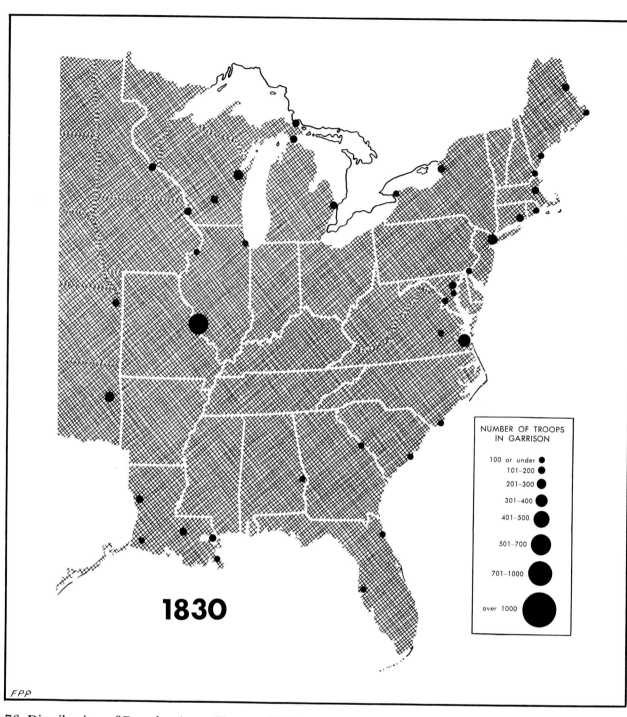

NUMBER OF TROOPS
IN GARRISON

100 or under ●
101–200 ●
201–300 ●
301–400 ●
401–500 ●
501–700 ●
701–1000 ●
over 1000 ●

1830

FPP

76. Distribution of Regular Army Troops: 1830

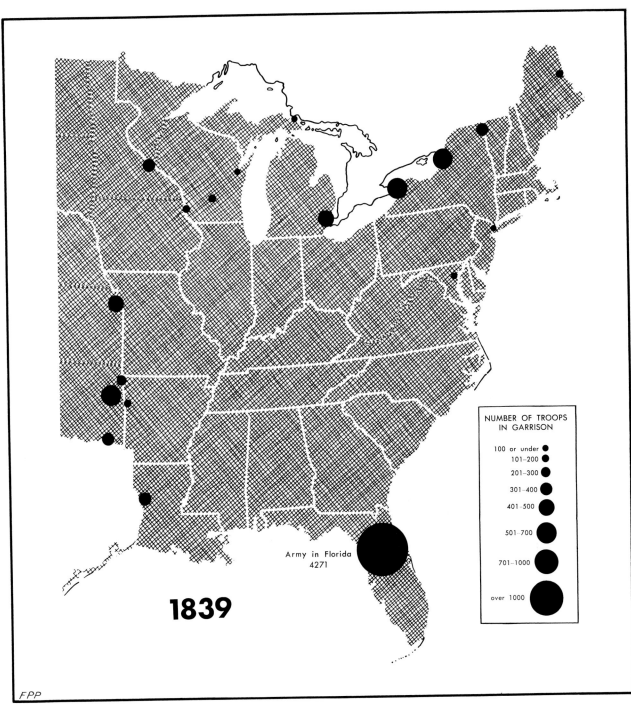

NUMBER OF TROOPS
IN GARRISON

100 or under
101–200
201–300
301–400
401–500
501–700
701–1000
over 1000

Army in Florida
4271

1839

FPP

77. Distribution of Regular Army Troops: 1839

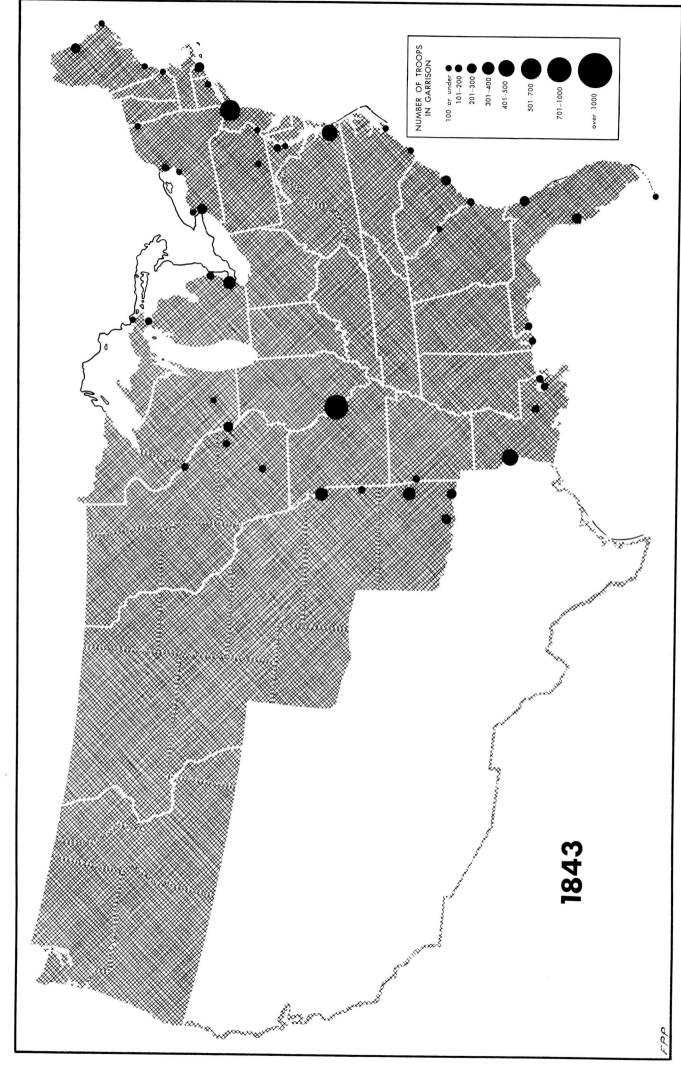

1843

78. Distribution of Regular Army Troops: 1843

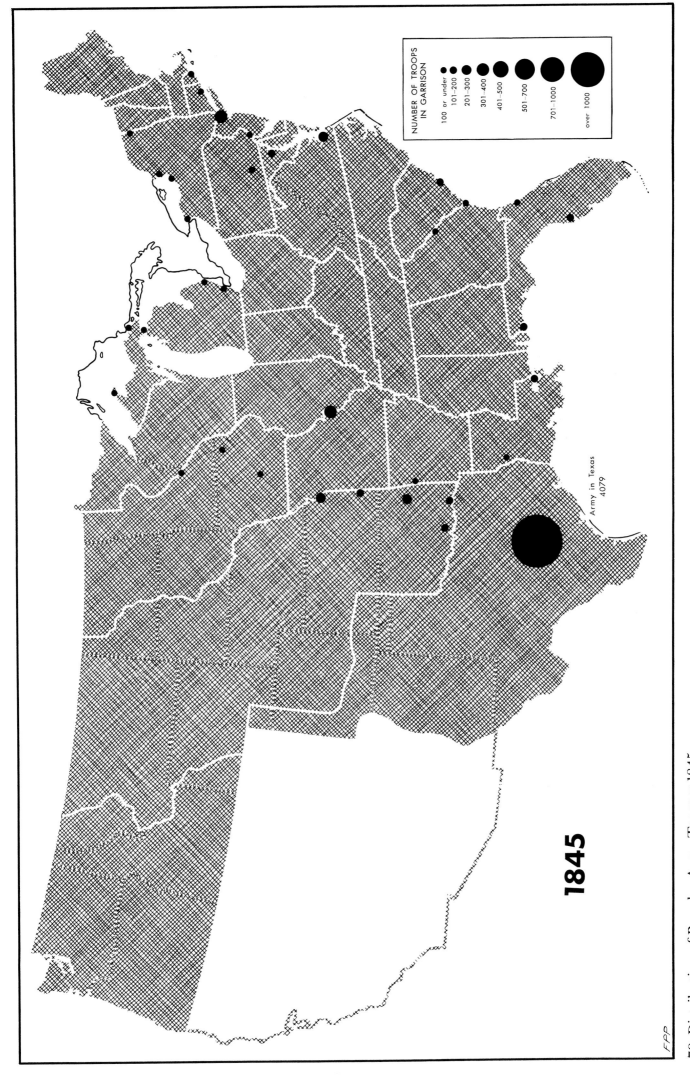

NUMBER OF TROOPS IN GARRISON

100 or under · 101–200 · 201–300 · 301–400 · 401–500 · 501–700 · 701–1000 · over 1000

Army in Texas 4079

1845

79. Distribution of Regular Army Troops: 1845

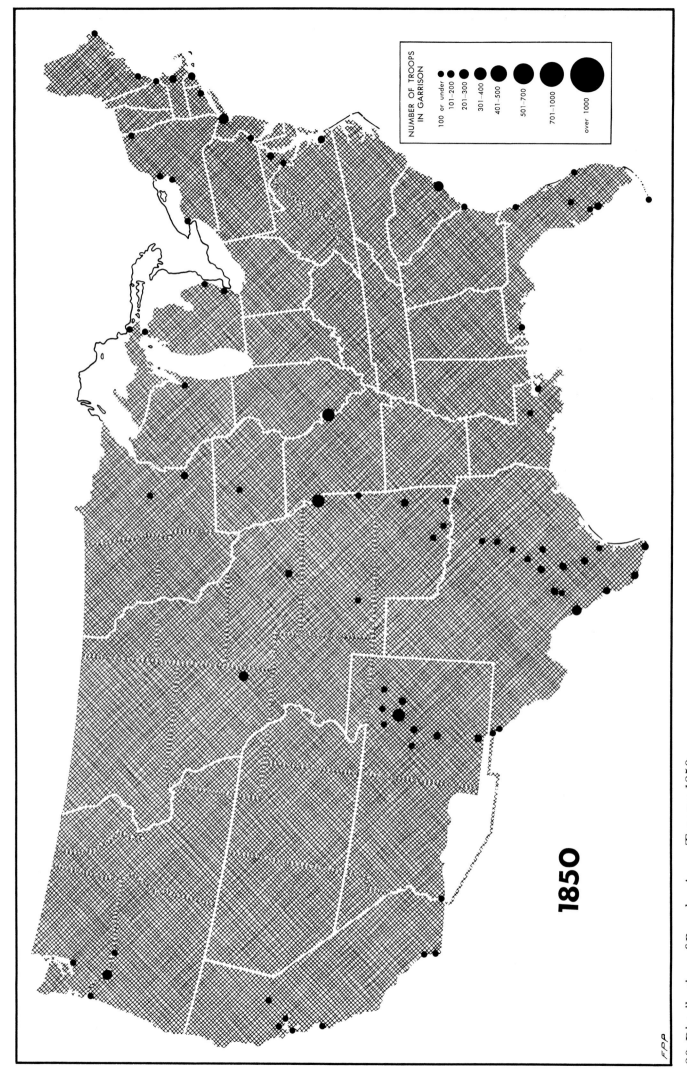

1850

80. Distribution of Regular Army Troops: 1850

NUMBER OF TROOPS
IN GARRISON

100 or under
101–200
201–300
301–400
401–500
501–700
701–1000
over 1000

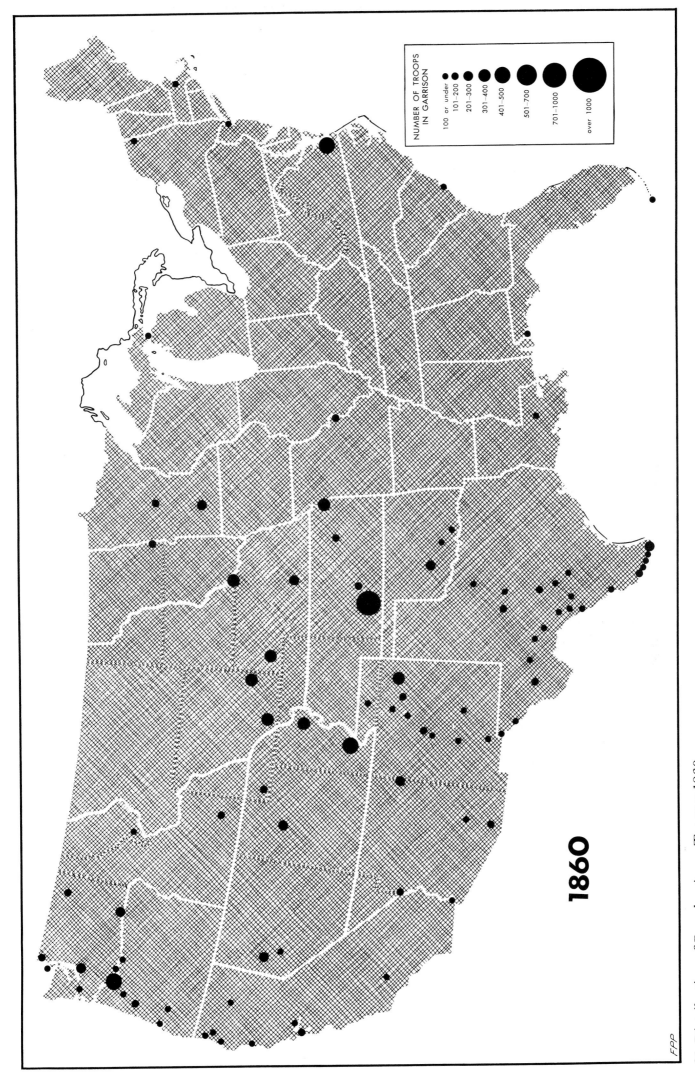

1860

81. Distribution of Regular Army Troops: 1860

NUMBER OF TROOPS IN GARRISON

100 or under · 101–200 · 201–300 · 301–400 · 401–500 · 501–700 · 701–1000 · over 1000

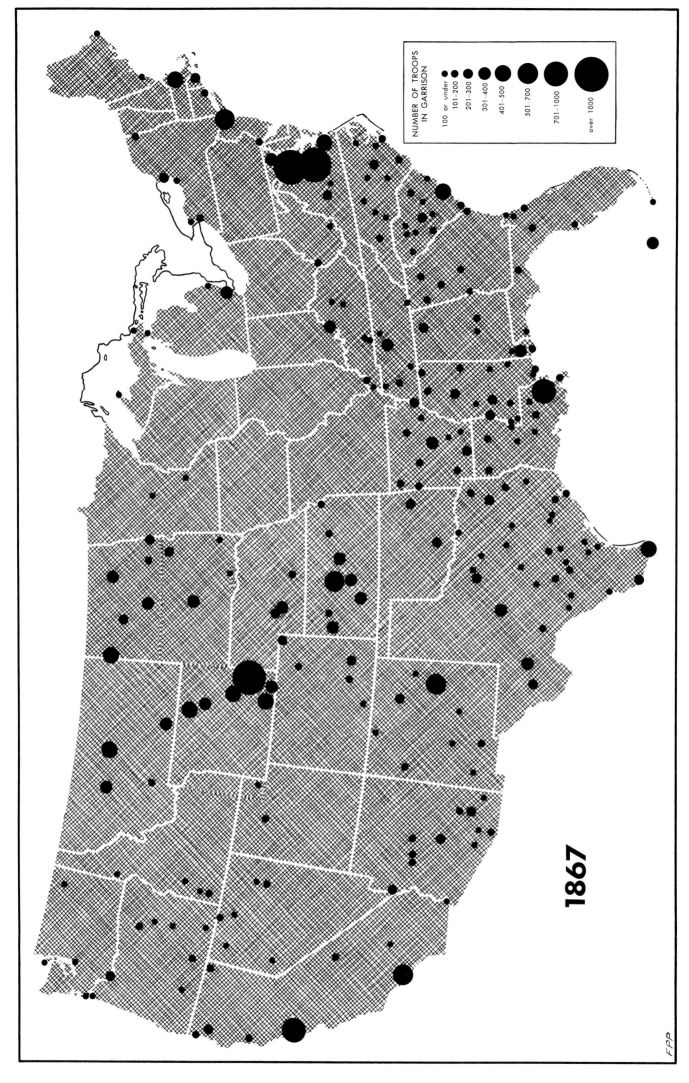

1867

NUMBER OF TROOPS
IN GARRISON

100 or under
101-200
201-300
301-400
401-500
501-700
701-1000
over 1000

FPP

82. Distribution of Regular Army Troops: 1867

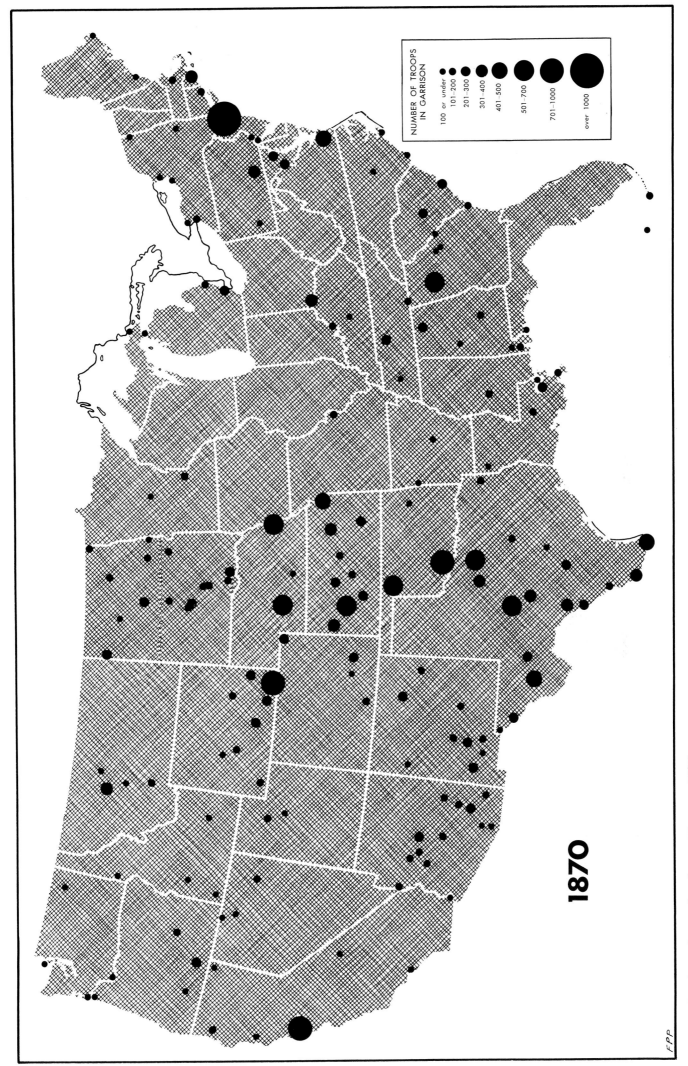

NUMBER OF TROOPS
IN GARRISON

100 or under	101–200	201–300	301–400	401–500	501–700	701–1000	over 1000

1870

F.P.P.

83. Distribution of Regular Army Troops: 1870

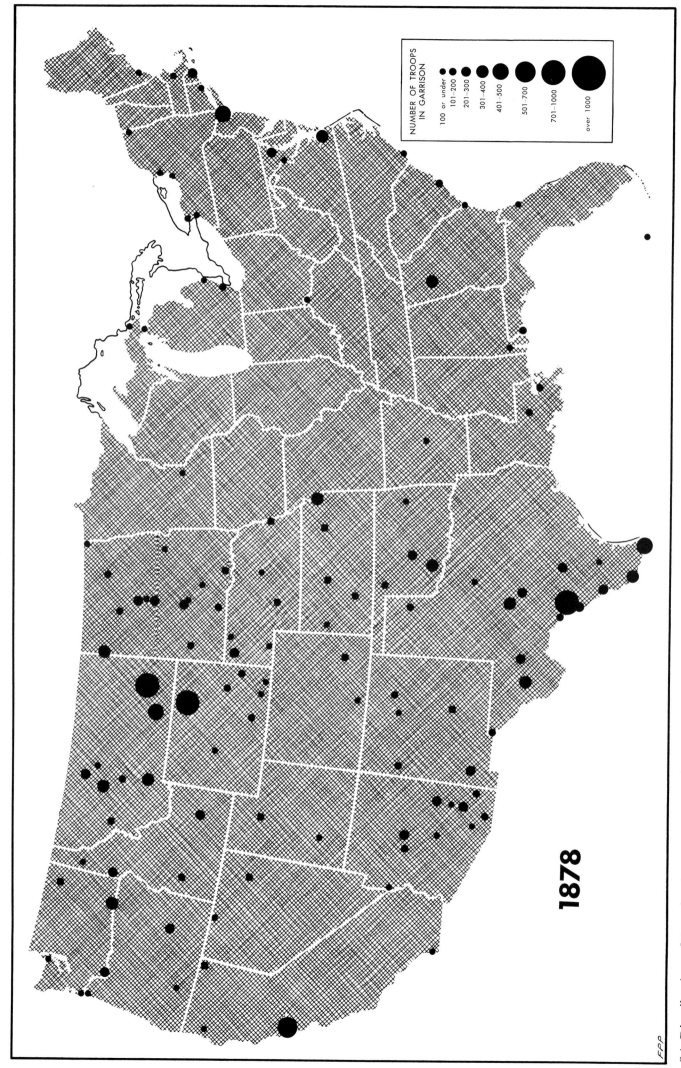

1878

84. Distribution of Regular Army Troops: 1878

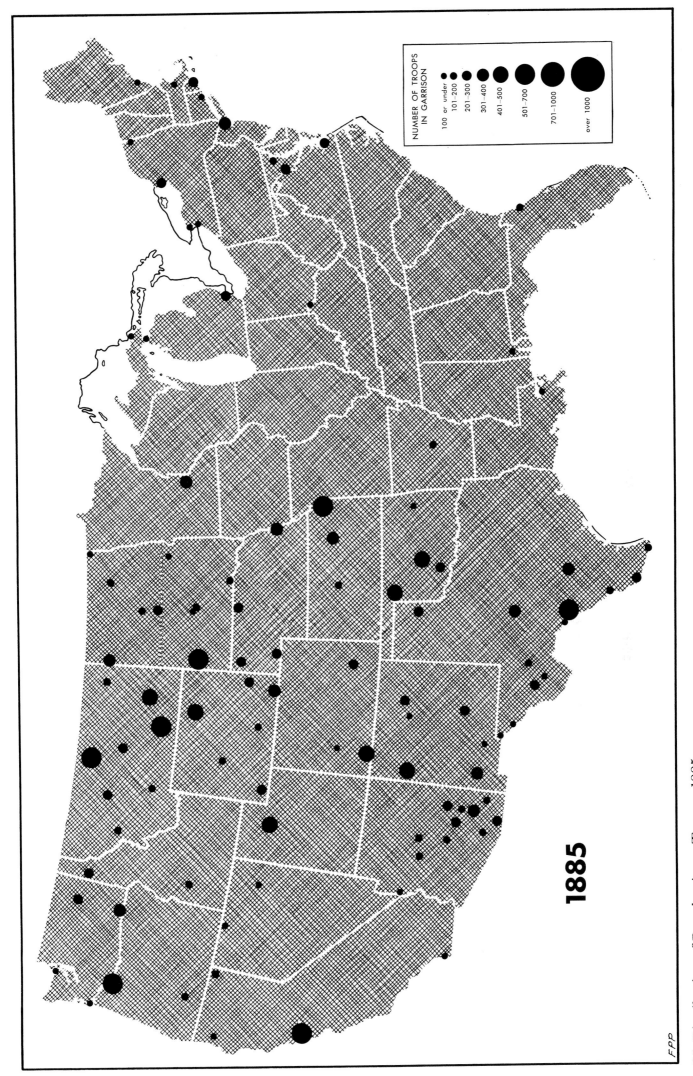

1885

NUMBER OF TROOPS
IN GARRISON

100 or under
101–200
201–300
301–400
401–500
501–700
701–1000
over 1000

85. Distribution of Regular Army Troops: 1885

FPP

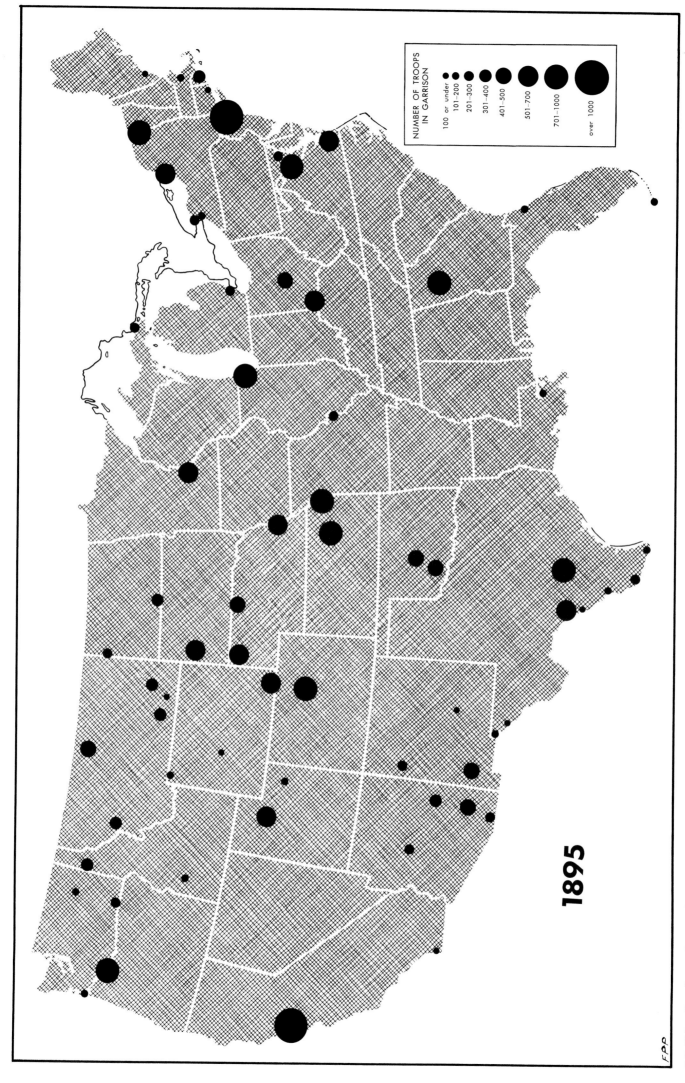

1895

86. Distribution of Regular Army Troops: 1895

NUMBER OF TROOPS IN GARRISON

100 or under
101–200
201–300
301–400
401–500
501–700
701–1000
over 1000

As the Indians in the East were moved to the West and as the United States acquired new territories, the federal installations and activities pertaining to Indians can be marked out on maps. The maps in this section follow the westward movement, from the early Indian frontier after the Revolutionary War to the frontiers in the Pacific Northwest and the Southwest after the mid-nineteenth century. These maps draw together a variety of information —army posts, military engagements, reservations, land cessions, and the like, for specific periods.

The last two maps deal with special topics in the Southwest: the enlargement of the Navajo Reservation and the division of the Hopi-Navajo Joint Use Area.

IX

Aspects of the Indian Frontier

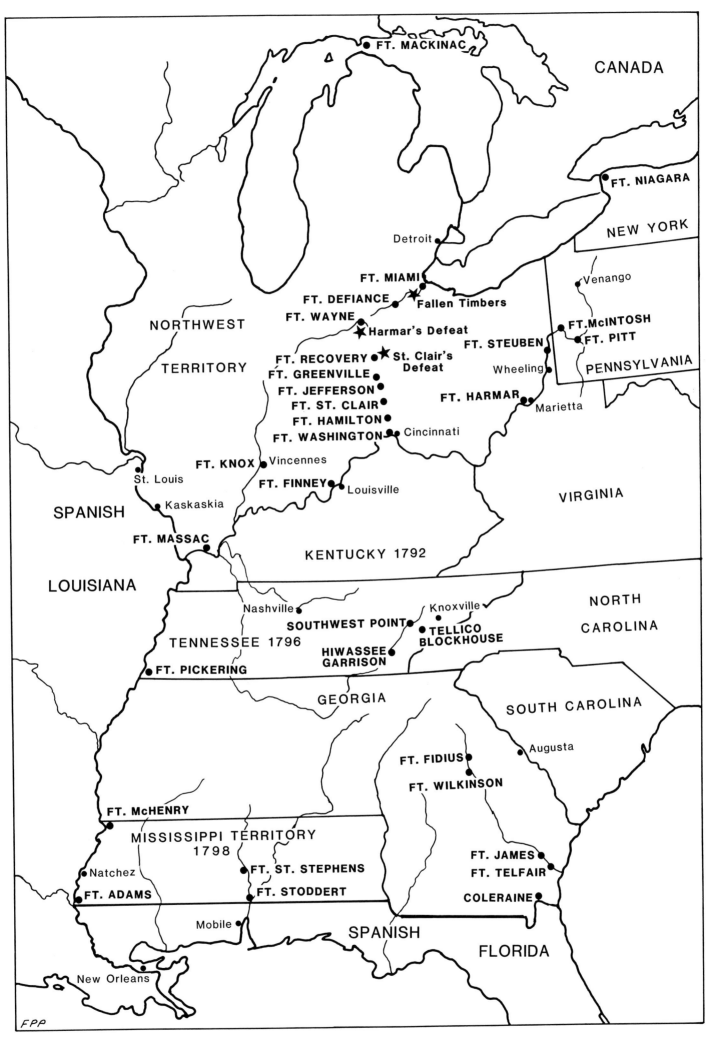

CANADA

FT. MACKINAC

FT. NIAGARA

NEW YORK

Detroit

Venango

FT. MIAMI

FT. DEFIANCE · Fallen Timbers

FT. WAYNE

★ Harmar's Defeat

FT.McINTOSH

FT. STEUBEN

FT. PITT

FT. RECOVERY · ★ St. Clair's Defeat

PENNSYLVANIA

NORTHWEST

TERRITORY

FT. GREENVILLE

Wheeling

FT. JEFFERSON

FT. ST. CLAIR

FT. HAMILTON

FT. HARMAR

FT. WASHINGTON · Cincinnati

Marietta

FT. KNOX · Vincennes

St. Louis

FT. FINNEY · Louisville

VIRGINIA

SPANISH

Kaskaskia

KENTUCKY 1792

FT. MASSAC

LOUISIANA

Nashville

Knoxville

NORTH

SOUTHWEST POINT

CAROLINA

TENNESSEE 1796

TELLICO BLOCKHOUSE

HIWASSEE GARRISON

FT. PICKERING

GEORGIA

SOUTH CAROLINA

Augusta

FT. FIDIUS

FT. WILKINSON

FT. McHENRY

MISSISSIPPI TERRITORY 1798

FT. JAMES

Natchez

FT. ST. STEPHENS

FT. TELFAIR

FT. ADAMS

FT. STODDERT

COLERAINE

Mobile

SPANISH

FLORIDA

New Orleans

FPP

87. Indian Frontier: 1785–1800

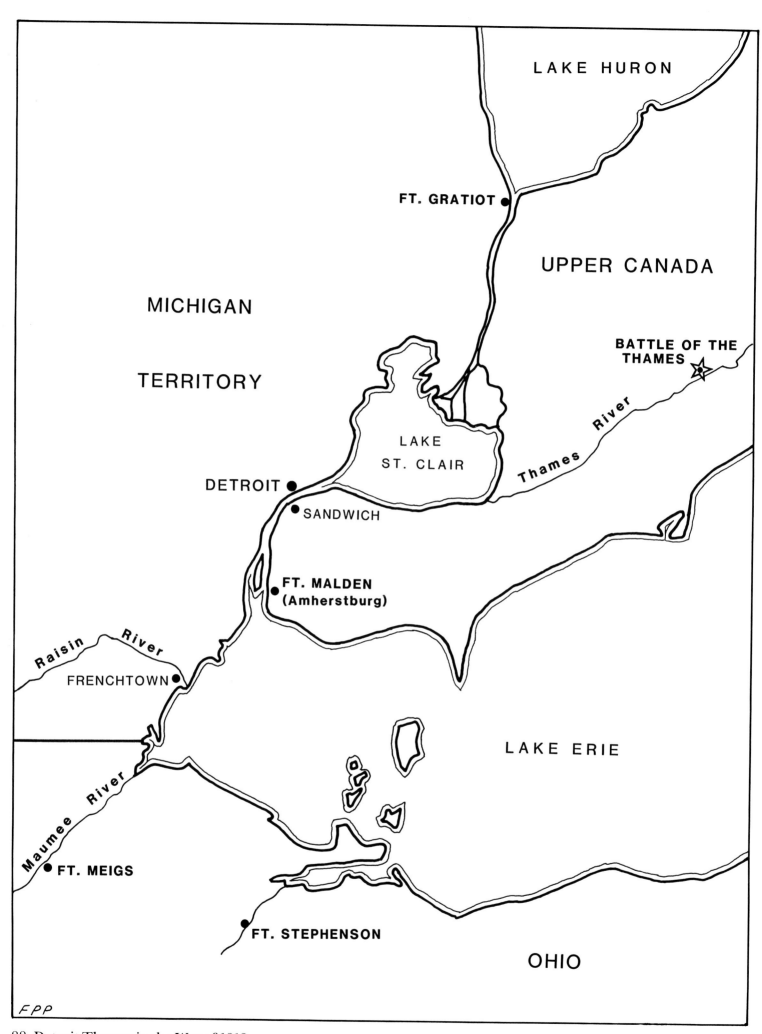

LAKE HURON

FT. GRATIOT

UPPER CANADA

MICHIGAN

TERRITORY

BATTLE OF THE
THAMES

LAKE
ST. CLAIR

Thames River

DETROIT

SANDWICH

FT. MALDEN
(Amherstburg)

Raisin River

FRENCHTOWN

LAKE ERIE

Maumee River

FT. MEIGS

FT. STEPHENSON

OHIO

FPP

88. Detroit Theater in the War of 1812

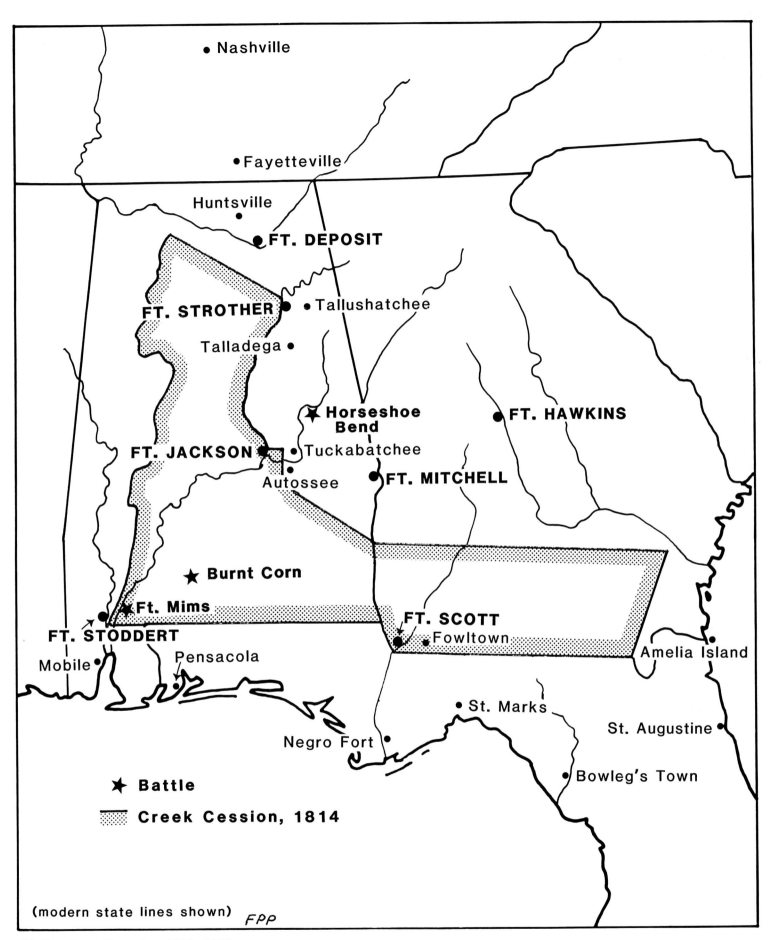

Nashville

Fayetteville

Huntsville

FT. DEPOSIT

FT. STROTHER

Tallushatchee

Talladega

★ **Horseshoe Bend**

FT. HAWKINS

FT. JACKSON

Tuckabatchee

Autossee

FT. MITCHELL

★ **Burnt Corn**

★ **Ft. Mims**

FT. STODDERT

Mobile

Pensacola

FT. SCOTT

Fowltown

Amelia Island

St. Marks

Negro Fort

St. Augustine

Bowleg's Town

★ **Battle**

▨ **Creek Cession, 1814**

(modern state lines shown) *FPP*

89. Southern Frontier: 1813–1818

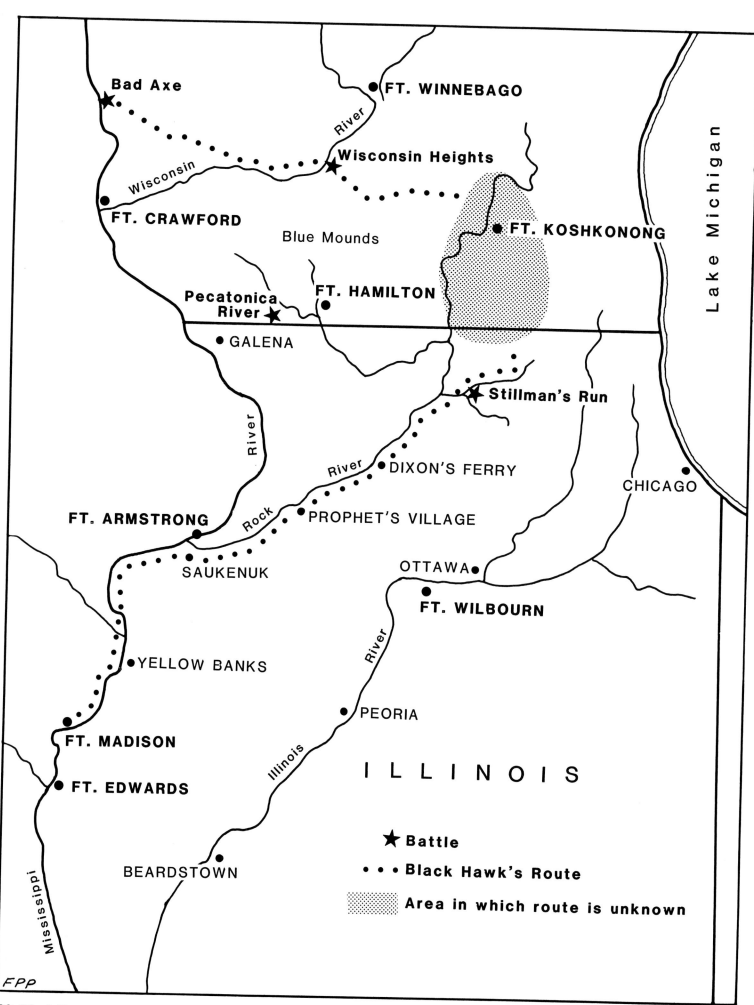

Lake Michigan

Bad Axe

● **FT. WINNEBAGO**

River

Wisconsin

Wisconsin Heights

● **FT. CRAWFORD**

Blue Mounds

● **FT. KOSHKONONG**

Pecatonica River ★

● **FT. HAMILTON**

● GALENA

River

★ **Stillman's Run**

River

● DIXON'S FERRY

FT. ARMSTRONG

Rock

● PROPHET'S VILLAGE

CHICAGO ●

SAUKENUK

OTTAWA ●

● **FT. WILBOURN**

● YELLOW BANKS

River

Illinois

● PEORIA

FT. MADISON

I L L I N O I S

● **FT. EDWARDS**

★ **Battle**

● ● ● **Black Hawk's Route**

Illinois

Mississippi

Area in which route is unknown

BEARDSTOWN ●

FPP

90. Black Hawk War

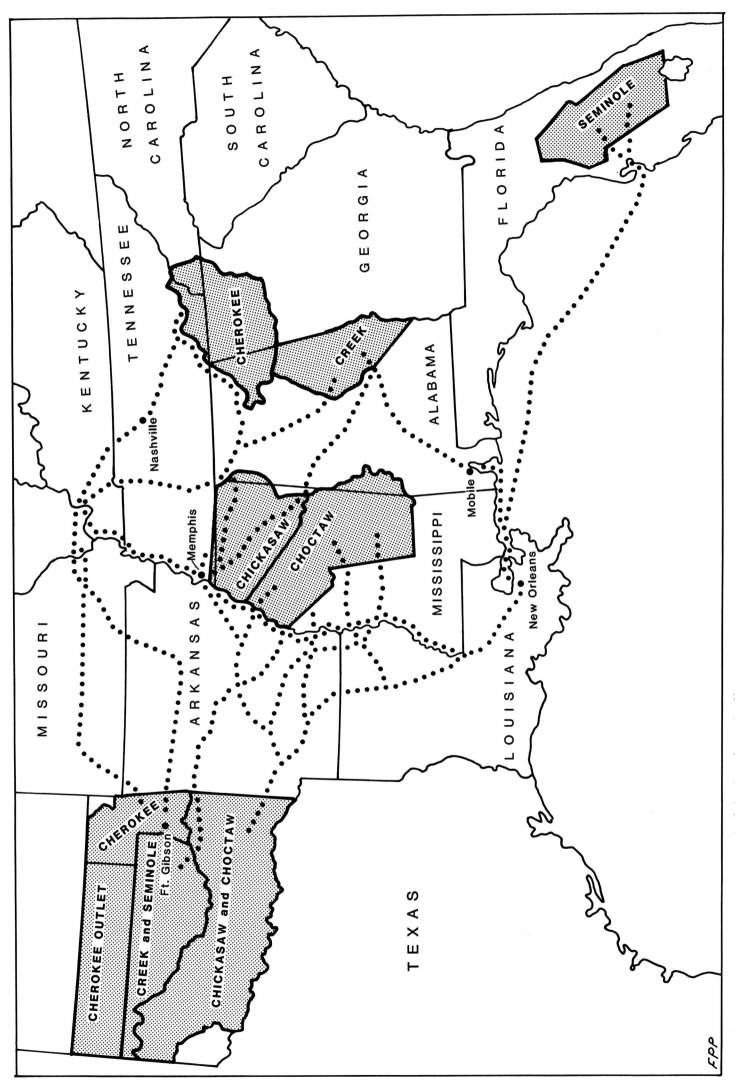

91. Emigration Routes in the Removal of the Southern Indians

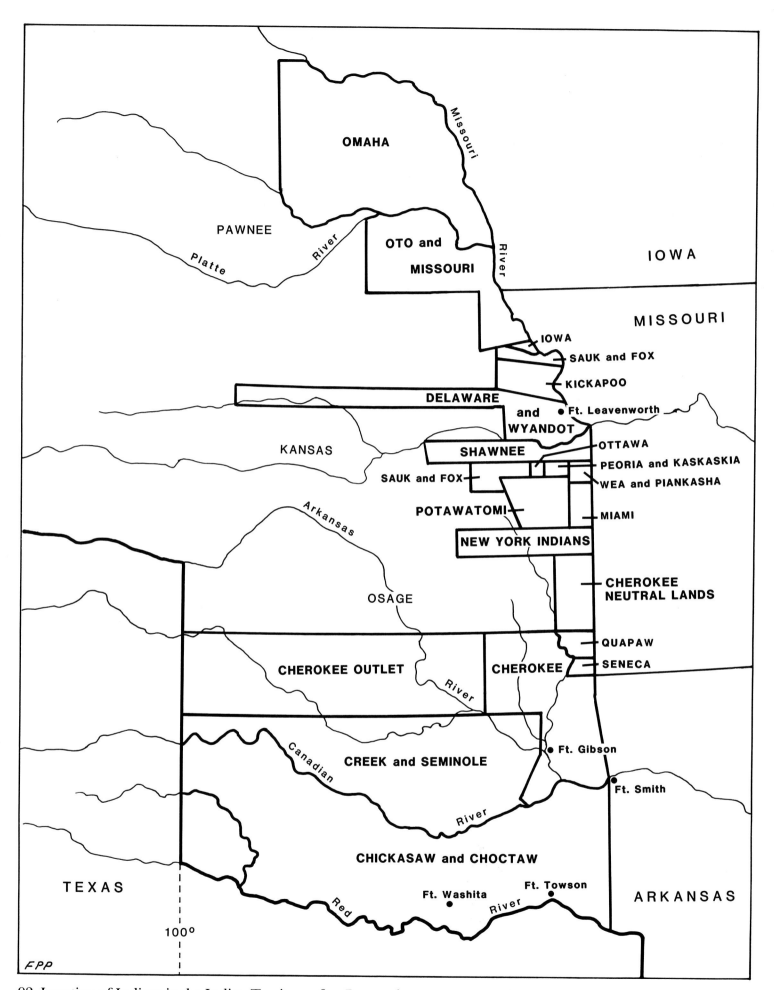

92. Location of Indians in the Indian Territory after Removal

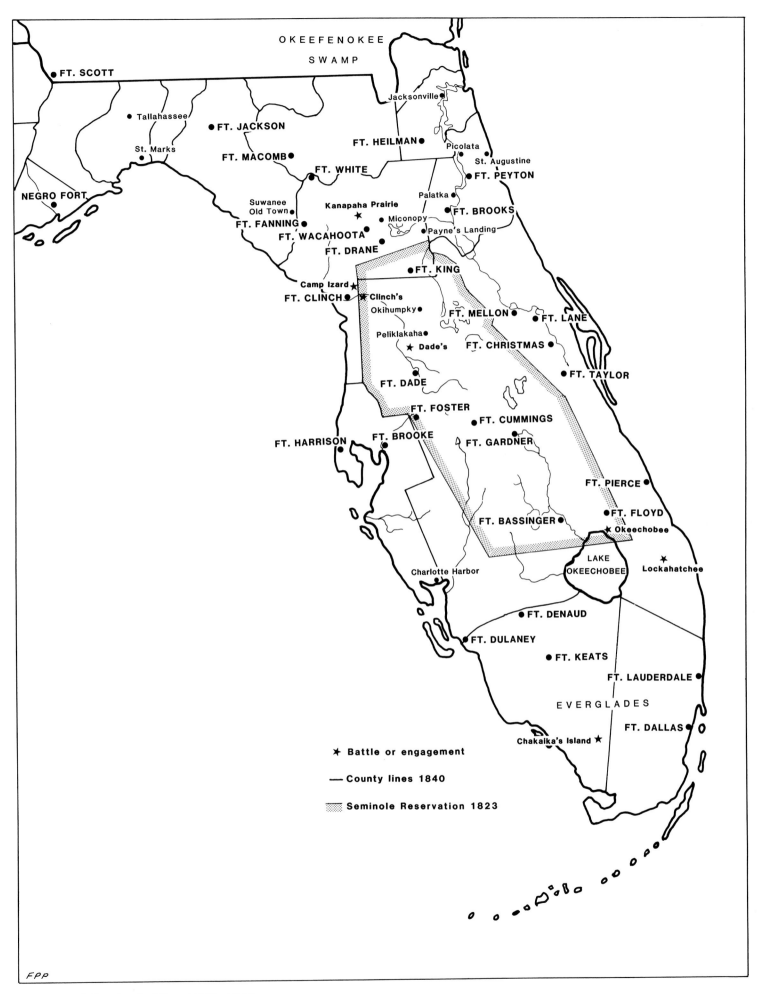

OKEEFENOKEE
SWAMP

● FT. SCOTT

● Tallahassee

● FT. JACKSON

St. Marks ●

FT. MACOMB ●

FT. WHITE

FT. HEILMAN ●

Jacksonville ●

Picolata

St. Augustine ●

● FT. PEYTON

NEGRO FORT

Suwanee
Old Town ●

Kanapaha Prairie ★

Palatka ●

● Miconopy

Payne's Landing

● FT. BROOKS

FT. FANNING ●

FT. WACAHOOTA ●

FT. DRANE ●

● FT. KING

Camp Izard ★

FT. CLINCH ● ★ Clinch's

Okihumpky ●

FT. MELLON ●

● FT. LANE

Peliklakaha ●

★ Dade's

FT. CHRISTMAS ●

● FT. DADE

● FT. TAYLOR

FT. FOSTER ●

● FT. CUMMINGS

FT. HARRISON ●

FT. BROOKE ●

FT. GARDNER ●

● FT. PIERCE

● FT. FLOYD

FT. BASSINGER ●

★ Okeechobee

LAKE
OKEECHOBEE

★ Lockahatchee

Charlotte Harbor ●

● FT. DENAUD

● FT. DULANEY

● FT. KEATS

FT. LAUDERDALE ●

EVERGLADES

● FT. DALLAS

Chakaika's Island ★

★ Battle or engagement

— County lines 1840

▒ Seminole Reservation 1823

FPP

93. Second Seminole War: 1835–1842

119

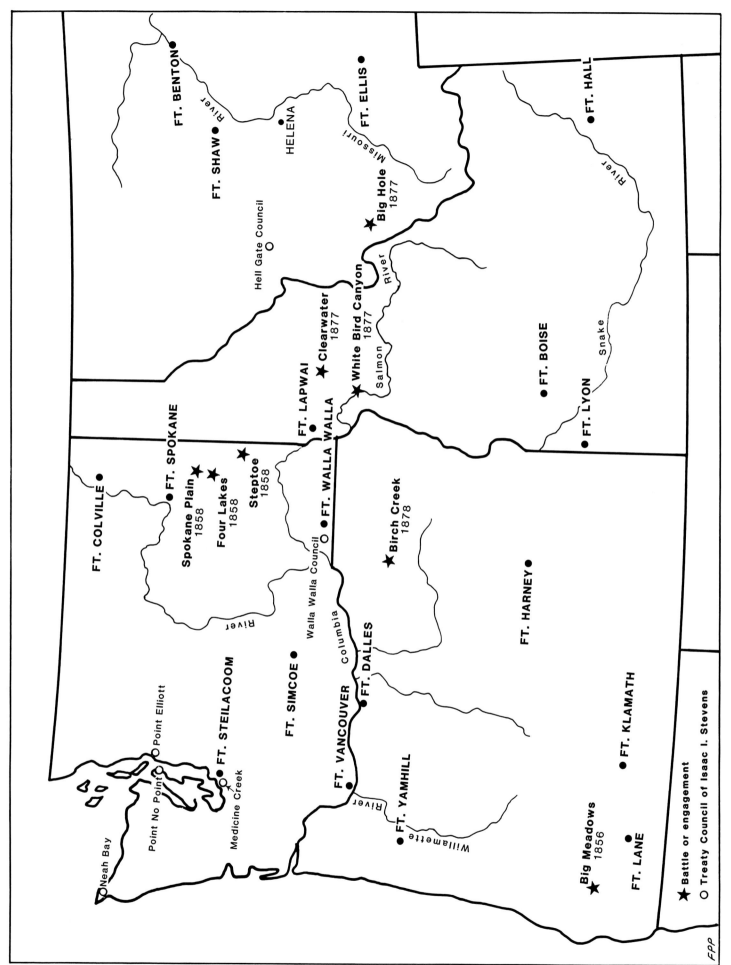

FT. BENTON ●

FT. SHAW ●   FT. ELLIS ●

HELENA ●

                                  Big Hole
                                  1877 ★

Hell Gate Council ○

FT. HALL ●

                 Clearwater
                 1877 ★
FT. LAPWAI ●   White Bird Canyon
                1877 ★

FT. SPOKANE ●

            Spokane Plain
            1858 ★
FT. COLVILLE ●   Four Lakes ★
            1858   Steptoe ★
                    1858

FT. BOISE ●

FT. LYON ●

Walla Walla Council ○   FT. WALLA WALLA

        Birch Creek ★
        1878

FT. HARNEY ●

FT. SIMCOE ●

Point Elliott ○
Point No Point ○
FT. STEILACOOM ●

Medicine Creek ○

FT. VANCOUVER ●   FT. DALLES ●

Neah Bay ○

FT. YAMHILL ●

FT. KLAMATH ●

Big Meadows ★
1856

FT. LANE ●

Columbia

River

River

Missouri River

Snake

Salmon River

Willamette River

★ Battle or engagement
○ Treaty Council of Isaac I. Stevens

94. Pacific Northwest: 1850–1880

FPP

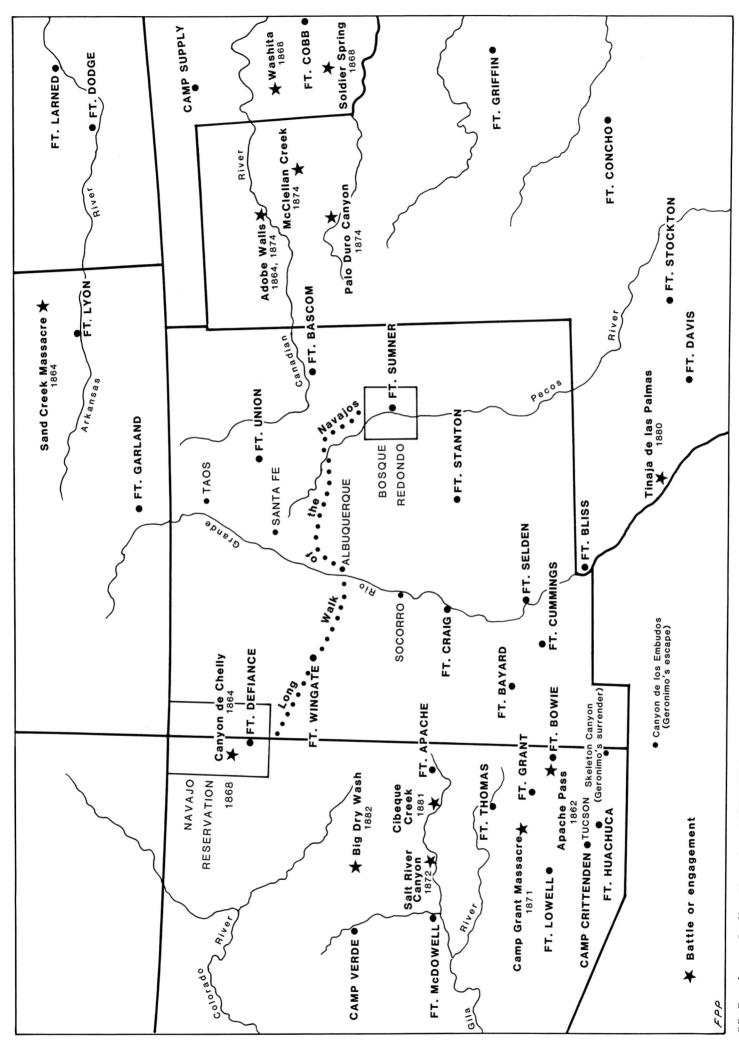

FT. LARNED ●

● FT. DODGE

CAMP SUPPLY ●

● Washita
  1868

● FT. COBB

Soldier Spring
  1868

● FT. GRIFFIN

★ Sand Creek Massacre
  1864

● FT. LYON

Arkansas

River

FT. GARLAND ●

● TAOS

River

McClellan Creek
  1874

Adobe Walls
  1864, 1874

Palo Duro Canyon
  1874

● FT. CONCHO

Canadian

● FT. BASCOM

● FT. UNION

● SANTA FE

Navajos

FT. SUMNER ●

BOSQUE
REDONDO

Pecos

River

● FT. STOCKTON

● FT. DAVIS

Tinaja de las Palmas
  1880
★

the

ALBUQUERQUE

● FT. STANTON

of

Grande

Rio

Walk

SOCORRO

● FT. SELDEN

● FT. BLISS

● FT. CUMMINGS

Canyon de Chelly
  1864

FT. DEFIANCE ●

★

Long

FT. WINGATE ●

FT. CRAIG ●

FT. BAYARD ●

● FT. BOWIE

● Canyon de los Embudos
  (Geronimo's escape)

NAVAJO
RESERVATION
  1868

Big Dry Wash
  1882 ★

Cibeque
Creek
  1881 ★

FT. APACHE ●

FT. THOMAS ●

FT. GRANT ●

Skeleton Canyon
(Geronimo's surrender)

Salt River
Canyon
  1872 ★

FT. McDOWELL ●

Camp Grant Massacre
  1871 ★

Apache Pass
  1862 ★

● TUCSON

CAMP CRITTENDEN ●

CAMP VERDE ●

River

Colorado

River

Gila

FT. LOWELL ●

FT. HUACHUCA ●

★ Battle or engagement

95. Southwest Indian Frontier: 1860–1890

FPP

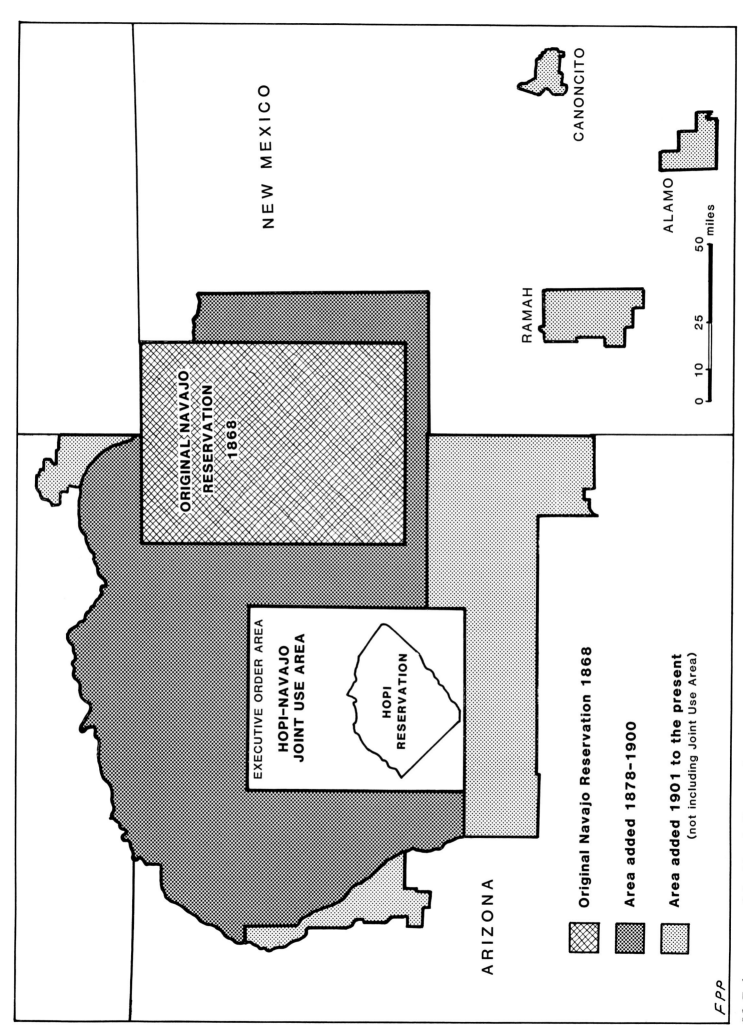

NEW MEXICO

CANONCITO

ALAMO

RAMAH

NAVAJO RESERVATION 1868

ORIGINAL NAVAJO RESERVATION 1868

EXECUTIVE ORDER AREA

HOPI-NAVAJO JOINT USE AREA

HOPI RESERVATION

ARIZONA

0   10   25   50
miles

Original Navajo Reservation 1868

Area added 1878–1900

Area added 1901 to the present
(not including Joint Use Area)

FPP

96. Enlargement of the Navajo Reservation

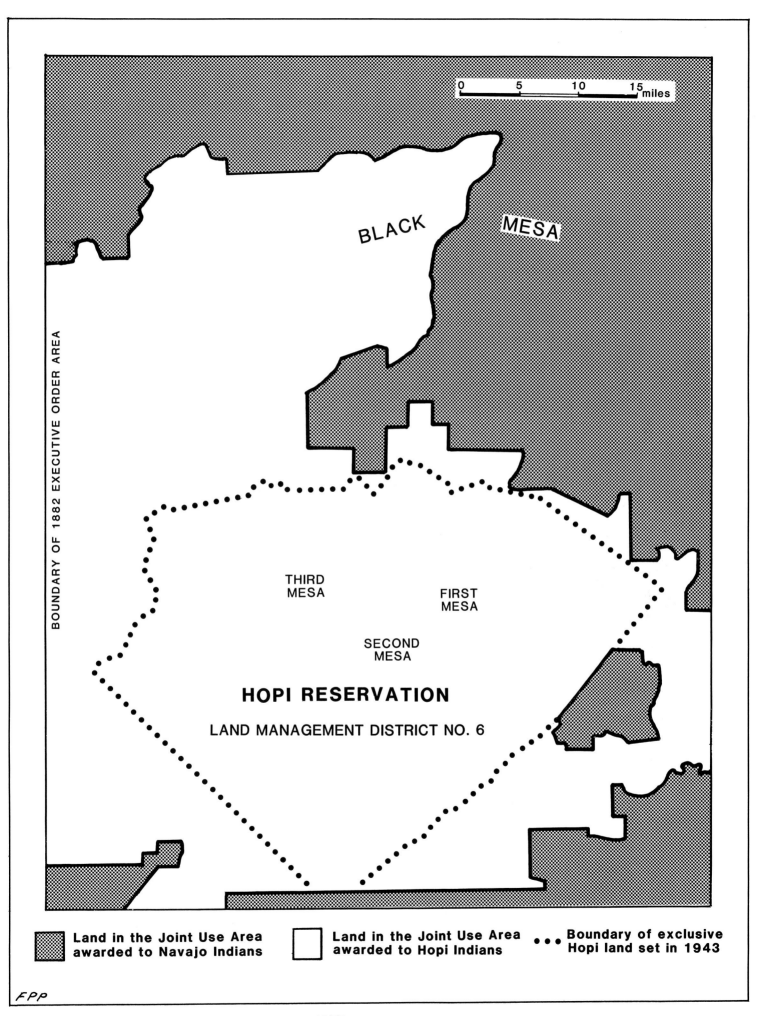

Within the map:

0 5 10 15 miles

BLACK MESA

BOUNDARY OF 1882 EXECUTIVE ORDER AREA

THIRD
MESA

FIRST
MESA

SECOND
MESA

HOPI RESERVATION

LAND MANAGEMENT DISTRICT NO. 6

Legend:

Land in the Joint Use Area awarded to Navajo Indians

Land in the Joint Use Area awarded to Hopi Indians

••• Boundary of exclusive Hopi land set in 1943

FPP

97. Division of the Hopi-Navajo Joint Use Area: 1977

The cartographer Rafael D. Palacios produced a series of twenty-one striking maps depicting military encounters with the Indians in the post–Civil War era for Ralph K. Andrist's *The Long Death: The Last Days of the Plains Indians* (1964). These maps present in careful detail the geographical setting of military engagements, sometimes with multiple maps for a single event (for example, the Battle of the Little Bighorn).

This portfolio presents a dozen of Palacios's maps, from the Sioux uprising of 1862 to Wounded Knee in 1890. They portray aspects of the army and the Indian frontier not shown on other maps of the atlas.

X

A Portfolio of Maps by Rafael D. Palacios

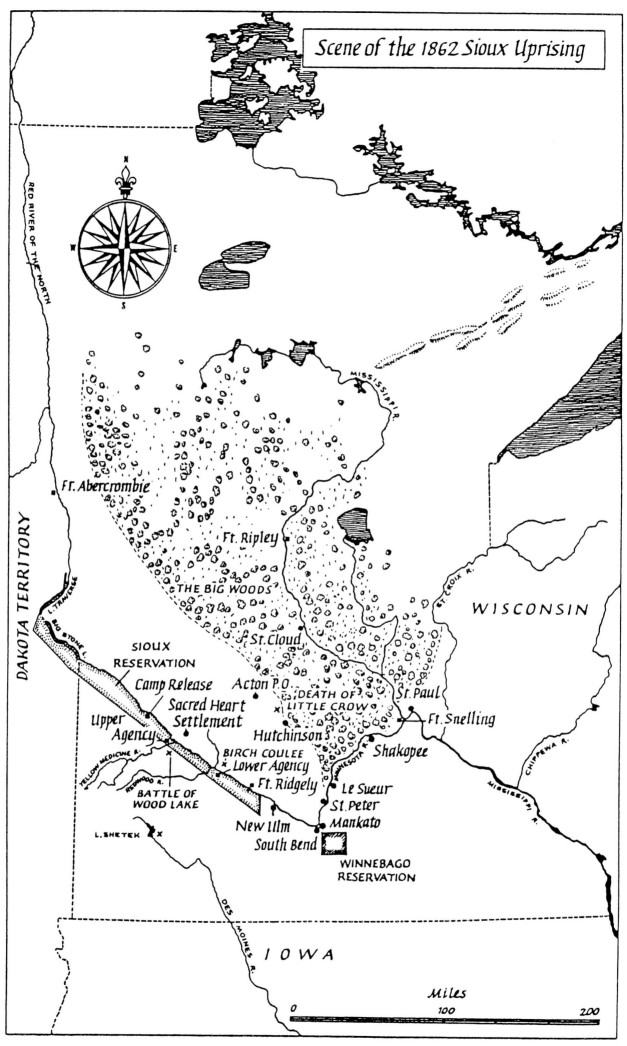

Scene of the 1862 Sioux Uprising

98. Scene of the 1862 Sioux Uprising

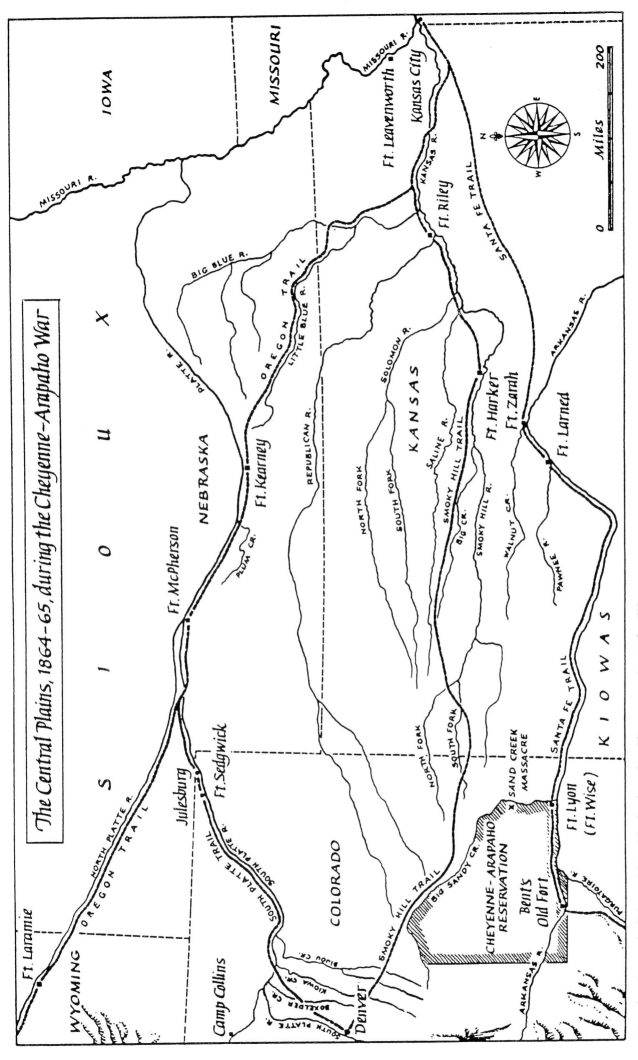

99. The Central Plains, 1864–65, during the Cheyenne-Arapaho War

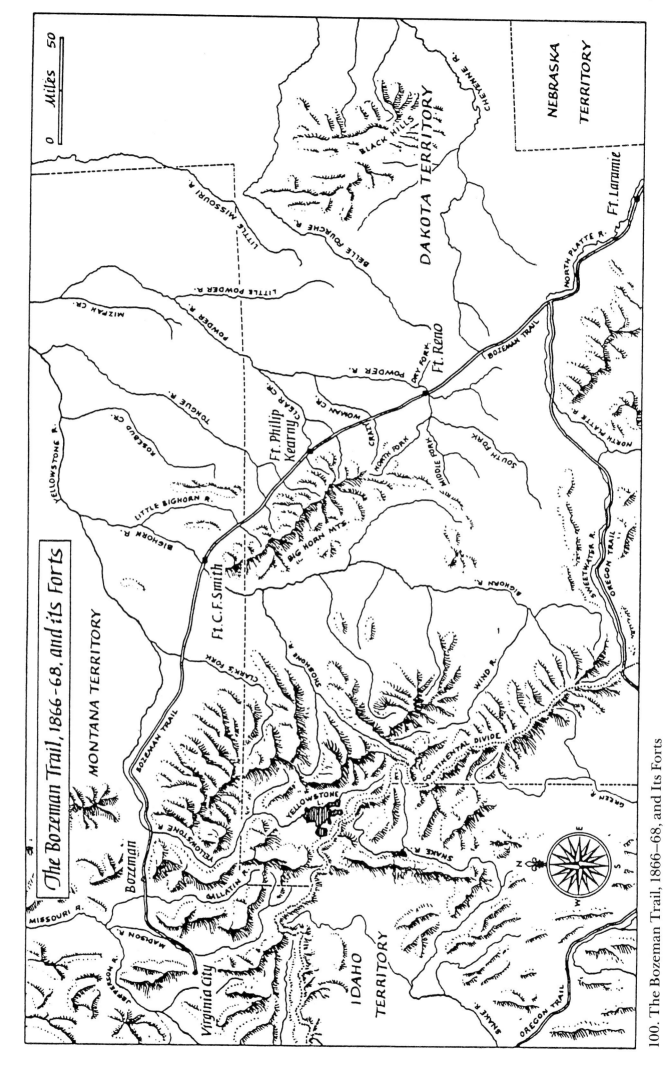

The Bozeman Trail, 1866–68, and its Forts

NEBRASKA TERRITORY

DAKOTA TERRITORY

MONTANA TERRITORY

IDAHO TERRITORY

Missouri R.
Jefferson R.
Madison R.
Gallatin R.
Yellowstone R.
Clark's Fork
Shoshone R.
Snake R.
Green R.
Wind R.
Bighorn R.
Sweetwater R.
North Platte R.
South Fork
Middle Fork
North Fork
Crazy
Woman Cr.
Clear Cr.
Powder R.
Dry Fork
Tongue R.
Rosebud Cr.
Little Bighorn R.
Bighorn R.
Little Powder R.
Mizpah Cr.
Little Missouri R.
Belle Fourche R.
Cheyenne R.
North Platte R.

BLACK HILLS
BIG HORN MTS.
CONTINENTAL DIVIDE
YELLOWSTONE

Virginia City
Bozeman
Ft. C. F. Smith
Ft. Philip Kearny
Ft. Reno
Ft. Laramie

BOZEMAN TRAIL
OREGON TRAIL

Miles
0   50

N S E W

100. The Bozeman Trail, 1866–68, and Its Forts

128

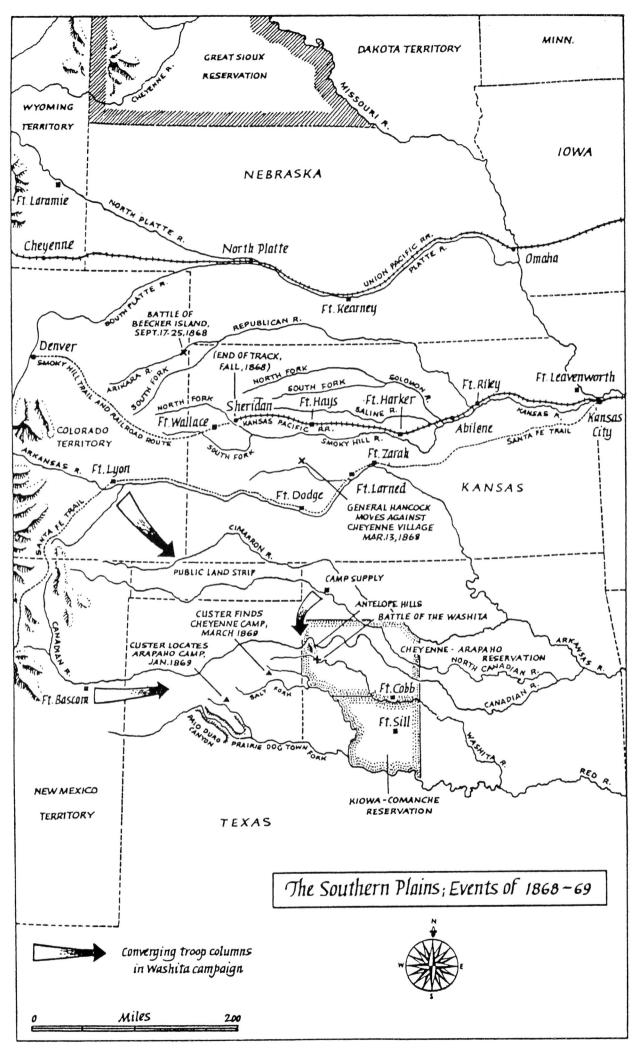

The Southern Plains; Events of 1868-69

Converging troop columns
in Washita campaign

Miles

101. The Southern Plains: Events of 1868–69

129

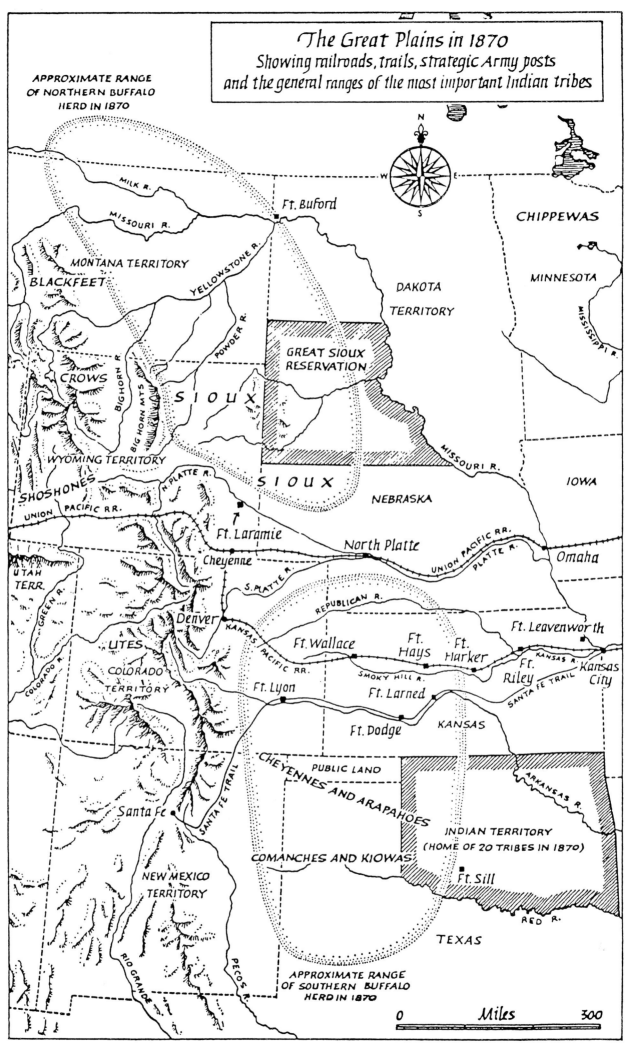

The Great Plains in 1870
Showing railroads, trails, strategic Army posts and the general ranges of the most important Indian tribes

APPROXIMATE RANGE OF NORTHERN BUFFALO HERD IN 1870

CHIPPEWAS

MILK R.

MISSOURI R.

MONTANA TERRITORY

BLACKFEET

YELLOWSTONE R.

DAKOTA TERRITORY

MINNESOTA

MISSISSIPPI R.

CROWS

BIGHORN R.

BIG HORN MTS

POWDER R.

S I O U X

GREAT SIOUX RESERVATION

WYOMING TERRITORY

SHOSHONES

N. PLATTE R.

S I O U X

MISSOURI R.

IOWA

UNION PACIFIC RR.

NEBRASKA

Ft. Laramie

North Platte

UNION PACIFIC RR.

PLATTE R.

Omaha

Cheyenne

UTAH TERR.

GREEN R.

S. PLATTE R.

Republican R.

UTES

Denver

KANSAS PACIFIC RR.

Ft. Wallace

Ft. Hays

Ft. Harker

Ft. Leavenworth

KANSAS R.

Ft. Riley

Kansas City

COLORADO R.

COLORADO TERRITORY

SMOKY HILL R.

SANTA FE TRAIL

Ft. Lyon

Ft. Larned

Ft. Dodge

KANSAS

SANTA FE TRAIL

CHEYENNES AND ARAPAHOES

PUBLIC LAND

ARKANSAS R.

Santa Fe

NEW MEXICO TERRITORY

COMANCHES AND KIOWAS

INDIAN TERRITORY (HOME OF 20 TRIBES IN 1870)

Ft. Sill

RIO GRANDE

PECOS R.

RED R.

TEXAS

APPROXIMATE RANGE OF SOUTHERN BUFFALO HERD IN 1870

0   Miles   300

102. The Great Plains in 1870

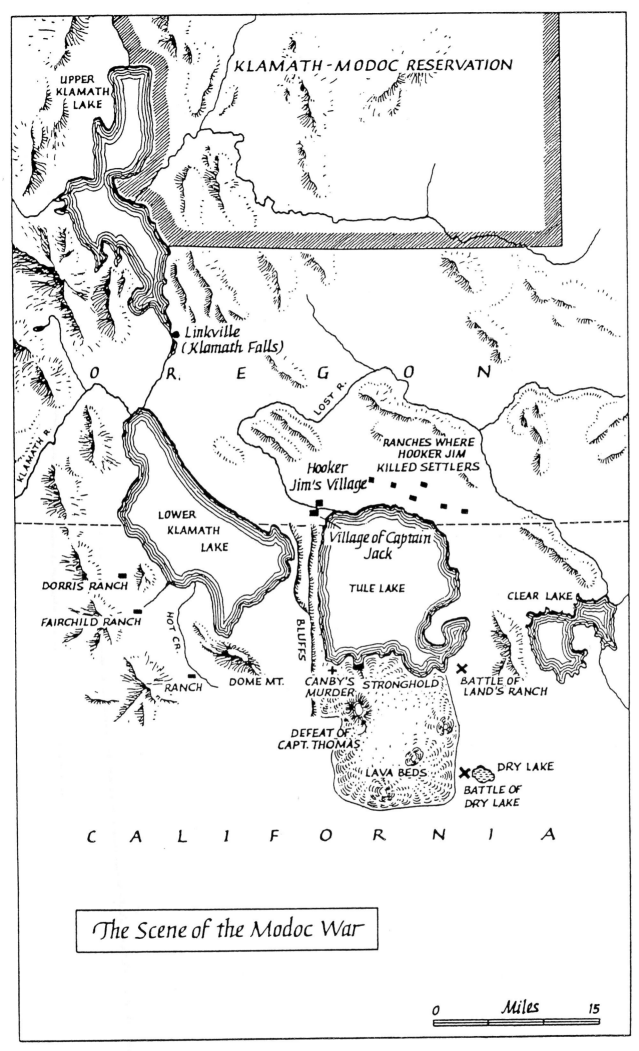

KLAMATH-MODOC RESERVATION

UPPER
KLAMATH
LAKE

Linkville
(Klamath Falls)

O   R.   E   G   O   N

KLAMATH R.

LOST R.

RANCHES WHERE
HOOKER JIM
KILLED SETTLERS

Hooker
Jim's Village

LOWER
KLAMATH
LAKE

Village of Captain
Jack

TULE LAKE

CLEAR LAKE

DORRIS RANCH

FAIRCHILD RANCH

HOT CR.

BLUFFS

RANCH

DOME MT.

Canby's
Murder

STRONGHOLD

BATTLE OF
LAND'S RANCH

DEFEAT OF
CAPT. THOMAS

LAVA BEDS

DRY LAKE

BATTLE OF
DRY LAKE

C   A   L   I   F   O   R   N   I   A

The Scene of the Modoc War

0   Miles   15

103. The Scene of the Modoc War

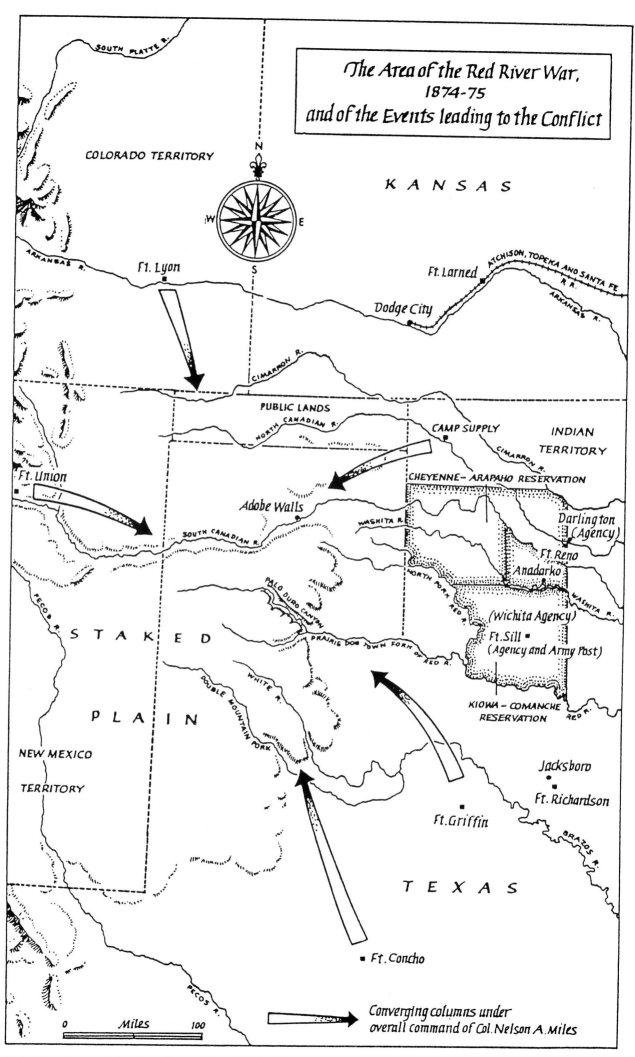

The Area of the Red River War, 1874-75 and of the Events leading to the Conflict

COLORADO TERRITORY

KANSAS

SOUTH PLATTE R.

ARKANSAS R.

Ft. Lyon

Ft. Larned

ATCHISON, TOPEKA AND SANTA FE R.R.

Dodge City

ARKANSAS R.

CIMARRON R.

PUBLIC LANDS

NORTH CANADIAN R.

CAMP SUPPLY

INDIAN TERRITORY

CIMARRON R.

Ft. Union

CHEYENNE - ARAPAHO RESERVATION

Adobe Walls

SOUTH CANADIAN R.

WASHITA R.

Darlington (Agency)

Ft. Reno

Anadarko

NORTH FORK RED R.

WASHITA R.

(Wichita Agency)

PALO DURO CANYON

S T A K E D

PECOS R.

PRAIRIE DOG TOWN FORK OF RED R.

Ft. Sill (Agency and Army Post)

WHITE R.

DOUBLE MOUNTAIN FORK

P L A I N

KIOWA - COMANCHE RESERVATION

RED R.

NEW MEXICO TERRITORY

Jacksboro

Ft. Richardson

Ft. Griffin

T E X A S

BRAZOS R.

Ft. Concho

PECOS R.

0   Miles   100

Converging columns under overall command of Col. Nelson A. Miles

104. The Area of the Red River War, 1874–75

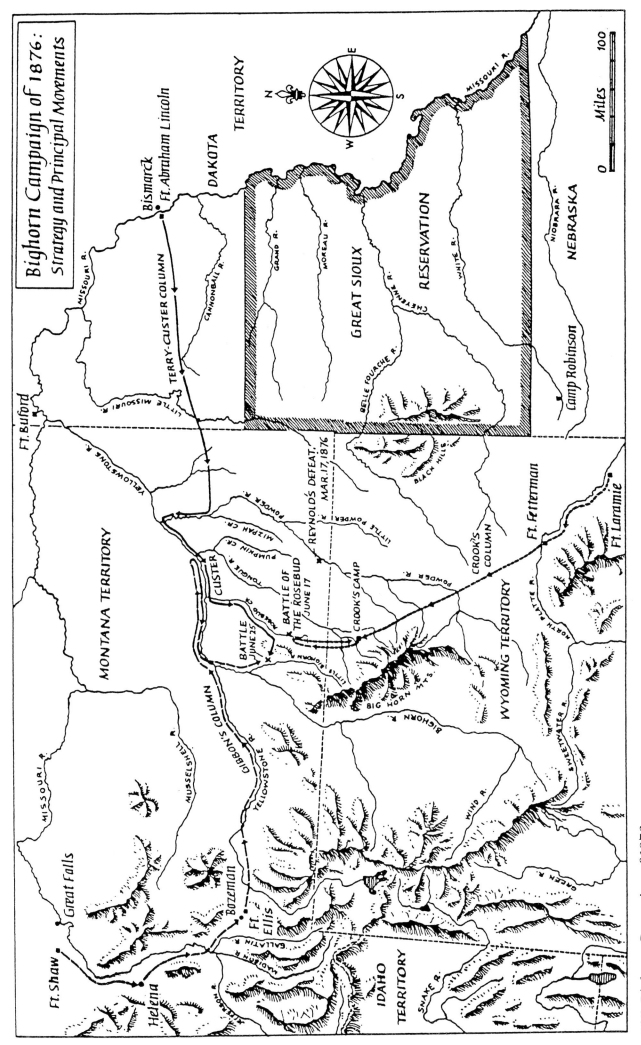

Bighorn Campaign of 1876:
Strategy and Principal Movements

Ft. Shaw

Great Falls

Helena

Ft. Buford

MISSOURI R.

MONTANA TERRITORY

MUSSELSHELL R.

Bozeman

Ft. Ellis

GALLATIN R.

MADISON R.

IDAHO TERRITORY

SNAKE R.

GIBBON'S COLUMN

YELLOWSTONE R.

CUSTER

PUMPKIN CR.

MIZPAH CR.

TONGUE R.

POWDER R.

BATTLE JUNE 25

BATTLE OF THE ROSEBUD JUNE 17

ROSEBUD CR.

LITTLE BIGHORN

CROOK'S CAMP

BIG HORN MTS.

BIGHORN R.

WIND R.

GREEN R.

REYNOLD'S DEFEAT, MAR. 17, 1876

LITTLE POWDER R.

POWDER R.

CROOK'S COLUMN

SWEETWATER R.

NORTH PLATTE R.

WYOMING TERRITORY

Ft. Fetterman

Ft. Laramie

BLACK HILLS

BELLE FOUACHE R.

Bismarck

Ft. Abraham Lincoln

DAKOTA TERRITORY

TERRY-CUSTER COLUMN

CANNONBALL R.

LITTLE MISSOURI R.

MISSOURI R.

GRAND R.

MOREAU R.

CHEYENNE R.

GREAT SIOUX RESERVATION

WHITE R.

NIOBRARA R.

NEBRASKA

Camp Robinson

MISSOURI R.

N E S W

Miles

0   100

105. Bighorn Campaign of 1876

106. Chief Joseph's Retreat, 1877

Flight of the Cheyennes

MONTANA TERRITORY

MISSOURI R.

BAND IS BROUGHT TO FORT KEOGH NEAR JUNCTION OF TONGUE WITH YELLOWSTONE

YELLOWSTONE R.

Ft. Keogh

Bismarck

NORTHERN PACIFIC RR.

Ft. Abraham Lincoln

MINNESOTA

LITTLE WOLF'S BAND IS CAPTURED BY U.S. TROOPS

CANNONBALL R.

SIOUX RESERVATION

DAKOTA TERRITORY

WYOMING TERR.

BELLE FOURCHE R.

CHEYENNE R.

THE LAST OF THE ESCAPING CHEYENNES ARE BROUGHT TO BAY AND KILLED OR CAPTURED

WHITE R.

Pine Ridge Agency

MISSOURI R.

CAPTIVITY AND ESCAPE FROM CAMP ROBINSON

Camp Robinson

IOWA

Ft. Laramie

NIOBRARA R.

LITTLE WOLF TAKES HIS BAND THROUGH THE WINTER ON LOST CHOKECHERRY CREEK

DULL KNIFE'S BAND CAPTURED BY ARMY FORCES

NORTH PLATTE R.

THE BANDS OF DULL KNIFE AND LITTLE WOLF SEPARATE

Omaha

NEBRASKA

PLATTE R.

UNION PACIFIC RR.

SOUTH PLATTE R.

Ft. Kearney

MISSOURI R.

REPUBLICAN R.

Denver

COLORADO

KANSAS PACIFIC RR.

Ft. Leavenworth

SOLOMON R.

Ft. Riley

Topeka

Ft. Wallace

Ft. Hays

KANSAS R.

Kansas City

Pueblo

SMOKY HILL R.

Ft. Larned

Ft. Lyon

ATCHISON, TOPEKA AND SANTA FE RR.

ARKANSAS R.

KANSAS

Dodge City

PUBLIC LAND

NORTH CANADIAN R.

INDIAN TERRITORY

ARKANSAS R.

CIMARRON R.

Ft. Reno

CANADIAN R.

TEXAS

CHEYENNE - ARAPAHO RESERVATION

Ft. Sill

MISSOURI

0 Miles 200

107. Flight of the Cheyennes, 1879

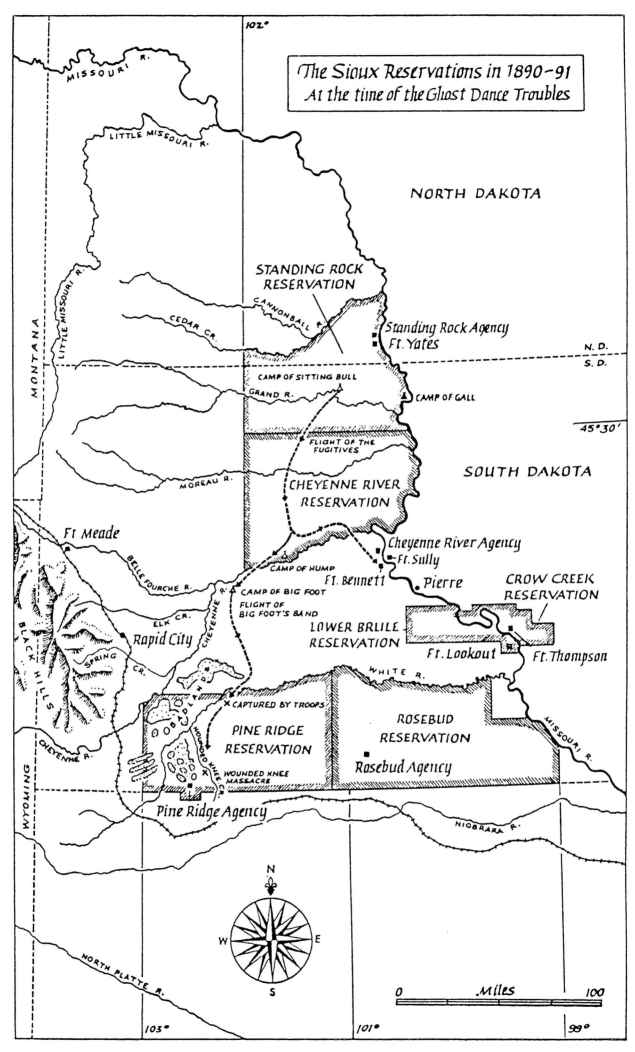

The Sioux Reservations in 1890–91
At the time of the Ghost Dance Troubles

MISSOURI R.

LITTLE MISSOURI R.

NORTH DAKOTA

MONTANA

LITTLE MISSOURI R.

CEDAR CR.

CANNONBALL R.

STANDING ROCK
RESERVATION

Standing Rock Agency
Ft. Yates

N. D.
S. D.

CAMP OF SITTING BULL

GRAND R.

CAMP OF GALL

45°30'

FLIGHT OF THE
FUGITIVES

SOUTH DAKOTA

MOREAU R.

CHEYENNE RIVER
RESERVATION

Ft. Meade

Cheyenne River Agency
Ft. Sully

BELLE FOURCHE R.

CAMP OF HUMP

Ft. Bennett

Pierre

CROW CREEK
RESERVATION

CHEYENNE R.

CAMP OF BIG FOOT

ELK CR.

FLIGHT OF
BIG FOOT'S BAND

LOWER BRULE
RESERVATION

BLACK HILLS

SPRING CR.

Rapid City

Ft. Lookout

Ft. Thompson

WHITE R.

MISSOURI R.

X CAPTURED BY TROOPS

BADLANDS

PINE RIDGE
RESERVATION

ROSEBUD
RESERVATION

CHEYENNE R.

WOUNDED KNEE CR.

WOUNDED KNEE
MASSACRE

Rosebud Agency

WYOMING

Pine Ridge Agency

NIOBRARA R.

NORTH PLATTE R.

N

W   E

S

Miles
0   100

102°

103°

101°

99°

108. The Sioux Reservations in 1890–91

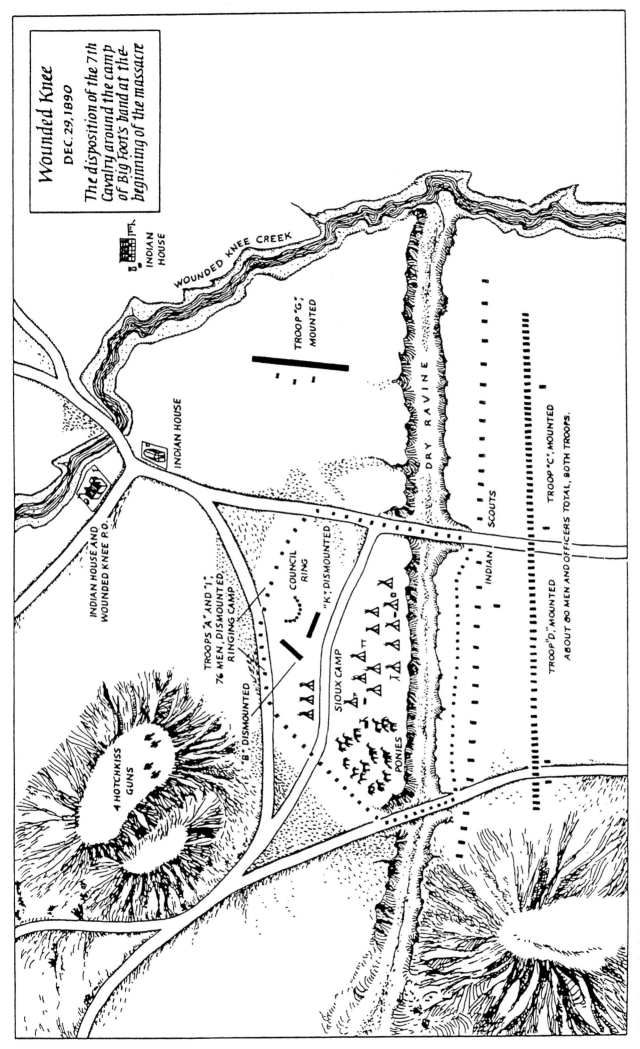

109. Wounded Knee, Dec. 29, 1890

Notes and References

On the spelling of names of Indian tribes, see the "Note on Indian Tribal Names" at the end of the Preface.

SECTION I
Indian Culture and Tribal Areas

Map 1. Indian Culture Areas

Harold E. Driver and William C. Massey, in *Comparative Studies of North American Indians,* Transactions of the American Philosophical Society, new series, vol. 47, part 2 (Philadelphia: American Philosophical Society, 1957), produced a series of maps, each one showing geographical distribution of a cultural trait—housing, food gathering, material culture, social organization, and the like. By a generalization of these features, they made a single map showing general culture areas (p. 170). This information was carried over into Harold E. Driver, *Indians of North America* (Chicago: University of Chicago Press, 1961), maps 1–37, following p. 612. Driver defines "culture area" as "a geographical area occupied by a number of peoples whose cultures show a significant degree of similarity with each other and at the same time a significant degree of dissimilarity with the culture of the people of other such areas" (p. 12).

Rather than use Driver's map of cultural areas, however, I have relied on a similar designation adopted by the Smithsonian Institution's *Handbook of North American Indians,* William C. Sturtevant, general editor, 20 vols. projected (Washington: Smithsonian Institution, 1978–). Eleven of the volumes are devoted to specific culture areas. The same general culture areas are used by the National Geographic Society, for example in its map *Indians of North America* (Washington: National Geographic Society, 1974), and its book *The World of the American Indian* (Washington: National Geographic Society, 1974). These maps differ from Driver's culture area map in that the latter divides the eastern United States into East and Prairies areas, while the former include much of the prairie area in the Great Plains and then divide the remainder of the eastern regions into Northeast and Southeast culture areas. See also the maps, "Early Indian Tribes, Culture Areas, and Linguistic Stocks," in *The National Atlas of the United States of America* (Washington: United States Department of the Interior, Geological Survey, 1970), 130–32.

The culture areas in Map 1 are drawn on a topographical base map (Erwin Raisz, *Landform Outline Map of the United States . . . without Lettering,* 1954, used with permission), in order to indicate in some detail the topographical nature of each area.

The culture areas of Alaska are shown on Map 63.

Map 2. Tribal Locations

It is difficult to show tribal locations accurately on a single map, first, because of the large number of tribes that have been identified historically, and, second, because many tribes moved from place to place. I have tried to indicate on this map a representative group of tribes, more or less where they were when they became important in United States history.

I have drawn on the "Key to Tribal Territories" maps in the published volumes of the Smithsonian Institution's *Handbook of North American Indians* (although in some cases the tribes are shown on those maps at an earlier period than suits my purposes), on maps 40–43 in Harold E. Driver, *Indians of North America* (Chicago: University of Chicago Press, 1961), on the map "Indian Tribes of North America" in *The American Heritage Pictorial Atlas of United States History* (New York: American Heritage Publishing Company, 1966), 23, and on the map *Indians of North America* (Washington: National Geographic Society, 1974). See also the maps, "Early Indian Tribes, Culture Areas, and Linguistic Stocks" in *The National Atlas of the United States of America* (Washington: United States Department of the Interior, Geological Survey, 1970), 130–32.

Map 3. Indian Land Areas Judicially Established

This map is a reduction of the large colored map included in the United States Indian Claims Commission's *Final Report* (Washington: Government Printing Office, 1979), inside back cover. The accompanying table contains data from the map area index in "Index to the Map Indian Land Areas Judicially Established" (pp. 127–37), written by Richard W. Yarborough, one of the commissioners, who edited the map and directed the compilation of data for it. The lines bounding various numbered subdivisions of the main tribal areas that appear on the original map are omitted here.

In determining areas with Indian or aboriginal title, the Indian Claims Commission looked at extent of use and occupancy, the exclusiveness of the use and occupancy, and whether the use continued for a long time. Some areas, especially in the region south of the Great Lakes, however, had joint title and are indicated on the map by parallel lines. The map also shows cases of "recognized title," in which by treaty or agreement the United States confirmed a section or reservation to a tribe out of a larger area held originally by Indian title.

The tribal names on the map and in the table are those of the original owners of the land, even though the plaintiffs before the Indian Claims Commission used a different designation. For reference, the map contains some names of tribes that did not have land areas adjudicated (the areas shown in gray on the map).

Many Indian homelands shifted with the passage of time. Yarborough says: "Every area mapped here is tied to a specific date, given in the Index, when that area was the tribe's by Indian title. The date usually coincides with the time when any of the title was first extinguished, by treaty of cession or otherwise. In general, the dates increase from east to west at the pace the country was settled" (p. 130).

The area numbers on the map do not correspond with the Royce Area numbers used by Charles C. Royce in *Indian Land Cessions in the United States* (see discussion of this work under Indian Land Cessions, p. 147 below). The work of the Indian Claims Commission was to determine what land was owned, not what was ceded, but some of the Royce Areas are found intact on this map.

Reduced and somewhat simplified versions of the Indian Claims Commission map are found in Carl Waldman, *Atlas of North American Indians* (New York: Facts on File Publications, 1985), 193, and in Imre Sutton, ed., *Irredeemable America: The Indians' Estate and Land Claims* (Albuquerque: University of New Mexico Press, 1985), figure P.1.

SECTION II
United States Census Enumeration of American Indians

Indians are difficult to count. A recent detailed study of Indian demography, which squarely faces the problems, is Russell Thornton, *American Indian Holocaust and Survival: A Population History since 1492* (Norman: University of Oklahoma Press, 1987). A useful bibliography and discussion of Indian demography is Henry F. Dobyns, *Native American Historical Demography: A Critical Bibliography* (Bloomington: Indiana University Press, 1976).

The table below shows census figures by states from 1890 to 1980. Because the methods of enumeration differed in different censuses, the figures must be used with caution for comparative purposes.

Indian Population by States, 1890–1980

State	1890	1900	1910	1920	1930	1940	1950	1960	1970	1980
US Total	248,253	237,196	265,683	244,437	332,397	333,969	343,410	523,591	792,730	1,365,676
Alabama	1,143	177	909	405	465	464	928	1,276	2,443	7,502
Alaska	—	—	—	—	—	—	14,089	14,444	16,276[1]	21,869[2]
Arizona	29,981	26,480	29,301	32,989	43,726	55,076	65,761	83,387	95,812	152,498
Arkansas	250	66	460	106	408	278	533	580	2,014	9,364
California	16,624	15,377	16,371	17,360	19,212	18,675	19,947	39,014	91,018	198,275
Colorado	1,092	1,437	1,482	1,383	1,395	1,360	1,567	4,288	8,836	17,734
Connecticut	228	153	152	159	162	201	333	923	2,222	4,431
Delaware	4	9	5	2	5	14	?	597	656	1,307
Dist. of Columbia	25	22	68	37	40	190	330	587	956	996
Florida	171	358	74	518	587	690	1,011	2,504	6,677	19,134
Georgia	68	19	95	125	43	106	333	749	2,347	7,442
Hawaii	—	—	—	—	—	—	?	472	1,126	2,655
Idaho	4,223	4,226	3,482	3,098	3,638	5,537	3,800	5,231	6,687	10,418
Illinois	98	16	188	194	469	624	1,443	4,704	11,413	15,846
Indiana	345	243	279	125	285	223	438	948	3,887	7,682
Iowa	457	382	471	529	660	733	1,084	1,708	2,992	5,369
Kansas	1,682	2,130	2,444	2,276	2,454	1,165	2,381	5,069	8,672	15,256
Kentucky	71	102	234	57	22	44	234	391	1,531	3,518
Louisiana	628	593	780	1,066	1,536	1,801	409	3,587	5,294	11,969
Maine	559	798	892	839	1,012	1,251	1,522	1,879	2,195	4,057
Maryland	44	3	55	32	50	73	314	1,538	4,239	7,823
Massachusetts	428	587	688	555	874	769	1,201	2,118	4,475	7,483
Michigan	5,625	6,354	7,519	5,614	7,080	6,282	7,000	9,701	16,854	39,734
Minnesota	10,096	9,182	9,053	8,761	11,077	12,528	12,533	15,496	23,128	34,831
Mississippi	2,036	2,203	1,253	1,105	1,458	2,134	2,502	3,119	4,113	6,131

Indian Population by States, 1890–1980 *(continued)*

State	1890	1900	1910	1920	1930	1940	1950	1960	1970	1980
Missouri	128	130	313	171	578	330	547	1,723	5,405	12,129
Montana	11,206	11,343	10,745	10,956	14,798	16,841	16,606	21,181	27,130	37,598
Nebraska	6,431	3,322	3,502	2,888	3,256	3,401	3,954	5,545	6,624	9,145
Nevada	5,156	5,216	5,240	4,907	4,871	4,747	5,025	6,681	7,933	13,306
New Hampshire	16	22	34	28	64	50	74	135	361	1,297
New Jersey	84	63	168	100	213	211	621	1,699	4,706	8,176
New Mexico	15,044	13,144	20,573	19,512	28,941	34,510	41,901	56,255	72,788	107,338
New York	6,044	5,257	6,046	5,503	6,973	8,651	10,640	16,491	28,355	38,967
N. Carolina	1,516	5,687	7,851	11,824	16,579	22,546	3,742	38,129	44,406	64,536
N. Dakota	8,174	6,968	6,486	6,254	8,387	10,114	10,766	11,736	14,369	20,120
Ohio	206	42	127	151	435	338	1,146	1,910	6,654	11,985
Oklahoma	64,456[3]	64,445[3]	74,825	57,337	92,725	63,125	53,769	64,689	98,468	169,292
Oregon	4,971	4,951	5,090	4,590	4,776	4,594	5,820	8,016	13,510	26,591
Pennsylvania	1,081	1,639	1,503	337	523	441	1,141	2,122	5,533	9,179
Rhode Island	180	35	284	110	318	196	385	932	1,390	2,872
S. Carolina	173	121	331	304	959	1,234	554	1,098	2,241	5,665
S. Dakota	19,834	20,225	19,137	16,384	21,833	23,347	23,344	25,794	32,365	44,948
Tennessee	146	108	216	56	161	114	339	638	2,276	5,013
Texas	708	470	702	2,109	1,001	1,103	2,736	5,750	17,957	39,740
Utah	3,456	2,623	3,123	2,711	2,869	3,611	4,201	6,961	11,273	19,158
Vermont	34	5	26	24	36	16	30	57	229	968
Virginia	349	354	539	824	779	198	1,056	2,155	4,853	9,211
Washington	11,181	10,039	10,997	9,061	11,253	11,394	13,816	21,076	33,386	58,186
W. Virginia	9	12	36	7	18	25	160	181	751	1,555
Wisconsin	9,930	8,372	10,142	9,611	11,548	12,265	12,196	14,297	18,924	29,320
Wyoming	1,844	1,686	1,486	1,343	1,845	2,249	3,237	4,020	4,980	7,057

Notes:
1. In addition, Alaska had 28,186 Eskimos and 6,352 Aleuts.
2. In addition, Alaska had 34,144 Eskimos and 8,090 Aleuts.
3. Includes Indian Territory.

Sources:
Figures for 1890–1930 are taken from *Fifteenth Census of the United States, 1930: The Indian Population of the United States and Alaska* (Washington: Government Printing Office, 1937), Table 2, "Indian Population by Divisions and States: 1890 to 1930," p. 3. Those for 1940–1980 are taken from the population censuses for those years, as follows:

1940: *Sixteenth Census of the United States, 1940, Population,* vol. 2, *Characteristics of the Population* (Washington: Government Printing Office, 1943), part 1, table 22, p. 52.

1950: *Census of Population: 1950,* vol. 2, *Characteristics of the Population,* part. 1, *United States Sum-*mary (Washington: Government Printing Office, 1953), p. 1-106.

1960: *United States Census of Population, 1960, General Population Characteristics, United States Summary* PC(1)-1B (Washington, Bureau of the Census, 1961), table 56, p. 1-164.

1970: *1980 Census of Population, Supplementary Reports: Race of the Population by States, 1980* (Washington: Bureau of the Census, 1981), table 3, 1970, p. 10.

1980: *1980 Census of Population, Supplementary Report: American Indian Areas and Alaska Native Villages, 1980,* PC80-S1-13 (Washington: Bureau of the Census, 1984), table 1, p. 14.

I have relied, too, on table 7–2, "American Indian Population of the Fifty States and the District of Columbia, 1900–1980," in Thornton, *American Indian Holocaust and Survival,* pp. 162–63, which cumulates the data given in the sources cited above.

It should be noted that different tables of population in a given census may show slightly different figures, depending upon whether corrected figures are used, whether samples rather than full enumeration are used, and so on.

See below under individual maps for further information about the statistics of a given census.

Map 4. Indian Population by States: 1890

In the Eleventh Census, 1890, the Bureau of the Census for the first time made an attempt to enumerate all Indians in the United States, including those on reservations, and it issued a voluminous report, *Report on Indians Taxed and Not Taxed in the United States (except Alaska) at the Eleventh Census: 1890* (Washington: Government Printing Office, 1894), which also provided a survey of Indian population figures before that date.

In *Indian Population in the United States and Alaska, 1910* (Washington: Government

Printing Office, 1915; reprint Millwood, New York: Kraus Reprint Company, 1973), the Bureau provided a series of tables on Indian population for the years 1890, 1900, and 1910. Table 11, "Indian Population of the United States, by Counties: 1910, 1900, and 1890," pp. 25–30, shows some population by counties for 1890, but for states with large Indian population the table indicates that the total Indian population shown for that year was not distributed by counties.

The data for Map 4 came from this volume. The same figures were repeated in *Fifteenth Census of the United States, 1930: Indian Population in the United States and Alaska* (Washington: Government Printing Office, 1937), Table 2, "Indian Population by Division and State: 1890 to 1930," p. 3.

Map 5. Indian Population by Counties: 1910

For the Thirteenth Census, 1910, the Bureau of the Census prepared a special report, *Indian Population in the United States and Alaska, 1910* (Washington: Government Printing Office, 1915; reprint Millwood, New York: Kraus Reprint Company, 1973). The data were derived in part from returns made on the general population schedule and in part from special schedules used in all districts containing Indians on reservations and in counties where at least 20 Indians had been counted in the census of 1900. Twelve topics are covered in the special report: population; proportion of mixed-bloods; sex distribution; age distribution; stocks and tribes, in detail by purity of blood, tribal mixture, sex, and age; fecundity and vitality; marital condition; school attendance; illiteracy; inability to speak English; occupations; and Indians taxed and not taxed.

The report indicates that "all persons of mixed white and Indian blood who have any appreciable amount of Indian blood are counted as Indians, even though the proportion of white blood may exceed that of Indian blood" (p. 10). Oklahoma, with 74,825 Indians, had by far the largest number, more than one-fourth of all the Indians in the United States.

The data for this map are taken from Table 11, "Indian Population of the United States, by Counties: 1910, 1900, and 1890," pp. 25–30. Population is shown only for counties having approximately 100 Indians or more.

Map 6. Indian Population by Counties: 1930

The 1930 enumeration of Indians is given in a special report: *Fifteenth Census of the United States, 1930: The Indian Population of the*

United States and Alaska (Washington: Government Printing Office, 1937). The data were derived incidentally from the regular census schedule, not from a special schedule, as was the case in 1910.

The enumerators in this census were to count as Indians not only those of full blood, but also those of mixed blood, except when the percentage of Indian blood was very small or when the person was regarded as a white person in the community. Persons of mixed Indian and black blood were counted as black unless Indian blood predominated and their status as Indians was generally accepted in their community.

The data for this map are taken from Table 8, "Indian Population by Counties: 1890 to 1930," pp. 10–32. The report includes a map of Indian population distribution by counties, with a dot representing 50 Indians (facing p. 1).

Population is shown on Map 6 only for counties having approximately 100 Indians or more.

Map 7. Indian Population by Counties: 1950

Data for this map are taken from *Census of Population: 1950*, vol. 2, *Characteristics of the Population*, state volumes, Table 47, "Indians, Japanese, and Chinese by Sex for Selected Counties and Cities: 1950." The figures in this table show counties and cities (of 10,000 or more inhabitants) with 10 or more Indians, Japanese, or Chinese in 1950. Since Map 7 shows population only for counties with approximately 100 Indians or more, the figures are adequate.

The Bureau of the Census in this census defined "American Indian" as follows: "This category includes fullblooded Indians, and persons of mixed white and Indian blood if they were enrolled on an Indian reservation or agency roll. Also included are persons of mixed Indian blood if the proportion of Indian blood is one-fourth or more, or if they are regarded as Indians in the community" (p. xvi in state volumes).

See also *Census of Population: 1950, Special Reports: Nonwhite Population by Race* (Washington: Government Printing Office, 1953), but this special report does not provide information on Indians by county.

The 1950 census does not show the concentration of Indians in North Carolina (centered in Robeson County) that earlier and later censuses show. The census says: "In 1950 for the first time, an attempt was made to identify persons of mixed white, Negro, and Indian ancestry living in certain communities in the eastern United States in a special category so they might be included in the categories 'Other races' and 'All other'

rather than being classified white, Negro, or Indian. This identification was accomplished with varying degrees of success, however. These groups are not shown separately, but they are included in the 'nonwhite' total" (p. xvi in state volumes).

The following comparison of figures for 1950 (other races) and 1960 (Indians) for selected counties in North Carolina indicates the peculiarity in the 1950 enumeration of persons in the state identified as Indians in other censuses.

County	1950 (other races)	1960 Indians
Columbus	468	854
Cumberland	458	1,078
Graham	211	255
Harnett	402	373
Hoke	764	1,462
Jackson	1,054	1,395
Person	168	172
Robeson	22,553	26,278
Sampson	786	893
Scotland	1,075	772
Swain	1,412	1,596
Warren	812	406

Sources: *Census of Population: 1950*, vol. 2, *Characteristics of the Population*, part 33, *North Carolina*, Table 42, "General Characteristics of the Population, for Counties: 1950"; and *U.S. Census of Population: 1960, General Population Characteristics, North Carolina*, PC(1)-35B, Table 28, "Characteristics of the Population, for Counties: 1960."

Map 8. Indian Population by Counties and SMSAs: 1960

This map is based upon the data in *U.S. Census of Population: 1960, General Population Characteristics*, state volumes, Table 21, "Characteristics of the Population, for Standard Metropolitan Statistical Areas, Urbanized Areas, and Urban Places of 10,000 or More: 1960," and Table 28, "Characteristics of the Population, for Counties: 1960."

The 1960 census defines "American Indian" in this way: "This category includes fullblooded Indians, and persons of mixed white and Indian blood if they were enrolled on an Indian reservation or agency roll. Also included are persons of mixed Indian blood if the proportion of Indian blood is one-fourth or more, or if they are regarded as Indians in the community." In this census the classification of mixed white-black-Indian persons as a separate category was abandoned. *U.S. Census of Population: 1960, Subject Reports: Nonwhite Population by Race,* Final Report, PC(2)-1c (Washington: Bureau of the Census, 1963), p. 3b-4.

Information for this census was obtained primarily through self-enumeration. Respondents could classify themselves with respect to race; nonrespondents were interviewed by telephone or direct visit. This method of enumeration differed from that in previous censuses, when classifications were made on the basis of observation by enumerators. For comparability of censuses through 1970, see *Census of Population: 1970, Subject Reports: American Indians,* Final Report, PC(2)-1F, pp. x–xi.

Population is shown on Map 8 only for counties and SMSAs having approximately 100 Indians or more.

Map 9. Indian Population by Counties and SMSAs: 1970

Data for this map were taken from *Census of Population: 1970, General Population Characteristics,* state volumes, PC(1)-b, Table 23, "Race by Sex, for Areas and Places: 1970," and Table 34, "Race by Sex, for Counties: 1970." See also *Census of Population: 1970, Subject Reports, American Indians,* Final Report, PC(2)-1f (Washington: Government Printing Office, 1973), which provides details about a good many social and economic characteristics.

The report says: "The concept of race used by the Bureau of the Census does not denote any scientific definition of biological stock. Rather, it reflects self-identification by respondents. Since the 1970 census obtained information on race primarily through self-enumeration, the data represent essentially self-classification by people according to the race with which they identify themselves. . . .

"The category 'American Indian' includes persons who indicated their race as 'Indian (Amer.),' as well as persons who did not classify themselves in one of the specific race categories on the questionnaire but who reported the name of an Indian tribe or had such entries as 'Mexican American–Indian,' 'Canadian–Indian,' or 'South American–Indian'" (pp. x–xi).

Critiques of the 1970 census in regard to Indians are Jeffrey S. Passel, "Provisional Evaluation of the 1970 Census Count of American Indians," *Demography* 13 (August 1976): 397–409, and Carl W. Meister, "The Misleading Nature of Data in the Bureau of the Census Subject Report on 1970 American Indian Population," *Indian Historian* 11 (December 1978): 12–19. Passel compares the census data with other demographic sources (e.g., count of births and deaths)

and says: "The increase of Indians as measured by the 1960 and 1970 censuses is 67,000 greater than the increase as measured by births and deaths. This excess cannot be accounted for by underregistration of births, overcounting of deaths, or net immigration from other countries. Net undercounts of Indians in the 1960 census can account for some of the difference, but excessive estimates of 1960 undercounts are required to explain all the increase. The large number of 'new' Indians appears, then, to be the result of a shift in racial self-identification, whereby many individuals designated as white in earlier censuses and records chose to classify themselves as Indian in 1970" (p. 407). Meister is critical of the sampling technique used by the census for certain data, especially about characteristics of the population, which he believes skews the results, especially for Indian groups with small populations.

Population is shown on Map 9 only for counties and SMSAs having approximately 100 Indians or more.

Map 10. Indian Population by Counties and SMSAs: 1980

Data for this map were taken from *1980 Census of Population,* vol. 1, *Characteristics of the Population,* chap. C, *General Social and Economic Characteristics,* PC80-1-C, state volumes, Table 58, "Race by Sex: 1980," which shows SMSAs and counties.

The Bureau of the Census also issued a special report: *1980 Census of Population, Supplementary Report, American Indian Areas and Alaska Native Villages: 1980* (Washington: Bureau of the Census, 1984), which supplies data (by states) on population for Indians living on and off identified reservations or identified tribal trust lands, as well as population figures (by states and counties) for Indians living on reservations and tribal trust lands. Comparable information is given for Indians, Aleuts, and Eskimos in Alaska. For the first time, the census includes information on Indians living in historic areas of Oklahoma (excluding urbanized areas). The report notes: "The American Indian population exceeded 1 million (1,366,676) in 1980 and showed an increase of about 574,000 persons or 72 percent over the decade. The substantially larger 1980 census count is the result of natural increase and overall improvements in census procedures, including modified enumeration procedures on American Indian reservations and the use of self-identification to obtain the race of respondents in all areas of the country. Also, a preliminary evaluation of the census results suggests that there may have been a greater frequency in 1980 than in 1970 for individ-

uals, especially those of mixed Indian and non-Indian descent, to report their race as American Indian" (p. 2).

In this census, race definition was as follows: "The categories 'American Indian,' 'Eskimo,' and 'Aleut' include persons who classified themselves as such in one of the specific race categories. In addition, persons who did not report themselves in one of the specific race categories, but entered the name of an American Indian tribe or reported entries such as Canadian Indian, French–American Indian, or Spanish–American Indian, were classified as American Indian" (p. 6).

In 1980 specific enumeration of Eskimos and Aleuts was made for all states and counties in the United States, rather than simply for Alaska, as was the case in 1970.

Additional details on Indians, Eskimos, and Aleuts in 1980 are found in *1980 Census of Population, Subject Reports: American Indians, Eskimos, and Aleuts on Identified Reservations and in the Historic Areas of Oklahoma (Excluding Urbanized Areas),* 2 parts, PC80-2-10, parts 1 and 2 (Washington: Bureau of the Census, 1985–1986); and *1980 Census of Population, Subject Reports: Characteristics of American Indians by Tribes and Selected Areas: 1980,* 2 sections, PC80-2-1C (Washington: Bureau of the Census, 1989). A more popular presentation of selected 1980 census data on Indians is the booklet *We, the First Americans* (Washington: Bureau of the Census, 1989).

A careful study and critique of the 1980 census data on Indians is Jeffrey S. Passel and Patricia A. Berman, "Quality of 1980 Census Data for American Indians," *Social Biology* 33 (Fall–Winter 1986): 163–82. The authors conclude: "The analysis of American Indian data from the 1980 census presented here suggest that users exercise considerable caution in using and interpreting data on the American Indian population. Users must be aware of the method of data collection and of the possible deficiencies in the data. Data for American Indians are probably of good quality in the areas we have delineated as 'Indian states' and in identified American Indian areas. Self-identification as American Indian in areas which historically have had substantial American Indian populations seems to provide a reasonable basis for defining the population.

"On the other hand, in areas which we have designated as 'non-Indian,' the 1980 census figures probably greatly overstate the American Indian population as defined with more objective measures. For these areas especially, users must exercise caution in interpreting and using 1980 census data on American Indians" (p. 182).

There is discussion of questions concerning the accuracy of 1980 census data for ethnic groups in James Paul Allen and Eugene James Turner, *We the People: An Atlas of American Ethnic Diversity* (New York: Macmillan Publishing Company, 1988), chap. 1, "Quality of the 1980 Census Data on Ethnicity," pp. 1–9. See also chap. 4, "People of Early North American Origin," pp. 25–37, which includes a map, "American Indians: Number of Persons by County—1980," p. 30, and an interesting series of cartograms of Indian tribal population, p. 31.

Population is shown on Map 10 only for counties and SMSAs having approximately 100 Indians or more.

For other maps showing population figures, see Map 61, "Oklahoma Indian Population by Counties and SMSAs: 1980"; Map 62, "Oklahoma, Showing Historic Indian Areas with Population: 1980"; Map 64, "Alaska Native Population: 1970"; Map 65, "Alaska Native Population: 1980"; and Map 66, "Population of Alaska Native Villages by Regional Corporations: 1980."

Map 11. Urban Indians, SMSAs with 1000 or More Indians: 1960

The data for this map came from *U.S. Census of Population: 1960, General Population Characteristics*, state volumes, Table 21, "Characteristics of the Population, for Standard Metropolitan Statistical Areas, Urbanized Areas, and Urban Places of 10,000 or More: 1960." For definition of "Indian" and method of enumeration in this census, see notes for Map 8.

Population figures for the SMSAs shown on the map are as follows:

Albuquerque	3,378
Baltimore	1,177
Buffalo	5,309
Chicago	4,153
Dallas	1,740
Denver	1,554
Detroit	2,195
Duluth–Superior	1,385
Fresno	1,083
Green Bay	1,289
Lawton	2,522
Los Angeles–Long Beach	8,839
Milwaukee	1,999
Minneapolis–St. Paul	3,285
New York	4,366
Oklahoma City	6,453
Philadelphia	1,577
Phoenix	8,136
Portland, OR	1,602
Reno	1,247
San Bernadino–Riverside–	
Ontario	3,566
San Diego	3,293
San Francisco–Oakland	3,883
Seattle	3,817
Syracuse	1,843
Tacoma	1,697
Tucson	7,307
Tulsa	7,608
Washington, DC	1,016
Wichita	1,062

Map 12. Urban Indians, SMSAs with 1000 or More Indians: 1970

The data for this map came from *Census of Population: 1970, General Population Characteristics, United States Summary*, Table 67, "Race of the Population for Areas and Places: 1970," pp. 324–26. For definition of "Indian" and method of enumeration in this census, see notes for Map 9.

Population figures for the SMSAs shown on the map are as follows:

Albuquerque	5,839
Anaheim–Santa Ana–	
Garden Grove	3,920
Appleton–Oshkosh	1,434
Bakersfield	2,039
Baltimore	2,553
Billings	1,063
Boston	2,132
Buffalo	5,775
Chicago	8,996
Cleveland	1,750
Dallas	5,022
Denver	4,348
Detroit	5,683
Duluth–Superior	1,781
Fayetteville, NC	3,199
Fort Smith	3,812
Fort Worth	1,610
Fresno	2,144
Grand Rapids	1,311
Great Falls	1,509
Green Bay	1,695
Greensboro–Winston Salem–	
High Point	1,169
Houston	3,215
Kansas City	2,402
Las Vegas	1,131
Lawton	3,343
Los Angeles–Long Beach	24,509
Miami	1,085
Milwaukee	4,075
Minneapolis–St. Paul	9,852
New York	12,160
Newark	1,214
Oklahoma City	13,033
Omaha	1,401
Oxnard–Ventura	1,150
Philadelphia	3,631
Phoenix	11,159
Portland, OR	4,011
Reno	1,926
Rochester, NY	1,446
Sacramento	3,559
St. Louis	1,931
Salem, OR	1,104
Salinas–Monterey	1,139
Salt Lake City	2,005
San Bernardino–Riverside–	
Ontario	6,378
San Diego	5,880
San Francisco-Oakland	12,011
San Jose	4,048
Santa Barbara	1,006
Santa Rosa	1,623
Seattle–Everett	9,496
Spokane	1,988
Stockton	1,218
Syracuse	2,458
Tacoma	3,343
Tucson	8,837
Tulsa	15,519
Vallejo–Napa	1,263
Washington, DC	3,300
Wichita	1,977

Map 13. Urban Indians, SMSAs with 1000 or More Indians: 1980

The data for this map came from *1980 Census of Population*, vol. 1, *Characteristics of the Population*, chap. C, *General Social and Economic Characteristics, United States Summary*, Table 69, "Persons by Race and Sex for Areas and Places: 1980," pp. 201–12. For definition of "Indian" and method of enumeration in this census, see notes for Map 10.

Population figures for the SMSAs shown on the map are as follows:

Albuquerque	20,721
Anaheim–Santa Ana–	
Garden Grove	12,782
Anchorage	3,565
Appleton–Oshkosh	2,202
Atlanta	2,870
Austin	1,378
Bakersfield	5,981
Baltimore	4,044
Bellingham	3,127
Billings	2,244
Bismarck	1,253
Boston	3,078
Bremerton	1,974
Buffalo	7,371
Charlotte–Gastonia, NC	1,837
Chicago	10,415
Chico	2,034
Cincinnati	1,160
Cleveland	1,958
Colorado Springs	1,767
Columbus, OH	1,433
Dallas–Ft. Worth	11,076
Denver–Boulder	8,973
Detroit	12,372
Duluth–Superior	3,388
El Paso	1,484

Eugene–Springfield, OR	2,382
Fayetteville, NC	3,644
Fayetteville–Springdale, AR	1,735
Flint	3,000
Fort Lauderdale–Hollywood	1,350
Fort Smith	9,292
Fresno	4,716
Grand Forks	1,059
Grand Rapids	2,461
Great Falls	2,656
Green Bay	2,429
Greensboro–Winston Salem–High Point	2,303
Honolulu	2,088
Houston	6,377
Indianapolis	1,442
Jacksonville	1,505
Joplin	1,122
Kalamazoo–Portage	1,111
Kansas City	4,580
Lansing–East Lansing	2,163
Las Vegas	2,994
Lawrence	1,742
Lawton	4,612
Little Rock–North Little Rock	1,227
Los Angeles–Long Beach	47,234
Louisville	1,046
Medford, OR	1,152
Miami	1,660
Milwaukee	6,489
Minneapolis–St. Paul	15,831
Mobile	1,580
Modesto	3,167
Muskegon–Norton Shores–Muskegon Heights	1,324
Nassau–Suffolk	2,797
New Orleans	2,465
New York	13,440
Newark	1,821
Norfolk–Virginia Beach–Portsmouth	1,952
Oklahoma City	24,695
Olympia	1,664
Omaha	2,355
Orlando	1,769
Oxnard–Simi Valley–Ventura	4,825
Pensacola	2,140
Philadelphia	5,176
Phoenix	22,788
Pittsburgh	1,465
Portland, OR	8,511
Providence–Warwick–Pawtucket	2,373
Provo–Orem	1,863
Redding, CA	2,610
Reno	3,377
Richmond	1,737
Riverside–San Bernardino–Ontario	17,107
Rochester, NY	2,227
Rock Hill, SC	1,251
Sacramento	10,944
St. Louis	3,206
Salem, OR	2,427
Salinas–Seaside–Monterey	2,889
Salt Lake City–Ogden	6,121
San Antonio	2,463
San Diego	14,355
San Francisco–Oakland	17,546
San Jose	8,312
Santa Barbara–Santa Maria–Lompoc	2,654
Santa Cruz	1,465
Santa Rosa	3,435
Seattle–Everett	15,162
Sioux City	1,344
Sioux Falls	1,115
Spokane	4,085
Springfield, MO	1,055
Stockton	3,419
Syracuse	3,720
Tacoma	5,619
Tampa–St. Petersburg	2,648
Toledo	1,205
Topeka	1,560
Tucson	14,880
Tulsa	38,463
Vallejo–Fairfield–Napa	2,662
Visalia–Tulare–Porterville	2,535
Washington, DC	6,409
Wichita	3,523
Yakima	6,600
Yuba City	1,724

SECTION III
Indian Land Cessions

The basic source for Indian land cessions, on which these maps ultimately rest is Charles C. Royce, *Indian Land Cessions in the United States,* Eighteenth Annual Report of the Bureau of American Ethnology, 1896–1897, part 2 (Washington: Government Printing Office, 1899). This indispensable volume has a "Schedule of Indian Land Cessions," pp. 648–948, which is arranged chronologically by treaty of cession, with a description of the pertinent cession or reservation and a designated serial number for each cession (known as a "Royce Area number"). Following the schedule is a series of sixty-seven state maps in color (for some states there is more than one map), on which the numbered cessions are clearly delineated. One can work from the schedule to the maps or from the maps to the schedule, using the Royce Area numbers as the key.

In addition there is a list of "Land Cessions by Tribes," pp. 951–64, which lists the tribes alphabetically with the dates of land cessions for each.

In preparing my maps, in addition to Royce's volume, I have relied upon Sam B. Hilliard, "Indian Land Cessions," Map Supplement Number Sixteen, cartography by Dan Irwin, in *Annals of the Association of American Geographers 62* (June 1972): 374 and map in pocket. The map is a large wall map that contains six maps of the United States showing 20-year intervals. The cessions shown on each map are divided into 5-year periods by use of separate colors. Permission to draw upon this source has kindly been given by Professor Hilliard and by the executive director of the Association of American Geographers.

Another series of maps showing Indian land cessions appears in *The American Heritage Pictorial Atlas of United States History* (New York: American Heritage Publishing Company: 1966), "Indian Cessions, 1794–1810," p. 119; "Indian Cessions, 1810–50," p. 148; and "Indian Cessions, 1850–90," p. 250. See also the three maps on Indian land transfers, 1775–1819, 1820–1864, 1865–1987, in *Handbook of North American Indians,* vol. 4, *History of Indian-White Relations,* ed. Wilcomb E. Washburn (Washington: Smithsonian Institution, 1988), 214–16.

A. National Maps

These maps show the major land cessions by decades. Some lands were claimed by several tribes, and the overlapping cessions cannot be shown on maps of this scale. In most cases only the first cession of an area is shown, with subsequent cessions covering the same area omitted, and very small cessions are not shown. Details on these matters can be found in Royce, *Indian Land Cessions.*

Map 14. Indian Land Cessions: 1784–1809
This map shows the first land cessions negotiated by the national government of the United States. Royce Area numbers 1–74, pp. 648–79.

Map 15. Indian Land Cessions: 1810–1819
Royce Area numbers 75–111, pp. 679–701.

Map 16. Indian Land Cessions: 1820–1829
Royce Area numbers 112–50, pp. 701–25.

Map 17. Indian Land Cessions: 1830–1839
Royce Area numbers 151–257, pp. 726–774.

Map 18. Indian Land Cessions: 1840–1849
Royce Area numbers 258–72, pp. 774–80. This was a decade of relatively little activity, following the decade of Indian removals.

Map 19. Indian Land Cessions: 1850–1859
Royce numbers 173–423, pp. 780–822. The map depicts the Indian land cessions in California enumerated by Royce and repeated in Robert F. Heizer, "Treaties," in *Handbook of North American Indians*, vol. 8, *California*, ed. Robert F. Heizer (Washington: Smithsonian Institution, 1978), 703.

Royce's map purports to show the lands ceded (all of California west of the Sierra Nevada) and the reservations established, but the map is based on faulty information and assumptions. Heizer's article, "Treaties," says: "There seems to be no basis whatsoever for this map beyond the vague impression of the U.S. Senate in 1852 that the California Indian tribes were agreeable to ceding to the United States the lands of California. Royce's map is, therefore, his own artifact deriving from the same assumption that the Senate made in 1852. But since it was already known in 1852 that many groups had not been treated with, either because they had not been encountered in the course of the wanderings of the three commissioners or because through lack of interpreters no communication was possible between the Americans and numbers of groups of native Californians, it must have been obvious that the 1851–1852 treaties did not, as was implied, cover the quieting of territorial claims ('title') of the Indians then living in the state" (pp. 702–4). And it should be noted that the treaties on which Royce based his cessions were never ratified.

Map 20. Indian Land Cessions: 1860–1869
Royce Area numbers 424–526, pp. 822–52.

Map 21. Indian Land Cessions: 1870–1879
Royce Area numbers 527–614, pp. 852–96.

Map 22. Indian Land Cessions: 1880–1890
Royce Area numbers 615–711, pp. 898–939.

B. Selected Tribal Cessions
A detailed accounting of cessions by tribe is in Royce, *Indian Land Cessions*, which indicates the cession areas on the maps and the treaties, agreements, and laws that provided for the cessions. The treaties and agreements are published in *United States Statutes at Large*. They are printed, as well, in Charles J. Kappler, comp., *Indian Affairs: Laws and Treaties*, 5 vols. (Washington: Government Printing Office, 1904–1941). Volume 2, *Treaties*, prints treaties from 1784 to 1868 and some agreements. The other volumes print laws, agreements, executive orders, etc., pertaining to Indian affairs. The pertinent references for the tribal cessions on the maps given here are indicated below.

Map 23. Cherokee Land Cessions: 1785–1835
Treaty of November 28, 1785 [Treaty of Hopewell], Royce Area number 3. *Statutes at Large*, 7:18–21; Kappler, *Treaties*, 8–11.

Treaty of July 2, 1791 [Treaty of Holston], Royce Area number 8. *Statutes at Large*, 7:39–43; Kappler, *Treaties*, 29–33.

Treaty of October 2, 1798, Royce Area number 42. *Statutes at Large*, 7:62–65; Kappler, *Treaties*, 51–55. The cession consisted of three detached tracts.

Treaty of October 24, 1804, Royce Area number 52. *Statutes at Large*, 7:228–29; Kappler, *Treaties*, 73–74. This treaty was misplaced in Washington and not proclaimed until 1824.

Treaty of October 25, 1805, Royce Area number 57. *Statutes at Large*, 7:93–94; Kappler, *Treaties*, 82–83.

Treaty of January 7, 1806, Royce Area number 64. *Statutes at Large*, 7:101–4; Kappler, *Treaties*, 90–92.

Treaty of March 22, 1816, Royce Area number 76. *Statutes at Large*, 7:139–40; Kappler, *Treaties*, 125–26.

Treaty of September 14, 1816, Royce Area number 79. *Statutes at Large*, 7:148–49; Kappler, *Treaties*, 133–34. This cession overlaps cessions by the Chickasaws of September 20, 1816, and October 20, 1832.

Treaty of July 8, 1817, Royce Area numbers 83–85. *Statutes at Large*, 7:156–60; Kappler, *Treaties*, 140–44. The cession in Royce Area number 83 overlaps the Creek cession of January 22, 1818.

Treaty of February 27, 1819, Royce Area numbers 101–3, 106. *Statutes at Large*, 7:195–200; Kappler, *Treaties*, 177–81. This cession was in three tracts. The treaty also provided for the cession of other small tracts not shown on the map.

Treaty of December 29, 1835 [Treaty of New Echota], Royce Area number 203. *Statutes at Large*, 7:478–89; Kappler, *Treaties*, 439–49.

There are good maps of Cherokee land cessions, including those made in colonial times, in Charles C. Royce, *The Cherokee Nation of Indians* (Chicago: Aldine Publishing Company, 1975), 260–64. The book, which is a reprinting of "The Cherokee Nation of Indians; A Narrative of Their Official Relations with the Colonial and Federal Governments," *Annual Report of the Bureau of Ethnology, 1883–1884* (Washington: Government Printing Office, 1887), 121–378, gives a treaty-by-treaty account.

Lands of the Cherokees in the West are shown on Maps 58–60.

Map 24. Creek Land Cessions: 1790–1832
Treaty of August 7, 1790 [Treaty of New York], Royce Area number 7. *Statutes at Large*, 7:35–38; Kappler, *Treaties*, 25–29.

Treaty of June 16, 1802, Royce Area number 44. *Statutes at Large*, 7:68–70; Kappler, *Treaties*, 58–59. The cession is in two detached tracts.

Treaty of November 14, 1805, Royce Area number 60. *Statutes at Large*, 7:96–98; Kappler, *Treaties*, 85–86.

Treaty of August 9, 1814 [Treaty of Fort Jackson], Royce Area number 75. *Statutes at Large*, 7:120–22; Kappler, *Treaties*, 107–10.

Treaty of January 22, 1818, Royce Area numbers 92–93. *Statutes at Large*, 7:171–72; Kappler, *Treaties*, 155–56. The cession of Royce Area number 93 overlaps the Cherokee cession of July 8, 1817.

Treaty of January 8, 1821 [Treaty of Indian Springs], Royce Area number 116. *Statutes at Large*, 7:215–16; Kappler, *Treaties*, 195–97.

Treaty of January 24, 1826, Royce Area numbers 127 and 131. *Statutes at Large*, 7:286–90; Kappler, *Treaties*, 264–68. By a supplementary article of March 31, 1836, the cession in Royce Area number 131 was enlarged.

Treaty of November 15, 1827, Royce Area number 141. *Statutes at Large*, 7:307–9; Kappler, *Treaties*, 284–86. This cession completed the cession of Creek lands in Georgia.

Treaty of March 24, 1832, Royce Area number 172. *Statutes at Large*, 7:366–68; Kappler, *Treaties*, 341–43.

Lands of the Creeks in the West, with significant changes as time passed, are shown on Maps 58–60.

Map 25. Chickasaw Land Cessions: 1805–1832, and Choctaw Land Cessions: 1801–1830
Chickasaw Cessions (top)
Treaty of July 23, 1805, Royce Area number 55. *Statutes at Large*, 7:89–90; Kappler, *Treaties*, 79–80. Part of this cession was claimed by the Cherokees; their claim was extinguished by a treaty of October 25, 1805.

Treaty of September 20, 1816, Royce Area number 80. *Statutes at Large*, 7:150–52; Kappler, *Treaties*, 135–37. Part of this cession was claimed by the Cherokees; their claim was extinguished by a treaty of September 14, 1816.

Treaty of October 19, 1818, Royce Area number 100. *Statutes at Large*, 7:192–95; Kappler, *Treaties*, 174–77.

Treaty of October 20, 1832 [Treaty of Pontitock Creek], Royce Area number 178. *Statutes at Large*, 7:381–91; Kappler, *Treaties*, 356–62. This cession overlaps the Cherokee cession of September 14, 1816.

Lands of the Chickasaws in the West are shown on Maps 58–60.

Choctaw Cessions (bottom)

Treaty of December 17, 1801, Royce Area number 43. *Statutes at Large*, 7:66–68; Kappler, *Treaties*, 56–58.

Treaty of October 17, 1802, Royce Area number 46. *Statutes at Large*, 7:73–74; Kappler, *Treaties*, 63–64. The treaty confirmed a cession previously made to Great Britain.

Treaty of November 16, 1805, Royce Area number 61. *Statutes at Large*, 7:98–100; Kappler, *Treaties*, 87–88.

Treaty of October 24, 1816, Royce Area number 82. *Statutes at Large*, 7:152; Kappler, *Treaties*, 137.

Treaty of October 18, 1820 [Treaty of Doak's Stand], Royce Area number 115. *Statutes at Large*, 7:210–14; Kappler, *Treaties*, 191–95.

Treaty of September 27–28, 1830 [Treaty of Dancing Rabbit Creek], Royce Area number 156. *Statutes at Large*, 7:333–42; Kappler, *Treaties*, 310–19.

Lands of the Choctaws in the West are shown on Maps 58–60.

Map 26. Seminole Land Cessions: 1823–1832

Treaty of September 18, 1823 [Treaty of Moultrie Creek], Royce Area number 118. *Statutes at Large*, 7:224–28; Kappler, *Treaties*, 203–5. This treaty was made with "The Florida tribes of Indians," and in it the Indians ceded all their claims in Florida. The northern boundary of the Indian claims is taken from the map "Indian Land Areas Judicially Established," in United State Indian Claims Commission, *Final Report* (Washington: Government Printing Office, 1979), inside back cover. This treaty provided for a reservation in central Florida, which was added to in 1824 and 1826. The addition is separated from the original reservation on the map by a dotted line.

Treaty of May 9, 1832 [Treaty of Payne's Landing], Royce Area number 173. *Statutes at Large*, 7:368–70; Kappler, *Treaties*, 344–45. This treaty provided that a delegation of Seminoles be sent to the West to approve the territory to be given to the Seminoles there. This approval appears in the Treaty of March 28, 1833 [Treaty of Fort Gibson]. *Statutes at Large*, 7:423–24; Kappler, *Treaties*, 394–95. The Seminole tribe rejected these treaties, and resistance to the removal directed by them resulted in the Second Seminole War of 1835–1842.

Lands of the Seminoles in the West, with significant changes, are shown on Maps 58–60.

Map 27. Potawatomi Land Cessions: 1807–1833

Some of these cessions were made by bands of Ottawa, Chippewa, and Potawatomi Indians, but the principal Indians were Potawatomis. In some of the treaties other tribes also were involved.

Treaty of November 17, 1807, Royce Area number 66. *Statutes at Large*, 7:105–7; Kappler, *Treaties*, 92–95.

Treaty of August 24, 1816, Royce Area numbers 77–78. *Statutes at Large*, 7:146–48; Kappler, *Treaties*, 132–33.

Treaty of September 29, 1817, Royce Area number 88. *Statutes at Large*, 7:160–70; Kappler, *Treaties*, 145–55.

Treaty of October 2, 1818, Royce Area number 98. *Statutes at Large*, 7:185–86; Kappler, *Treaties*, 168–69.

Treaty of August 29, 1821, Royce Area number 117. *Statutes at Large*, 7:218–21; Kappler, *Treaties*, 198–201.

Treaty of October 16, 1826, Royce Area numbers 132–33. *Statutes at Large*, 7:295–99; Kappler, *Treaties*, 273–77. This treaty provided for the cession of two distinct tracts.

Treaty of September 20, 1828, Royce Area number 146. *Statutes at Large*, 7:317–20; Kappler, *Treaties*, 294–97. Two separate tracts were ceded.

Treaty of July 29, 1829, Royce Area numbers 147–48. *Statutes at Large*, 7:378–81; Kappler, *Treaties*, 353–56.

Treaty of October 26, 1832, Royce Area number 180. *Statutes at Large*, 7:394–97; Kappler, *Treaties*, 367–70.

Treaty of October 27, 1832, Royce Area number 181. *Statutes at Large*, 7:399–403; Kappler, *Treaties*, 372–75.

Treaty of September 26–27, 1833 [Treaty of Chicago], Royce Area numbers 187 and 190. *Statutes at Large*, 7:431–48; Kappler, *Treaties*, 402–15. The treaty also included another small cession in Michigan, not shown on the map.

There is a map of major Potawatomi land cessions in R. David Edmunds, *The Potawatomis: Keepers of the Fire* (Norman: University of Oklahoma Press, 1978), 245.

The cessions on these maps did not end the land changes for the Potawatomis. Some of the movements were complicated; they can be traced in Royce, *Indian Land Cessions*. See Maps 60 and 92 for the location of Potawatomis in the West.

Map 28. Sauk and Fox Land Cessions: 1804–1842

Treaty of November 3, 1804, Royce Area number 50. *Statutes at Large*, 7:84–87; Kappler, *Treaties*, 74–77.

Treaty of July 15, 1830 [Treaty of Prairie du Chien], Royce Area number 152. *Statutes at Large*, 7:328–32; Kappler, *Treaties*, 305–10.

Treaty of September 21, 1832, Royce Area number 175. *Statutes at Large*, 7:374–76; Kappler, *Treaties*, 349–51.

Treaty of September 28, 1836, Royce Area number 226. *Statutes at Large*, 7:520–23; Kappler, *Treaties*, 476–78.

Treaty of October 21, 1837, Royce Area number 244. *Statutes at Large*, 7:543–44; Kappler, *Treaties*, 497–98.

Treaty of October 11, 1842, Royce Area number 262. *Statutes at Large*, 7:596–600; Kappler, *Treaties*, 546–49. The dotted line on the map separates the area ceded at once and the area to the west to be ceded after three years.

There is a map of Sauk and Fox land cessions in William T. Hagan, *The Sac and Fox Indians* (Norman: University of Oklahoma Press, 1958), 228.

Later land changes of the Sauks and Foxes can be traced in Royce, *Indian Land Cessions*. See Maps 60 and 92 for the locations of the tribes in the West.

Map 29. Lake Superior Chippewa Land Cessions: 1837–1854

Treaty of July 29, 1837, Royce Area number 242. *Statutes at Large*, 7:536–38; Kappler, *Treaties*, 491–93.

Treaty of October 4, 1842, Royce Area number 261. *Statutes at Large*, 7:591–95; Kappler, *Treaties*, 542–45.

Treaty of September 30, 1854, Royce Area number 332. *Statutes at Large*, 10:1109–15; Kappler, *Treaties*, 648–52.

There is a map showing land cessions in Edmund Jefferson Danziger, Jr., *The Chippewas of Lake Superior* (Norman: University of Oklahoma Press, 1979), following p. xiv.

Map 30. Blackfeet Land Cessions: 1873–1896, and Crow Land Cessions: 1868–1904

Gros Ventre, Piegan, Blood, Blackfeet, and River Crow Indians (top)

Executive Order, July 5, 1873, Kappler, *Indian Affairs: Laws and Treaties*, 1:855–56. It set aside a reservation in northern Montana for these Indians, Royce Area number 565, and excluded Royce Area number 399, which had been assigned to these Indians by a Treaty of October 17, 1855.

Executive Order, August 19, 1874, Kappler, *Indian Affairs: Laws and Treaties*, 1:856. The order restored to the public domain the land included in Royce Area number 574, land not embraced in the Act of April 15, 1874, which confirmed the lands of these Indians. *Statutes at Large*, 18, pt. 3, pp. 28–29.

Act of May 1, 1888, which ratifed agreements with the Indians of December 28, 1886–February 11, 1887. *Statutes at Large*, 25:113–33; Kappler, *Indian Affairs: Laws and*

Treaties, 1:261–66. By the act reservations were established for the Indians of Fort Peck Agency, Indians of Fort Belknap Agency, and Indians of Blackfeet Agency; all the remaining lands were ceded, Royce Area number 692.

Act of June 10, 1896, which ratified an agreement with the Blackfeet of September 26, 1895. *Statutes at Large,* 29:353–58; Kappler, *Indian Affairs: Laws and Treaties,* 1:604–9.

There are maps of cessions by the Blackfeet in John C. Ewers, *The Blackfeet: Raiders on the Northwestern Plains* (Norman: University of Oklahoma Press, 1958), 271, 305.

Crow Indians (bottom)

Treaty of May 7, 1868 [Treaty of Fort Laramie], Royce Area number 517. *Statutes at Large,* 15: 649–53; Kappler, *Treaties,* 1008–11.

Act of April 11, 1882, which ratified an agreement of June 12, 1880, Royce Area number 619. *Statutes at Large,* 22:42–43; Kappler, *Indian Affairs: Laws and Treaties,* 1:195–97.

Act of March 3, 1891, which ratified an agreement of December 8, 1890, Royce Area number 714. *Statutes at Large,* 26:1039–43; Kappler, *Indian Affairs: Laws and Treaties,* 1:432–36.

Act of April 27, 1904, which ratified an agreement of August 14, 1899. *Statutes at Large,* 33:352–62; Kappler, *Indian Affairs: Laws and Treaties,* 3:87–97.

Map 31. Ute Land Cessions: 1868–1880

Treaty of March 2, 1868, Royce Area number 515. *Statutes at Large,* 15:619–27; Kappler, *Treaties,* 990–96.

Act of April 29, 1874, which ratified an agreement of September 13, 1873, Royce Area number 566. *Statutes at Large,* 18, pt. 3, pp. 36–41; Kappler, *Indian Affairs: Laws and Treaties,* 1:151–52.

Act of June 15, 1880, which ratified an agreement of March 6, 1880, Royce Area number 616. *Statutes at Large,* 21:199–205; Kappler, *Indian Affairs: Laws and Treaties,* 1:180–86.

Map 32. Teton Sioux Land Cessions: 1877–1889

Act of February 28, 1877, which ratified agreements of September 23–October 27, 1876, with Sioux and Northern Cheyenne and Arapaho Indians, by which the Indians ceded all claims to the area described in Article 16 of the treaty of April 29, 1868, Royce Area number 597.

Act of February 28, 1877, which ratified an agreement of September 26, 1876, by which Royce Area number 598 was ceded. This area included the Black Hills.

Act of March 2, 1889, which established the reservations for the Pine Ridge Sioux, the Rosebud Sioux, the Standing Rock Sioux, the Cheyenne River Sioux, the Lower Brule Sioux, and the Crow Creek Sioux. The remaining lands, Royce Area number 699, were ceded. *Statutes at Large,* 25:888–99; Kappler, *Indian Affairs: Laws and Treaties,* 1:328–39.

Act of May 27, 1910, which opened that part of the Pine Ridge Reservation lying in Bennett County to sale and disposition. The United States Court of Appeals, Eighth Circuit, decided on October 29, 1975, in *United States* v. *Parkinson,* that "Bennett County, South Dakota, was severed from the Pine Ridge Indian Reservation by the Act of May 27, 1910, and became part of the public domain of the State of South Dakota." *Federal Reporter,* 2d series, 525:120–24. Certiorari was denied by the United States Supreme Court, April 25, 1977, *United States Reports,* 430:982.

Act of April 23, 1904, ratifying an agreement of September 14, 1901, which opened Gregory County, South Dakota, *Statutes at Large,* 33:254–58; Act of March 2, 1907, which opened Tripp County, South Dakota, *Statutes at Large,* 34:1230–32; and Act of May 30, 1910, which opened Mellette County, South Dakota, *Statutes at Large,* 36:448–52. The United States Supreme Court in *Rosebud Sioux Tribe* v. *Kneip,* decided April 4, 1977, declared that the acts of 1904, 1907, and 1910 disestablished the designated parts of the Rosebud Reservation. *United States Reports,* 430:584–633.

SECTION IV
Indian Reservations

A. National Maps

Map 33. Western Indian Reservations: 1880

This map is based on "Map Showing Indian Reservations in the United States West of the 84th Meridian and Number of Indians Belonging Thereto, 1880," included in the Report of the Commissioner of Indian Affairs, 1880, *House Executive Document* no. 1, part 5, 46th Congress, 3d session, serial 1959. The original map shows Indian agencies and stations occupied by United States troops as well as the reservations, and for most of the reservations the number of Indians is given.

The table opposite the map is based on "Schedule Showing the Names of Indian Reservations in the United States . . . ," in the Report of the Commissioner of Indian Affairs, 1880, 350–59. The schedule indi-

cates also the agency and the church denomination connected with each reservation, the tribe or tribes occupying the reservation, the area in square miles and in acres, and references to pertinent treaties, statutes, and executive orders. Spelling from the commissioner's report is followed.

The gray areas on the map indicate white population of two persons or more per square mile, as designated by the United States census. The census map for 1880 appears in *Statistical Atlas of the United States,* Eleventh Census, plate 5. I have used an adaptation of this map in Charles O. Paullin, *Atlas of the Historical Geography of the United States* (Washington: Carnegie Institution of Washington, and New York: American Geographical Society of New York, 1932), plate 78A. Another modern presentation of the 1880 population map is in Randall D. Sale and Edwin D. Karn, *American Expansion: A Book of Maps* (Homewood, Illinois: Dorsey Press, 1962; reprint Lincoln: University of Nebraska Press, 1979), 21.

Map 34. Western Indian Reservations: 1890

This map is based on "Map Showing Indian Reservations within the Limits of the United States, Compiled under the Direction of the Hon. T. J. Morgan, Commissioner of Indian Affairs, 1890," in Report of the Commissioner of Indian Affairs, 1890, *House Executive Document* no. 1, part 5, 51st Congress, 2d session, serial 2841. The original map shows agencies, military stations, and Indian schools as well as reservations. It also includes reservations in New York and North Carolina not shown on this map.

The table opposite the map is based on data in "Schedule Showing the Names of Indian Reservations in the United States . . . ," in Report of the Commissioner of Indian Affairs, 1890, pp. 434–45. The schedule for 1890 contains the same kind of information as that for 1880, except that religious denominations are no longer shown. Spelling from the commissioner's report is followed.

The gray areas on the map indicate white population of two persons or more per square mile, as shown in *Statistical Atlas of the United States,* Eleventh Census, plate 6. I have used the adaptation of this map in Paullin's *Atlas of the Historical Geography of the United States,* plate 78B. See also Sale and Karn, *American Expansion,* 23.

Map 35. Major Indian Reservations: 1987

This map shows the general distribution and size of Indian reservations in the United States in 1987. It is based on the map *Indian Land Areas* (Washington: Bureau of Indian Affairs, 1987), compiled by the

Smithsonian Institution's *Handbook of North American Indians,* in cooperation with the Bureau of Indian Affairs, and prepared by the U.S. Geological Survey. In addition to federal Indian reservations, this BIA map shows state reservations, federal Indian groups without reservations, and Bureau of Indian Affairs area offices.

Some reservations, too small to show on a map of this scale, are omitted; for more detail on the reservations, see Maps 36–45.

The base map used in this plate is *Landform Outline Map of the United States . . . without Lettering,* by Erwin Raisz, used with permission. It enables the reader to see the topographical situation of the reservations.

The heavy line indicates the eastern and western limits of the region in which there is less than twenty inches of annual rainfall. The line is approximate and is adapted from *The National Atlas of the United States* (Washington: United States Geological Survey, 1970), plate 97, "Mean Annual Precipitation," and from Paullin's *Atlas of the Historical Geography of the United States,* plate 5G, "Rainfall: Average, Annual."

B. Maps by Geographical Areas

The following maps, arranged by convenient geographical areas, show federal Indian reservations as of 1987. Reservations with fewer than 500 Indians in the 1980 census are indicated by a black dot. For reservations with a population of more than 500 Indians in the 1980 census, an outer square indicates the total population (all races) on the reservation, and an inner shaded square indicates the Indian population on the reservation.

Population figures, given below for each map, indicate the total for all races, the number of American Indians, and the percent American Indian of all races. The statistics are taken from the *1980 Census of Population, Supplementary Report: American Indian Areas and Alaska Native Villages, 1980,*

PC80-S1-13 (Washington: Bureau of the Census, 1984), Table 4, "Total and American Indian Persons for Identified Reservations and Identified Tribal Trust Lands by States and Counties: 1980," pp. 21–15. Some of these are corrected figures and thus may differ from those published in the *1980 Census of Population, General Population Characteristics,* PC80-1-B.

The *Supplementary Report* notes: "The concept of race as used by the Census Bureau reflects self-identification by respondents; it does not denote any clear-cut scientific definition of biological stock" (p. 1). The reservations and their boundaries were identified by the Bureau of Indian Affairs and state governments. For detailed explanations of the data in the tables, see the *Supplementary Report,* "Introduction," "Definitions and Explanations," and "Limitations of the Data," pp. 1–13.

The location and boundaries of the reservations shown on the maps are based on the map *Indian Land Areas* (Washington: Bureau of Indian Affairs, 1987).

The reservations on the 1987 map show changes that occurred after the 1980 census data were gathered, so there may be slight discrepancies between the reservations shown on the maps and the reservations listed with population figures by the Census Bureau.

It should be noted that there are non-Indian land holdings within the boundaries of the reservations. Allotment of land in severalty to Indians in the late nineteenth and early twentieth centuries, with subsequent disposal of "surplus lands" and eventual alienation of many allotments, resulted in a checkerboard pattern within the reservations. Maps of land ownership status of the reservations (at a scale of 2 inches = 1 mile) are maintained by the Land Title and Records Office of the Area Offices of the Bureau of Indian Affairs. These maps distinguish, where applicable, nine types of land ownership: (1) trust lands owned by in-

dividual Indians; (2) trust lands tribally owned; (3) trust lands tribally owned in reserve status; (4) fee lands; (5) tribal fee lands; (6) land owned by the Bureau of Indian Affairs; (7) submarginal BIA lands; (8) land owned by other federal agencies; and (9) lands in the public domain. I have examined examples of these maps from the Aberdeen Area Office; they are too detailed, however, to reproduce at the scale of the maps used in this atlas.

Examples of checkerboarding can be seen on the maps accompanying studies of land ownership on selected reservations; see Harold Hoffmeister, "The Consolidated Ute Indian Reservation," *Geographical Review 35* (October 1945): 601–23; C. W. Loomer, *Land Tenure Problems in the Bad River Indian Reservation of Wisconsin,* University of Wisconsin Agricultural Experiment Station, Research Bulletin 188, December 1955; and Jack Hunt, "Land Tenure and Economic Development on the Warm Springs Indian Reservation," *Journal of the West 9* (January 1970): 93–109. See also the map "Ownership Status of Land on the Lac du Flambeau Indian Reservation, Wisconsin, 1933," published by John Collier in *Indians at Work: Reorganization Number* (1936).

Two volumes that present current statistical and other information for each Indian reservation are *Federal and State Indian Reservations and Indian Trust Areas* (Washington: United States Department of Commerce, 1974), and *Indian Reservations: A State and Federal Handbook,* compiled by the Confederation of American Indians (Jefferson, North Carolina: McFarland & Company, 1986). For an earlier period see the wealth of information in "Report with Respect to the House Resolution Authorizing the Committee on Interior and Insular Affairs to Conduct an Investigation of the Bureau of Indian Affairs," *House Report* no. 2503, 82d Congress, 2d session, serial 11582 (1952).

Map 36. Indian Reservations in Washington and Oregon, with 1980 Population

States and Reservations	All races	Am. Indian	% Am. Indian of all races
WASHINGTON	4,132,156	58,186	1.4
Total on reservations	79,043	16,440	20.8
Chelalis Reservation	405	200	49.4
Colville Reservation	7,047	3,500	49.7
Hoh Reservation	67	46	68.7
Kalispel Reservation	106	98	92.5

States and Reservations	All races	Am. Indian	% Am. Indian of all races
Lower Elwha Reservation	64	47	73.4
Lummi Reservation	2,274	1,259	55.4
Makah Reservation	1,245	803	64.5
Muckleshoot Reservation	2,991	375	12.5
Nisqually Reservation	254	42	16.5
Nooksack Reservation	—	—	—
Ozette Reservation	6	1	16.7
Port Gamble Reservation	302	266	88.1

States and Reservations	All races	Am. Indian	% Am. Indian of all races
Port Madison Reservation	3,415	148	4.3
Puyallup Reservation	25,188	856	3.4
Quileute Reservation	327	273	83.5
Quinault Reservation	1,501	943	62.8
Sauk-Suiattle Reservation	—	—	—
Shoalwater Reservation	33	28	84.8
Skokomish Reservation	483	305	63.1
Spokane Reservation	1,475	1,050	71.2
Squaxin Island Reservation	56	35	62.5
Swinomish Reservation	1,390	414	29.8
Tulalip Reservation	5,046	768	15.2
Upper Skagit Reservation	5	—	—
Yakima Reservation	25,363	4,983	19.6
OREGON	2,633,105	26,591	1.0
Total on reservations	5,030	3,072	61.1
Burns Reservation	167	160	95.8
Fort McDermit Reservation (pt.)	—	—	—
Umatilla Reservation	2,619	908	34.7
Warm Springs Reservation	2,244	2,004	89.3

Source:
1980 Census of Population, Supplementary Report: American Indian Areas and Alaska Native Villages, 1980, 24–25.

Map 37. Indian Reservations in California and Nevada, with 1980 Population

Although in 1980 California had more Indians than any other state (198,275), relatively few of them (9,265) lived on the numerous small reservations or rancherias scattered across the state. The number of Indians at some of these sites was very small, but the units were nevertheless considered by the federal government to have "government-to-government relations" with the United States.

States and Reservations	All races	Am. Indian	% Am. Indian of all races
CALIFORNIA	23,667,902	198,275	0.8
Total on reservations	30,590	9,265	30.3
Agua Caliente Reservation	13,743	65	0.5
Alturas Rancheria	7	7	100.0
Augustine Reservation	—	—	—
Barona Rancheria	300	222	74.0
Benton Paiute Reservation	12	12	100.0
Berry Creek Rancheria	—	—	—
Big Bend Rancheria	11	8	72.7
Big Lagoon Rancheria	11	8	72.7

States and Reservations	All races	Am. Indian	% Am. Indian of all races
Big Pine Rancheria	396	269	67.9
Bishop Rancheria	1,125	784	69.7
Bridgeport Colony	55	47	85.5
Cabazon Reservation	815	8	1.0
Cachil Dehe Rancheria	17	17	100.0
Cahuilla Reservation	56	29	51.8
Campo Reservation	100	86	86.0
Capitan Grande Reservation	—	—	—
Cedarville Rancheria	6	6	100.0
Chemehuevi Reservation	265	23	8.7
Cold Springs Rancheria	65	63	96.9
Colorado River Reservation (pt.)	1,233	24	1.9
Cortina Rancheria	6	2	33.3
Coyote Valley Rancheria	9	—	—
Cuyapaipe Reservation	2	2	100.0
Dry Creek Rancheria	46	41	89.1
Enterprise Rancheria	16	16	100.0
Fort Bidwell Reservation	98	93	94.9
Fort Independence Reservation	61	31	50.8
Fort Mojave Reservation (pt.)	36	—	—
Fort Yuma Reservation (pt.)	2,346	959	40.9
Grindstone Creek Rancheria	73	72	98.6
Hoopa Valley Reservation	2,041	1,502	73.6
Hoopa Valley Extension Reservation	1,082	411	38.0
Hopland Rancheria	13	10	76.9
Inaja-Cosmit Reservation	—	—	—
Jackson Rancheria	15	15	100.0
La Jolla Reservation	151	141	93.4
La Posta Reservation	1	1	100.0
Laytonville Rancheria	111	105	94.6
Likely Rancheria	—	—	—
Lone Pine Rancheria	248	172	69.4
Lookout Rancheria	13	12	92.3
Los Coyotes Reservation	51	45	88.2
Manchester Rancheria	81	77	95.1
Manzanita Reservation	14	13	92.9
Mesa Grande Reservation	—	—	—
Middletown Rancheria	40	39	97.5
Montgomery Creek Rancheria	1	1	100.0
Morongo Reservation	414	313	75.6

States and Reservations	All races	Am. Indian	% Am. Indian of all races
Pala Reservation	559	433	77.5
Pauma Reservation	89	86	96.6
Pechanga Reservation	141	117	83.0
Ramona Reservation	—	—	—
Resighini Rancheria	21	18	85.7
Rincon Reservation	490	297	60.6
Roaring Creek Rancheria	25	24	96.0
Round Valley Reservation	1,268	528	41.6
Rumsey Rancheria	13	11	84.6
San Manuel Reservation	31	24	77.4
San Pasqual Reservation	209	133	63.6
Santa Rosa Rancheria	169	117	69.2
Santa Rosa Reservation	12	12	100.0
Santa Ynez Reservation	133	120	90.2
Santa Ysabel Reservation	196	181	92.3
Sheep Ranch Rancheria	2	2	100.0
Sherwood Valley Rancheria	19	17	89.5
Shingle Springs Rancheria	—	—	—
Soboba Reservation	258	230	89.1
Stewart's Point Rancheria	75	72	96.0
Sulphur Bank Rancheria	115	115	100.0
Susanville Reservation	90	82	91.1
Sycuan Reservation	61	48	78.7
Torres-Martinez Reservation	278	11	4.0
Trinidad Rancheria	63	47	74.6
Tule River Reservation	453	424	93.6
Tuolumne Rancheria	93	73	78.5
Twenty-nine Palms Reservation	—	—	—
Viejas Rancheria	209	142	67.9
Woodfords Community	308	126	40.9
XL Ranch Reservation	24	24	100.0
NEVADA	800,493	13,306	1.7
Total on reservations	5,248	4,400	83.8
Carson Colony	227	213	93.8
Dresslerville Colony	129	127	98.4
Duck Valley Reservation (pt.)	846	744	87.9
Duckwater Reservation	106	103	97.2
Ely Colony	78	67	85.9
Fallon Colony	64	46	71.9
Fallon Reservation	279	258	92.5
Fort McDermit Reservation (pt.)	472	463	98.1
Fort Mojave Reservation (pt.)	—	—	—

States and Reservations	All races	Am. Indian	% Am. Indian of all races
Goshute Reservation (pt.)	25	25	100.0
Las Vegas Colony	113	106	93.8
Lovelock Colony	126	117	92.9
Moapa River Reservation	185	182	98.4
Pyramid Lake Reservation	853	720	84.4
Reno-Sparks Colony	463	451	97.4
Summit Lake Reservation	15	15	100.0
Te-Moak Reservation	91	91	100.0
Walker River Reservation	571	471	82.5
Washoe Reservation	87	4	4.6
Winnemucca Colony	37	35	94.6
Yerington Reservation	421	105	24.9
Yomba Reservation	60	57	95.0

Source:

1980 Census of Population, Supplementary Report: American Indian Areas and Alaska Native Villages, 1980, 21–23.

Map 38. Indian Reservations in Idaho, Montana, and Wyoming, with 1980 Population

States and Reservations	All races	Am. Indian	% Am. Indian of all races
IDAHO	943,935	10,418	1.1
Total on reservations	27,735	4,771	17.2
Coeur d'Alene Reservation	4,911	538	11.0
Duck Valley Reservation (pt.)	195	188	96.4
Fort Hall Reservation	4,783	2,542	53.1
Kootenai Reservation	40	40	100.0
Nez Perce Reservation	17,806	1,463	8.2
MONTANA	786,690	37,598	4.8
Total on reservations	49,564	24,043	48.5
Blackfeet Reservation	6,660	5,525	83.0
Crow Reservation	5,973	3,953	66.2
Flathead Reservation	19,628	3,771	19.2
Fort Belknap Reservation	2,060	1,870	90.8
Fort Peck Reservation	9,921	4,273	43.1
Northern Cheyenne Reservation	3,664	3,101	84.6
Rocky Boy's Reservation	1,650	1,549	93.9
WYOMING	469,557	7,057	1.5
Total on reservations	23,166	4,159	18.0
Wind River Reservation	23,166	4,159	18.0

Source:

1980 Census of Population, Supplementary Report: American Indian Areas and Alaska Native Villages, 1980, 22–23, 25.

Map 39. Indian Reservations in Utah and Arizona, with 1980 Population

States and Reservations	All races	Am. Indian	% Am. Indian of all races
UTAH	1,461,037	19,158	1.3
Total on reservations	21,979	6,868	31.2
Goshute Reservation (pt.)	80	80	100.0
Navajo Reservation (pt.)	4,787	4,539	94.8
Skull Valley Reservation	13	13	100.0
Southern Paiute Reservation	190	186	97.9
Uintah and Ouray Reservation	16,909	2,050	12.1
ARIZONA	2,718,215	152,498	5.6
Total on reservations	129,254	113,763	88.0
Camp Verde Reservation	200	173	86.5
Cocopah Reservation	355	349	98.3
Colorado River Reservation (pt.)	6,640	1,941	29.2
Fort Apache Reservation	7,774	6,880	88.5
Fort McDowell Reservation	349	345	98.9
Fort Mojave Reservation (pt.)	183	127	69.4
Fort Yuma Reservation (pt.)	2,815	146	5.2
Gila Bend Reservation	—	—	—
Gila River Reservation	7,380	7,067	95.8
Havasupai Reservation	282	267	94.7
Hopi Reservation	6,896	6,591	95.6
Hualapai Reservation	849	809	95.3
Kaibab Reservation	173	93	53.8
Maricopa Reservation	397	375	94.5
Navajo Reservation (pt.)	76,052	71,677	94.2
Papago Reservation	7,203	6,959	96.6
Pascua Yaqui Reservation	562	551	98.0
Payson Community of Yavapai-Apache	—	—	—
Salt River Reservation	4,089	2,624	64.2
San Carlos Reservation	6,104	5,872	96.2
San Xavier Reservation	875	851	97.3
Yavapai Reservation	76	66	86.8

Source:
1980 Census of Population, Supplementary Report: American Indian Areas and Alaska Native Villages, 1980, 21, 24.

Map 40. Indian Reservations in Colorado, New Mexico, and Texas (part), with 1980 Population

States and Reservations	All races	Am. Indian	% Am. Indian of all races
COLORADO	2,889,964	17,734	0.6
Total on reservations	6,877	1,966	28.6
Southern Ute Reservation	5,739	855	14.9
Ute Mountain Reservation (pt.)	1,138	1,111	97.6
NEW MEXICO	1,302,894	107,338	8.2
Total on reservations	84,860	61,876	72.9
Acoma Pueblo	2,359	2,268	96.1
Alamo Reservation	1,072	1,062	99.1
Canoncito Reservation	978	969	99.1
Cochiti Pueblo	839	613	73.1
Isleta Pueblo	2,412	2,289	94.9
Jemez Pueblo	1,515	1,504	99.3
Jicarilla Apache Reservation	1,996	1,715	85.9
Laguna Pueblo	3,791	3,564	94.0
Mescalero Apache Reservation	2,101	1,922	91.5
Nambe Pueblo	1,097	188	17.1
Navajo Reservation (pt.)	29,604	28,762	97.2
Picuris Pueblo	1,539	125	8.1
Pojoaque Pueblo	1,143	94	8.2
Ramah Community	1,237	1,163	94.0
Sandia Pueblo	2,509	227	9.0
San Felipe Pueblo	2,266	1,789	78.9
San Ildefonso Pueblo	1,491	488	32.7
San Juan Pueblo	4,149	851	20.5
Santa Ana Pueblo	409	407	99.5
Santa Clara Pueblo	8,658	1,839	21.2
Santo Domingo Pueblo	2,162	2,139	98.9
Taos Pueblo	4,227	1,034	24.5
Tesuque Pueblo	369	236	64.0
Ute Mountain Reservation (pt.)	—	—	—
Zia Pueblo	524	524	100.0
Zuni Pueblo	6,291	5,988	95.2
TEXAS	14,229,191	39,740	0.3
Total on reservations	1,007	859	85.3
Tigua Reservation	503	365	72.6

(See also Map 42)

Source:
1980 Census of Population, Supplementary Report: American Indian Areas and Alaska Native Villages, 1980, 22–24

Map 41. Indian Reservations in North Dakota, South Dakota, Nebraska, and Kansas, with 1980 Population

States and Reservations	All races	Am. Indian	% Am. Indian of all races
NORTH DAKOTA	652,717	20,120	3.1
Total on reservations	18,790	11,287	60.1
Fort Berthold Reservation	5,577	2,640	47.3
Fort Totten Reservation	3,313	2,261	68.2
Sisseton Reservation (pt.)	1,969	24	1.2
Standing Rock Reservation (pt.)	3,620	2,341	64.7
Turtle Mountain Reservation	4,311	4,021	93.3
SOUTH DAKOTA	690,768	44,948	6.5
Total on reservations	48,716	28,468	58.4
Cheyenne River Reservation	1,826	1,529	83.7
Crow Creek Reservation	1,787	1,474	82.5
Flandreau Reservation	169	158	93.5
Lower Brule Reservation	1,023	850	83.1
Pine Ridge Reservation	13,229	11,946	90.3
Rosebud Reservation	7,328	5,688	77.6
Sisseton Reservation (pt.)	11,617	2,676	23.0
Standing Rock Reservation (pt.)	5,196	2,459	47.3
Yankton Reservation	6,541	1,688	25.8
NEBRASKA	1,569,825	9,145	0.6
Total on reservations	9,477	2,846	30.0
Iowa Reservation (pt.)	19	7	36.8
Omaha Reservation (pt.)	5,459	1,275	23.4
Sac and Fox Reservation (pt.)	531	4	0.8
Santee Reservation	914	420	46.0
Winnebago Reservation	2,554	1,140	44.6
KANSAS	2,363,679	15,256	0.6
Total on reservations	1,845	715	38.8
Iowa Reservation (pt.)	93	19	20.4
Kickapoo Reservation	461	356	77.2
Pottawatomi Reservation	985	331	33.6
Sac and Fox Reservation (pt.)	306	9	2.9

Source:
1980 Census of Population, Supplementary Report: American Indian Areas and Alaska Native Villages, 1980, 22–24.

Map 42. Indian Reservations in Oklahoma, Louisiana, and Texas (part), with 1980 Population

Although Oklahoma in 1980 ranked second (after California) in number of Indians, there was only one reservation, the Osage. The 1980 Census, for the first time, noted Indian population in "Historic Areas of Oklahoma (Excluding Urbanized Areas)" by county. This information is shown on Map 62.

States and Reservations	All races	Am. Indian	% Am. Indian of all races
OKLAHOMA	3,025,290	169,292	5.6
Total on reservations	39,327	4,749	12.1
Osage Reservation	39,327	4,749	12.1
LOUISIANA	4,205,900	11,969	0.3
Total on reservations	1,381	210	15.2
Chitamacha Reservation	1,300	185	14.2
Coushatta Reservation	18	18	100.0
Tunica-Biloxi Reservation	63	7	11.1
TEXAS	14,229,191	39,740	0.3
Total on reservations	1,007	859	85.3
Alabama-Coushatta Reservation	504	494	98.0

(See also Map 40)

Source:
1980 Census of Population, Supplementary Report: American Indian Areas and Alaska Native Villages, 1980, 22, 24.

Map 43. Indian Reservations in Minnesota, Wisconsin, Iowa, and Michigan, with 1980 Population

States and Reservations	All races	Am. Indian	% Am. Indian of all races
MINNESOTA	4,075,970	34,831	0.9
Total on reservations	25,441	9,901	38.9
Bois Forte Reservation (Nett Lake)	416	392	94.2
Deer Creek Reservation	219	7	3.2
Fond du Lac Reservation	2,853	514	18.0
Grand Portage Reservation	281	187	66.5
Leech Lake Reservation	8,441	2,759	32.7
Lower Sioux Community	79	65	82.3
Mille Lacs Reservation	307	293	95.4
Prairie Island Community	111	80	72.1
Red Lake Reservation	2,979	2,823	94.8
Sandy Lake Reservation	—	—	—
Shakopee Community	105	77	73.3
Upper Sioux Community	54	51	94.4
Vermillion Lake Reservation	110	103	93.6
White Earth Reservation	9,486	2,550	26.9

States and Reservations	All races	Am. Indian	% Am. Indian of all races
WISCONSIN	4,705,767	29,320	0.6
Total on reservations	24,017	9,361	39.0
Bad River Reservation	916	699	76.3
Lac Courte Oreilles			
Reservation	1,699	1,145	67.4
Lac du Flambeau			
Reservation	2,211	1,092	49.4
Menominee Reservation	2,672	2,377	89.0
Oneida Reservation	13,389	1,821	13.6
Potawatomi Reservation	244	220	98.2
Red Cliff Reservation	686	589	85.9
St. Croix Reservation	427	392	91.8
Sokaogon Chippewa Community	105	95	90.5
Stockbridge Reservation	1,272	582	45.8
Wisconsin Winnebago			
Reservation	416	349	83.9
IOWA	2,913,679	5,369	0.2
Total on reservations	509	492	96.7
Omaha Reservation (pt.)	—	—	—
Sac and Fox Reservation	509	492	96.7
MICHIGAN	9,262,078	39,734	0.4
Total on reservations	27,217	1,607	5.9
Bay Mills Reservation	322	283	87.9
Hannahville Community	211	206	97.6
Isabella Reservation	23,373	517	2.2
L'Anse Reservation	3,289	581	17.7
Ontonagon Reservation	—	—	—
Pine Creek Reservation	22	20	90.0
Sault Ste. Marie Reservation	—	—	—

Source:
1980 Census of Population, Supplementary Report: American Indian Areas and Alaska Native Villages, 1980, 22, 25.

States and Reservations	All races	Am. Indian	% Am. Indian of all races
Poospatuck Reservation	203	94	46.3
St. Regis Mohawk			
Reservation	1,802	1,763	97.8
Shinnecock Reservation	297	194	65.3
Tonawanda Reservation	467	438	93.8
Tuscarora Reservation	921	873	94.8
MAINE	1,124,660	4,057	0.4
Total on reservations	1,430	1,235	86.4
Indian Township			
Reservation	423	333	78.7
Penobscot Reservation	458	398	86.9
Pleasant Point Reservation	549	504	91.8
MASSACHUSETTS	5,737,037	7,483	0.1
Total on reservations	1	1	100.0
Hassanamisco Reservation	1	1	100.0
Wampanoag Reservation	—	—	—
CONNECTICUT	3,107,576	4,431	0.1
Total on reservations	62	27	43.5
Eastern Pequot Reservation	29	16	55.2
Golden Hill Reservation	3	3	100.0
Schaghticoke Reservation	6	2	33.3
Western Pequot Reservation	24	6	25.0
NORTH CAROLINA	5,881,766	64,536	1.1
Total on reservations	5,717	4,844	84.7
Eastern Cherokee			
Reservation	5,717	4,844	84.7
SOUTH CAROLINA	3,121,820	5,665	0.2
Total on reservations	998	728	72.9
Catawba Reservation	998	728	72.9

Source:
1980 Census of Population, Supplementary Report: American Indian Areas and Alaska Native Villages, 1980, 22, 24.

Map 44. Indian Reservations in New York, New England, North Carolina, and South Carolina, with 1980 Population

States and Reservations	All races	Am. Indian	% Am. Indian of all races
NEW YORK	17,558,072	39,967	0.2
Total on reservations	13,967	6,734	48.2
Allegany Reservation	7,681	925	12.0
Cattaraugus Reservation	1,994	1,855	93.0
Oil Springs Reservation	6	—	—
Onondaga Reservation	596	592	99.3

Map 45. Indian Reservations in Mississippi, Georgia, and Florida, with 1980 Population

States and Reservations	All races	Am. Indian	% Am. Indian of all races
MISSISSIPPI	2,520,638	6,131	0.2
Total on reservations	2,866	2,756	96.2
Mississippi Choctaw Reservation	2,866	2,756	96.2
GEORGIA	5,463,105	7,442	0.1
Total on reservations	33	30	90.9
Tama Reservation	33	30	90.9

States and Reservations	All races	Am. Indian	% Am. Indian of all races
FLORIDA	9,746,324	19,134	0.2
Total on reservations	3,593	1,303	36.3
Big Cypress Reservation	387	351	90.7
Brighton Reservation	338	323	95.6
Hollywood Reservation	2,592	416	16.0
Miccosukee Reservation	276	213	77.2

Source:
1980 Census of Population, Supplementary Report: American Indian Areas and Alaska Native Villages, 1980, 22–23.

SECTION V
Agencies, Schools, and Hospitals

Map 46. Government Trading Houses (Factories): 1795–1822

This map follows the map and table in Francis Paul Prucha, *The Great Father: The United States Government and the American Indians,* 2 vols. (Lincoln: University of Nebraska Press, 1984), 1:123–24, which drew data from Ora Brooks Peake, *A History of the United States Indian Factory System, 1795–1822* (Denver: Sage Books, 1954); Aloysius Plaisance, "The United States Government Factory System, 1796–1822" (Ph.D. dissertation, Saint Louis University, 1954); and Herman J. Viola, *Thomas L. McKenney: Architect of America's Early Indian Policy, 1816–1830* (Chicago: Swallow Press, 1974), 6–70. Information on individual factories and other documentation relating to the factory system can be found in the footnotes to chapter 4, "Government Trading Houses (Factories)," in *The Great Father,* 1:115–34.

Map 47. Indian Agencies: 1824

The system of Indian agents and their agencies grew haphazardly in the early national period. First appointed as "temporary agents" for particular tribes, the agents soon became a fundamental part of Indian administration, even though there was no official regularization of their appointment until 1818. When a Bureau of Indian Affairs was established by Secretary of War John C. Calhoun in the War Department in 1824, the head of the bureau became responsible for the agencies and for the broader geographical administrative units called superintendencies.

The list of agencies in 1824 used for this map was compiled from Edward E. Hill, *The Office of Indian Affairs, 1824–1880: Historical Sketches* (New York: Clearwater Publishing Company, 1974).

In this period subagencies were not subordinated to any agency but were independent entities that were judged less important than full agencies.

Map 48. Indian Agencies: 1837

In 1834 Congress revamped the Indian department, making explicit provision for Indian agents and codifying Indian policy as it had been embodied in a series of trade and intercourse laws. See "An act to provide for the organization of the department of Indian affairs," June 30, 1834, *United States Statutes at Large,* 4:735–36. By 1837 the new system was in place; this map shows the distribution of agencies and subagencies at that date.

Information was taken from "Regulations Concerning Superintendencies, Agencies, and Subagencies, April 13, 1837," in *Office Copy of the Laws, Regulations, Etc., of the Indian Bureau, 1850* (Washington: Gideon and Company, 1850), and from Edward E. Hill, *The Office of Indian Affairs, 1824–1880: Historical Sketches* (New York: Clearwater Publishing Company, 1974). See also "Revised Regulations, No. II, Concerning Superintendencies, Agencies, and Sub-Agencies," April 13, 1837, in Report of the Commissioner of Indian Affairs, 1837, *Senate Document* no. 1, 25th Congress, 2d session, serial 314, pp. 611–15.

Subagencies were not subordinated to any agency but were independent entities. Commissioner of Indian Affairs C. A. Harris wrote in his report of December 1, 1837: "The titles imply a distinction in rank and duties, which the clause just quoted [that no subagent shall reside within the limits of any agency where there is an agent appointed], repudiates: for it makes the sub-agent equally independent, as an office, with the agent. The distinction, however, exists, in an essential particular, the pay of the former being only one-half of that of the latter. In point of fact, the duties and responsibilities of both are alike, and, with few exceptions, they are equal" (p. 528).

The map shows the Mackinac Agency located at Detroit. Hill, *Office of Indian Affairs,* says: "In 1836 the Mackinac and Sault Ste. Marie agent was made acting superintendent of the Michigan Superintendency. He was expected to spend the summers at Mackinac and the winters at Detroit. Gradually he spent less and less time at Mackinac, until Detroit became the headquarters of the agency and only occasional trips were made to Mackinac" (p. 90).

Map 49. Indian Agencies: 1846–1859

The period between the Mexican War and the Civil War was one of dramatic extension of American Indian affairs, as Indians in Texas, Oregon, and the Mexican Cession (including California and Utah) demanded attention.

This map shows the new agencies established in this period, with the date of founding for each. It presents a graphic picture of the spread of federal responsibility for Indian in the West. The heavy lines indicate the territorial additions.

Information for this map was compiled from Edward E. Hill, *The Office of Indian Affairs, 1824–1880: Historical Sketches* (Washington: Clearwater Publishing Company, 1974).

Map 50. Indian Agencies, with Assignment to Churches: 1872

As part of President Grant's "Peace Policy," Indian agencies were assigned to church bodies, which assumed the responsibility for nominating agents and other agency personnel. The practice began first with the Quakers in 1869 and then spread to other major denominations. By 1872 the system was pretty well in place.

This map shows the agencies in 1872 and indicates the denomination that was responsible for each. The two separate groups of Quakers are indicated as "Friends, O" for the Orthodox Friends and "Friends, H" for the Hicksite Friends. The information was taken from "Statement exhibiting the names and locations of Indian agencies . . ." in Report of the Commissioner of Indian Affairs, 1872, *House Executive Document* no. 1, 42d Congress, 3d session, serial 1560, pp. 456–59. A summary and recapituation by denomination is given in the commissioner's narrative report, ibid., 461–62.

Detailed information on the Protestant agencies can be found in Robert H. Keller, Jr., *American Protestantism and United States Indian Policy, 1869–82* (Lincoln: University of Nebraska Press, 1983); see especially Appendix 1, "Denominational Appointments," pp. 219–22, and the series of maps by denominations following page 46.

There is a map showing Indian reservations and the church groups to which they were assigned in 1874 in Charles Lewis Slattery, *Felix Reville Brunot, 1820–1898: A Civilian in the War for the Union, President of the First Board of Indian Commissioners* (New York: Longmans, Green, and Company, 1901), 152.

Map 51. Indian Agencies: 1880

By 1880 most of the churches had given up their responsibilities for agencies, and the agents again became political appointees. The agents served the Indians on the reservations that represented the remnants of land still in Indian hands after the land cessions of the preceding decades.

Information for this map came from Edward E. Hill, *The Office of Indian Affairs, 1824–1880: Historical Sketches* (New York: Clearwater Publishing Company, 1974). The Report of the Commissioner of Indian Affairs, 1880, *House Executive Document* no. 1, 46th Congress, 3d session, serial 1959, shows the agencies in "Table of statistics relating to population, education, &c., by tribes and their respective agencies," pp. 360–79.

Map 52. BIA Area Offices and Indian Agencies: 1988

Government officials and humanitarian reformers at the end of the nineteenth and the beginning of the twentieth century asserted that as the Indians adapted to white society (especially with the individual allot-

ment of land), there would be less and less need for reservations and formal federal concern for the Indians. The Bureau of Indian Affairs with all its field offices, in the language of that day, would "wither away."

In fact, that was far from the case. The bureau seemed unable to relinquish control, and Indian agencies continued. The renewal of tribal governments after 1934 increased the need for some agencies of the federal government to deal with individual tribal governments or groups of tribes.

In 1949, in order to decentralize administration, the secretary of the interior established eleven area offices, to which the reservation superintendents and other officers would report. They were located at Juneau, Alaska; Phoenix, Arizona; Window Rock, Arizona; Sacramento, California; Minneapolis, Minnesota; Billings, Montana; Albuquerque, New Mexico; Anadarko, Oklahoma; Muskogee, Oklahoma; Portland, Oregon; Aberdeen, South Dakota.

An additional Eastern Area Office, in Washington, D.C., deals with certain eastern Indian groups.

This map is based on Bureau of Indian Affairs, *Directory of Field Offices*, February 1988. The *Directory* gives the names of officers in charge, post office addresses, and telephone numbers and is arranged by area office, with the agencies that report to each one.

A general map showing the boundaries of the area offices is in *Handbook of North American Indians*, vol. 4, *History of Indian-White Relations*, ed. Wilcomb E. Washburn (Washington: Smithsonian Institution, 1988), 274.

Map 53. Government Indian Schools: 1899

The education of the Indians for many decades was largely in the hands of missionary organizations, often enough supported by federal funds. Toward the end of the nineteenth century, however, demands (largely from white Protestant reformers) arose for a full-scale national school system for the Indians. Off-reservation boarding schools (patterned on the Carlisle Indian Industrial School established by Richard Henry Pratt in 1879) were established throughout the West, and many government boarding schools appeared on the reservations. Day schools were another element in the system.

The annual reports of the commissioners of Indian affairs provide data on the schools, but in 1899 a special report was issued: *Statistics on Indian Tribes, Indian Agencies, and Indian Schools of Every Character* (Washington: Government Printing Office, 1899). This report, which for most schools gives a precise location, furnished the basic

data for this map. The report also includes information on school capacity, on the use and character of the buildings, and on the extent of farming land. Day schools as well as boarding schools are listed in the report, though only the numbers of such schools by states, not their locations, are shown on the map.

Data in the special report can be augmented with the information on the tribes entitled "Statistics as to Indian Schools during the year ended June 30, 1899," in Report of the Commissioner of Indian Affairs, 1899, *House Document* no. 5, 56th Congress, 1st session, serial 3915, pp. 548–61. The final table in this series gives the following summary information:

Government schools	Enrollment
Nonreservation boarding	6,880
Reservation boarding	8,881
Reservation day	4,951
Contract schools	
Boarding	2,468
Day	42
Contract, specially appropriated for	393
Mission schools	
Boarding	1,079
Day	182
Public day	326
Total	25,202

The commissioner's report for 1899 includes a map entitled "Map Showing Indian Reservations within the Limits of the United States, Compiled under the Direction of the Hon. W. A. Jones, Commissioner of Indian Affairs, 1899," which locates by symbols nonreservation schools, boarding schools, day schools, contract schools, and public schools under contract with the Indian bureau. Unfortunately, it is difficult to decipher some of this information on the map, and in some cases the map does not seem to correspond with the data in the tables.

A detailed description of each school that was still in operation in 1903 is given in another special report: *Statistics of Indian Tribes, Agencies, and Schools, 1903* (Washington: Government Printing Office, 1903; reprint, Millwood, New York: Kraus Reprint Company, 1976).

Map 54. Government Indian Schools: 1919

The Bureau of Indian Affairs in 1919 produced a map in color entitled *Indian Reservations West of the Mississippi River, 1919*, which by symbols of varied shapes and colors located day schools, boarding schools, mission schools, mission contract boarding schools, and nonreservation schools, as well as other entities. I have taken the data for Map 54 from this map (the copy preserved in the Cartographic Branch of the National Archives, Alexandria, Virginia, Record Group 75, Administrative Maps) and from Table 18, "Location, capacity, enrollment, and attendance, etc., of schools during fiscal year ended June 30, 1919," in Report of the Commissioner of Indian Affairs, 1919, *House Document* no. 409, 66th Congress, 2d session, serial 7706, pp. 156–65. Where there is a discrepancy between the two sources, I followed the table in the commissioner's report.

The distribution of schools in 1919 conformed closely to the geographical pattern of government schools established in the 1890s. There were more Indian students enrolled in school, however, and a large number of Indians attended public schools, as the summary of data from the commissioner's report shows (Table 17, "Indian and school population . . . ., Recapitulation," p. 154):

Government schools	Enrollment
Nonreservation boarding	10,852
Reservation boarding	9,660
Day	5,813
Mission schools	
Contract boarding	1,859
Noncontract	
Boarding	2,892
Day	690
Private schools: contract boarding	102
Public schools	29,021
Total	60,889

Map 55. Government Indian Schools: 1989

Although in 1989 the great majority of Indian students were enrolled in public schools, the Bureau of Indian Affairs still was responsible for many boarding schools, especially in the Southwest. A large proportion of these schools, however, were effectively under Indian control.

This map shows a variety of schools, as follows:

BIA on-reservation boarding school: an elementary and/or secondary school.
BIA off-reservation boarding school: an elementary and/or secondary school.
Grant or contract boarding school: an elementary or secondary school operated by a tribe or tribal organization under a grant authorized by P.L. 100–297 (funded by the federal government but Indian controlled) or an elementary and/ or secondary school located either on or off a reservation operated by a tribe or tribal organization under a contract authorized by P.L. 93–638.

Contract off-reservation boarding school: an elementary and/or secondary school located off-reservation operated by a tribe or tribal organization under a contract authorized by P.L. 93–638.
Cooperative boarding school: an elementary and/or secondary school operated under a cooperative agreement between the BIA and a state. Board and lodging are provided for both Indian and non-Indian students.
BIA post-secondary school: junior college level school.
Tribally controlled community college: a two-year or four-year college operated by a tribe or a tribal organization under the Tribally Controlled Community College Act of 1978 or related acts (see *United States Statutes at Large*, 92:1325–31).

The information for this map came from Bureau of Indian Affairs, Office of Indian Education Programs, *Education Directory*, 1989. The *Directory* lists also peripheral dormitories (both BIA operated and tribally operated under contract), which are facilities that provide board and lodging during the school year for students attending public schools, and day schools (shown on the map only as the number of schools in each state). For each school it provides the area office and agency under which the school falls, address and telephone number, person in charge, and range of grades taught.

Help in locating the schools on the Navajo Reservation came from Map 43, "Educational Facilities," in James M. Goodman, *The Navajo Atlas: Environments, Resources, People, and History of the Diné Bikeyah* (Norman: University of Oklahoma Press, 1982), 86–87.

Statistics for enrollment of Indian students in 1988 in BIA-funded schools, broken down into BIA-operated schools and schools operated by tribes under contract, are given in Table 1, "Numbers of Indian Children Attending BIA-Funded Elementary and Secondary Schools, Excluding Peripheral Dormitories and Alaska Schools," in Office of Indian Education Programs, Bureau of Indian Affairs, *Report on BIA Education*, Final Review Draft, March 1988, p. xi:

BIA-operated schools	Enrollment
Boarding	9,126
Day	17,589
Contract schools	
Boarding	2,138
Day	9,064
Total	37,917

The table shows comparable figures for selected years from 1930 to 1988. The *Report* describes the changes:

"In the early 1980s, more than 3,000 students in BIA-operated schools in Alaska became part of the public school system of Alaska. Excluding Alaska schools, total recorded enrollment in BIA-funded schools has risen by about 2,600 students since 1965. . . . Total enrollment outside Alaska reached a peak of 40,280 in 1978. Since then, there has been a small decline in enrollment to 37,917 students in 1987–1988.

"The comparative stability of enrollments has been maintained despite an increasing number of contract schools and contract school enrollments. Total contract school enrollment rose from 2,299 students in 1973 to 11,202 students in 1988. At the same time, enrollment in BIA-operated schools declined from 33,532 students to 26,715 students.

"Boarding schools include significant numbers of day attendees, as well as actual boarders. Counting only the latter, total boarding enrollment has declined sharply, from 24,051 boarding students in 1965 to 11,264 boarding students in 1988, as boarding schools were closed outright or transformed into day schools. A moderate increase in contract boarding attendance (from 500 boarding students in 1973 to 2,138 boarding students in 1988) has been overwhelmed by the decline in boarding students attending BIA-operated schools. However, enrollment in day schools operated by the BIA has risen from 11,235 students in 1965 to 17,589 students in 1988—an indication of the strength of tribal support for converting boarding schools to day schools.

"Over time, BIA-funded schools have educated a smaller percentage of the total number of Indian students attending elementary and secondary schools in the United States. Within BIA areas of service responsibility the percentage of students attending BIA-funded schools fell from 39 percent in 1930 to 23 percent in 1977 (the last year BIA reported this statistic), due partly to the movement of some Indian families off-reservation to seek employment. By 1977, more than two-thirds of Indian students within BIA areas of service responsibility were attending public schools.

"Many Indian students live in urban areas where they have no connection with BIA or its services. Nationwide there were 391,937 Indian students enrolled in schools of all kinds in 1986. However, students enrolled in BIA-funded schools were slightly less than 10 percent of all Indian students in the United States." (Pp. x–xii)

Map 56. Indian Hospitals: 1919

After 1900 the federal government paid increasing attention to Indian health, as evidence mounted of devastating morbidity, especially tuberculosis and trachoma (an eye disease).

The Bureau of Indian Affairs map entitled *Indian Reservations West of the Mississippi, 1919* includes symbols showing the location of hospitals. It, together with Table 15, "Hospitals and sanatoria in Indian Service, fiscal year ended June 30, 1919," in Report of the Commissioner of Indian Affairs, 1919, *House Document* no. 409, 66th Congress, 2d session, serial 7706, pp. 141–44, furnished the information for this map. The table makes a distinction between agency hospitals, school hospitals, combined agency and school hospitals, and sanatoria. The Indian Insane Asylum at Canton, South Dakota, is a separate category.

Map 57. Indian Health Facilities: 1985

In 1954 Congress transferred responsibility for Indian health services from the Bureau of Indian Affairs to the Public Health Service (now in the Department of Health and Human Services), which directs a variety of health facilities. Indian participation in the provision of health care is provided by the Indian Self-Determination and Education Assistance Act of 1975 and the Indian Health Care Improvement Act of 1976.

This map is based on *Indian Health Facilities*, published by the Indian Health Service about 1985. It shows IHS hospitals and health centers, tribally-run hospitals and health centers, school health centers, rural-tribal health programs in California, and urban Indian health programs, but it does not include IHS-funded alcoholism programs and environmental health field stations.

See also *IHS and Tribally Operated Facilities List as of October 1, 1988,* issued by the Division of Program Statistics, Indian Health Service.

SECTION VI
Oklahoma (Indian Territory)

Map 58. Indian Territory: Removal to 1855

This is a standard map, which shows the land holdings of the Five Civilized Tribes in the West after removal. It appears in a number of publications. I have used the following sources: John W. Morris, Charles R. Goins, and Edwin C. McReynolds, *Historical Atlas of Oklahoma*, 3d ed. (Norman: University of Oklahoma Press, 1986), Map 23, "Indian Territory, 1830–1855"; Roy Gittinger, *The Formation of the State of Oklahoma, 1803–1906* (Norman: University of Oklahoma

Press, 1939), "Territory of the Southern Indians before 1855," opposite p. 60; and Edward Everett Dale and Morris L. Wardell, *History of Oklahoma* (New York: Prentice-Hall, 1948), "Indian Territory, 1837–1855," p. 124.

Map 59. Indian Territory: 1855–1866

The Choctaws and the Chickasaws (who originally settled on the western section of Choctaw lands) agreed to a separation of their lands, which was confirmed by a treaty concluded in Washington in 1855. By this treaty the two tribes leased to the United States their lands jointly claimed west of the 98th meridian. This Leased District was intended for the settlement of Wichita Indians and other tribes. See treaties with Choctaws and Chickasaws, November 4, 1854, and June 22, 1855, in Charles J. Kappler, *Indian Affairs: Laws and Treaties*, vol. 2, *Treaties* (Washington: Government Printing Office, 1904), 652–63, 706–14.

Similarly, the Seminoles, who settled on Creek lands, were unhappy with the arrangement, and in 1856 they were separated from the Creeks. See treaty with Creeks and Seminoles, August 7, 1856, in Kappler, *Treaties,* 756–63.

Greer County was claimed by Texas because of a dispute about the true course of the Red River. Finally, on March 16, 1896, the Supreme Court decided against Texas's claim (*United States* v. *Texas,* 162 *U.S. Reports* 1–91).

This map is based on maps published in the books indicated above in the note for Map 58: Morris and others, *Historical Atlas of Oklahoma,* Map 26, "Indian Territory, 1855–1866"; Gittinger, *State of Oklahoma,* "The Indian Territory, 1855–1866," opposite p. 84; and Dale and Wardell, *Oklahoma,* "Indian Territory, 1856–1860," p. 149.

Map 60. Indian Territory: 1866–1889

Under the Reconstruction treaties after the Civil War, the Five Civilized Tribes in Indian Territory lost the western part of their lands, which were then opened to other Indian tribes, as shown on this map. See Kappler, *Treaties,* 910–15 (Seminole); 918–31 (Choctaw and Chickasaw); 931–36 (Creek); 942–50 (Cherokee).

This map is based on the following maps: Morris and others, *Historical Atlas of Oklahoma,* Map 33, "Indian Territory, 1866–1889"; Gittinger, *State of Oklahoma,* "The Indian Territory in 1889," opposite p. 186; Dale and Wardell, *Oklahoma,* "Indian Territory, 1885," p. 197.

Map 61. Oklahoma Indian Population by Counties and SMSAs: 1980

This map reproduces data used on the gen-

eral Indian population map for 1980 (Map 10). The population distribution, by counties and SMSAs, is shown here on a different scale, which eliminates overlapping of circles. The data came from *1980 Census of Population,* vol. 1, *Characteristics of the Population,* chap. C, *General Social and Economic Characteristics,* part 38, *Oklahoma,* Table 58, "Race by Sex: 1980."

In 1984, Bureau of Indian Affairs offices in Oklahoma reported the following tribal populations for the state:

Five Nations	
Cherokee	42,992
Creek	37,679
Choctaw	19,660
Chickasaw	8,507
Seminole	3,719
Small Tribes in Northeastern Oklahoma	
Quapaw	1,193
Delaware	989
Seneca-Cayuga	670
Wyandotte	440
Peoria	355
Miami	350
Ottawa	336
Eastern Shawnee	335
Modoc	150
Plains Tribes	
Citizen Potawatomi	11,094
Kiowa	9,197
Cheyenne-Arapaho	8,309
Comanche	8,126
Osage	5,612
Caddo	2,947
Pawnee	2,325
Absentee Shawnee	2,297
Sac and Fox	2,145
Ponca	2,024
Kickapoo	1,741
Oto-Missouri	1,334
Wichita	1,169
Apache	1,001
Kaw	331
Fort Sill Apache	302
Iowa	280
Tonkawa	212

John W. Morris, Charles R. Goins, and Edwin C. McReynolds, *Historical Atlas of Oklahoma,* 3d ed. (Norman: University of Oklahoma Press, 1986), Map 76, "Population: Distribution of Indians, 1980."

Map 62. Oklahoma, Showing Historic Indian Areas, with Population: 1980

The Bureau of the Census in 1980, for the first time, enumerated Indians in what it called "Historic Indian Areas of Oklahoma (Excluding Urbanized Areas)." These areas were defined as follows: "The historic areas of Oklahoma (excluding urbanized areas) consist of the former reservations which had legally established boundaries during the period 1900–1907. These reservations were dissolved during the two- to three-year period preceding the statehood of Oklahoma in 1907." The map shows historical Indian areas in white; the urban areas are drawn with a heavy line.

The data were taken from *1980 Census of Population, Supplementary Report, American Indian Areas and Alaska Native Villages: 1980,* PC80-S1-13, map on page vi and Table 5, "Total and American Indian Persons and Housing Unit Counts for the Identified Historic Areas of Oklahoma (Excluding Urbanized Areas) by County: 1980," p. 27.

SECTION VII
Alaska

Map 63. Culture Areas and Tribal Areas in Alaska

Alaska is part of three general cultural areas: Arctic, Subarctic, and Northwest Coast, as culture areas are delineated in the Smithsonian Institution's *Handbook of North American Indians* and the National Geographic Society's *The World of the American Indian* (Washington: National Geographic Society, 1974) and its map *Indians of North America* (Washington: National Geographic Society, 1974). For discussion of culture areas, see the notes for Map 1.

Map 63 shows not only the three culture areas (marked by a heavy line), but also tribal areas within each culture area. There is less agreement about these than about the culture areas. I have relied on the maps, "Key to Tribal Territories," in *Handbook of North American Indians,* vol. 6, *Subarctic,* ed. June Helm (Washington: Smithsonian Institution, 1981), ix; and vol. 5, *Arctic,* ed. David Damas (Washington: Smithsonian Institution, 1984), p. ix. See also map "Indian Tribes of North America" in Harold E. Driver and William C. Massey, *Comparative Studies of North American Indians,* Transactions of the American Philosophical Society, new series, vol. 47, pt. 2 (Philadelphia: American Philosophical Society, 1957), inside back cover.

There is a map of Alaska showing culture areas, tribal areas, and linguistic stocks in *The National Atlas of the United States of America* (Washington: Department of the Interior, Geological Survey, 1970), 132.

Map 64. Alaska Native Population: 1970

Because Alaska is not divided into counties, census enumeration was based on organized boroughs and on census divisions agreed upon by the state and the Bureau of the Census. This map shows the census areas used in 1970 and for each indicates by an outer circle the total number of Alaska Natives (Indians, Eskimos, and Aleuts) and by an inner solid circle the number of Indians only. Data were taken from *Census of Population: 1970, General Population Characteristics,* pt. 3, *Alaska,* Table 34, "Race by Sex, for Census Divisions: 1970." Table 34 does not list Eskimos and Aleuts separately but combines them under "all other races," and I have used that enumeration.

Alaska population, on a choropleth map, is included in the map *Number of American Indians by Counties of the United States: 1970* (Washington: Bureau of the Census, 1973).

Map 65. Alaska Native Population: 1980

Data for this map were taken from *1980 Census of Population,* vol. 1, *Characteristics of the Population,* chap. C, *General Social and Economic Characteristics,* pt. 3, *Alaska,* Table 58, "Race by Sex: 1980." The map shows the boroughs and other census areas for 1980 and for each indicates by an outer circle the total number of Alaska Natives (Indians, Eskimos, and Aleuts) and by an inner solid circle the number of Indians only. In 1980 Eskimos and Aleuts were enumerated separately and not counted under "all other races"; the census counts were based on self-classification as to race.

Table 7, "Persons by Race for Identified Alaska Native Villages by Boroughs and Census Areas: 1980," in *1980 Census of Population, Supplementary Report, American Indian Areas and Alaska Native Villages: 1980* (Washington: Bureau of the Census, 1984), gives slightly different figures, based on corrections made after the final census tabulations were completed.

Map 66. Alaska Native Villages by Regional Corporations: 1980

The Alaska Native Claims Settlement Act of 1971 divided Alaska into twelve regional corporations and recognized villages within each of the regions. These categories were the basis for one enumeration of Alaska population in the 1980 census, which furnished the data for this map and the accompanying table. The data are printed in *1980 Census of Population, Supplementary Report, American Indian Areas and Alaska Native Villages: 1980,* Table 8, "Persons by Race for Identified Alaska Native Villages by Regional Corporations: 1980."

Regional corporation boundaries and the location of the villages within each region were taken chiefly from the maps in Robert D. Arnold and others, *Alaska Native Land Claims* (Anchorage: Alaska Native Foundation, 1976): a large folded map inside back cover, entitled simply "Alaska," which shows boroughs, regional corporations, and villages; and a series of twelve maps (one for each regional corporation) printed in the text of the book. I was helped in locating villages by the large folded map "Native Communities of Alaska," in *Alaska Natives and the Land* (Anchorage: Federal Field Committee for Development Planning in Alaska, 1968), and the large map (42 x 60 inches) entitled "Alaska" prepared by the Bureau of the Census and showing boundaries and locations as of 1980. This second map was distributed by the Superintendent of Documents (C362/6:AL13/980).

SECTION VIII
The Army and the Indian Frontier

Maps 67–73. United States Military Posts, 1789–1895

These maps were published originally as plates 14–20 in Francis Paul Prucha, *A Guide to the Military Posts of the United States, 1789–1895* (Madison: State Historical Society of Wisconsin, 1964). The remarkable topographical map by Erwin Raisz, "Landforms of the United States," serves as the base map.

It was difficult to pinpoint precisely the location of some of these nineteenth-century installations. Sometimes they changed locations several times, and often the early maps that show the locations are inaccurate in their geographical features. Similarly, the dating of the establishment and abandonment of military posts was fraught with difficulties. Whenever the information was available, the maps show the date when the troops first arrived at the site and the date when they left, but it should be noted that the dates of troop arrival, of orders officially establishing a fort, and of orders naming the post do not always coincide. And abandonment might be dated from the time that caretakers left the site or when the army turned the military reservation over to the Department of the Interior or when the government sold the property to some private individual. A careful study of published government and other lists and maps and of the federal records and cartographic materials in the National Archives, however, has resulted in reasonably complete and accurate information.

Posts that were still in use in 1895 do not have a terminal date indicated.

A number of published lists of regular army military installations are available, which vary in completeness and in accuracy. The following were useful in the compilation of data for these maps.

"List of Military Forts, Arsenals, Camps, Barracks, &c," in Thomas H.S. Hamersly, *Complete Regular Army Register of the United States for One Hundred Years (1778–1879)* (Washington: T.H.S. Hamersly, 1880), part II, pp. 122–62.

"List of Forts, Batteries, Named Camps, Redoubts, Reservations, General Hospitals, National Cemeteries, etc., Established or Erected in the United States from Its Earliest Settlement to Date," in Francis B. Heitman, *Historical Register and Dictionary of the United States Army, from Its Organization, September 29, 1789, to March 2, 1903*, 2 vols. (Washington: Government Printing Office, 1903), 2:475–559.

List of Military Posts, etc., Established in the United States from Its Earliest Settlement to the Present Time (Washington: Government Printing Office, 1902).

Outline Index of Military Forts and Stations. A compilation of data in 26 folio volumes in manuscript, in Records of the Adjutant General's Office, Record Group 94, National Archives.

In addition there are official listings of military posts at given dates. These include tables prepared by the adjutant general and published in the annual reports of the secretary of war and the following special reports.

"Geographical Positions of the Military Posts, with Their Local Topography and Altitudes Above the Sea," in *Statistical Report on the Sickness and Mortality in the Army of the United States, Compiled from the Records of the Surgeon General's Office, Embracing a Period of Sixteen years, from January, 1839, to January, 1855 (Senate Executive Document* no. 96, 34th Congress, 1st session, serial 827), pp. 498–508.

A Report on Barracks and Hospitals, with Descriptions of Military Posts, Circular no. 4 (Washington: Office of the Surgeon General, 1870).

A Report on the Hygiene of the United States Army, with Descriptions of Military Posts, Circular no. 8 (Washington: Office of the Surgeon General, 1875).

Outline Description of U.S. Military Posts and Stations in the Year 1871 (Washington, 1872).

Outline Descriptions of the Posts and Stations of Troops in the Geographical Divisions and Departments of the United States, compiled by Inspector General R. B. Marcy, by order of the General in Chief of the Army (Washington, 1872).

Also of use were a variety of official lists for particular geographical divisions.

When all these resources failed, it was necessary to use manuscript records in the National Archives, such as post or department returns, special lists of forts, inspection reports, medical histories, and letter books. These are found in Records of the Adjutant General's Office (Record Group 94), Records of the Headquarters of the Army (Record Group 108), Records of the Office of the Inspector General (Record Group 159), Records of the Office of the Secretary of War (Record Group 107), and Records of United States Army Commands (Record Group 98). The Cartographic Branch of the National Archives, with its rich collection of manuscript maps, has many materials concerning military posts.

For a more detailed listing and discussion of all these source materials, see Prucha, *Guide to Military Posts,* 159–78.

Maps Showing Distribution of Regular Army Troops

The following chronological series of maps showing distribution of regular army troops at selected dates (Maps 74–86) was published originally in Prucha, *Guide to the Military Posts of the United States,* plates 1–13. They were based on data drawn from the annual reports of the secretary of war, as noted below for each map.

The relative size of the garrison at each post is indicated by the size of the black dot marking the posts. The names of the posts, listed according to present-day states, and the number of soldiers at each are given below for each map. Some arsenals are omitted from the maps and from the lists.

By reference to Maps 67–73, one can determine the names of the specific posts shown graphically on these maps. Sources for the location of the posts are listed above.

Map 74. Distribution of Regular Army Troops: 1817

After the War of 1812, during which western posts on the Indian frontiers were destroyed or evacuated, the War Department began a program of regarrisoning, hoping especially to block the channels through which British traders moved into the Mississippi and Missouri river valleys from Canada. In 1816 Fort Dearborn was reestablished at Chicago, Fort Howard built at Green Bay, and three new posts established on the upper Mississippi.

The concentration of troops along the St. Lawrence boundary and in the South in the vicinity of Mobile and New Orleans reflected a carry-over from the deployments of the war. But the fanning out of troops into the Northwest is evident. Fort Osage was the farthest outpost, but the region of the upper Mississippi and the Great Lakes was well provided with small garrisons. The War Department was concerned also about coastal defenses, and Secretary of War John C. Calhoun worried about their effectiveness in a future war.

Distribution of the Army, 1817

State	Post	Number of troops
Alabama	Fort Bowyer	28
	Fort Charlotte	52
	Fort Crawford	97
	Fort Hampton	67
	Fort Montgomery	421
	Cantonment Montpelier	350
Connecticut	Fort Trumbull	73
Georgia	Point Petre	83
	Fort Scott	42
Illinois	Fort Armstrong	132
	Fort Clark	30
	Fort Dearborn	93
	Fort Edwards	64
Indiana	Fort Harrison	76
	Fort Wayne	56
Kentucky	Newport	22
Louisiana	Baton Rouge	217
	Covington	124
	Natchitoches	182
	New Orleans	63
	Petite Coquille	69
	Fort St. Philip	79
Maine	Fort George	60
	Fort Preble	118

State	Post	Number of troops
Maryland	Fort McHenry	105
	Fort Severn	88
	Fort Washington	187
Massachusetts	Fort Independence	290
	Fort Sewall	76
	Fort Warren	51
Michigan	Cantonment Detroit	249
	Fort Gratiot	49
	Grosse Isle	55
	Michilimackinac	175
	Fort Shelby	65
Mississippi	Pass Christian	332
Missouri	Belle Fontaine	159
	Fort Osage	49
New Hampshire	Fort Constitution	236
New York	New York Harbor	
	Fort Columbus	194
	Fort Lewis	78
	Fort Wood	74
	Greenbush	71
	Fort Niagara	179
	Fort Pike	101
	Plattsburg	428
	Sackett's Harbor	460
North Carolina	Fort Johnston	67
Pennsylvania	Fort Mifflin	108
	Pittsburgh	35
Rhode Island	Fort Adams	53
	Fort Wolcott	65
South Carolina	Charleston Harbor (Fort Moultrie, Fort Johnson)	74
Virginia	Craney Island	43
	Fort Nelson	64
	Fort Norfolk	50
	Richmond	34
Wisconsin	Fort Crawford	218
	Fort Howard	224

Source:

Table, "Distribution of the Army of the United States, Showing the Strength of Posts and Garrisons," December 1, 1817, *American State Papers: Military Affairs*, vol. 1 (Washington: Gales and Seaton, 1832), 671–72.

Map 75. Distribution of Regular Army Troops: 1822

The advance into the West that was part of Secretary of War John C. Calhoun's plan to promote the fur trade and to vindicate American sovereignty resulted in new posts, even though the army was reduced in size in 1821. The most important of the new posts were Fort Snelling, at the confluence of the Minnesota and Mississippi rivers; Fort Atkinson, on the Missouri above present-day Omaha; Fort Smith, on the Arkansas; and Fort Jesup, in northwestern Louisiana. The string of small posts along the Great Lakes and the Atlantic coast remained.

Distribution of the Army, 1822

State	Post	Number of troops
Alabama	Mobile	43
Arkansas	Fort Smith	239
	Sulphur Fork	41

State	Post	Number of troops
Connecticut	Fort Trumbull	56
Florida	Pensacola	491
	St. Augustine	121
	St. Mark's	89
Georgia	Augusta Arsenal	35
	Fort Jackson	46
Illinois	Fort Armstrong	55
	Chicago (Fort Dearborn)	90
	Fort Edwards	54
Louisiana	Baton Rouge	315
	Cantonment Jesup	141
	Petite Coquille	51
Maine	Fort Preble	54
	Fort Sullivan	50
Maryland	Fort McHenry	53
	Fort Severn	47
	Fort Washington	64
Massachusetts	Fort Independence	112
Michigan	Mackinac	56
	Saganaw	93
	Sault Ste. Marie	274
	Fort Shelby	48
Minnesota	Falls of St. Anthony (Fort Snelling)	315
Nebraska	Council Bluffs (Fort Atkinson)	490
New Hampshire	Fort Constitution	44
New York	New York Harbor	112
	Niagara	42
	Plattsburg	69
	Sackett's Harbor	179
	Watervliet Arsenal	37
North Carolina	Fort Johnston	43
Pennsylvania	Fort Mifflin	51
	Pittsburgh Arsenal	44
Rhode Island	Fort Wolcott	51
South Carolina	Charleston Harbor	75
Virginia	Norfolk Harbor	108
	Richmond Arsenal	39
Wisconsin	Fort Crawford	105
	Green Bay (Fort Howard)	243

Source:

Tables C and D (dated November 9, 1822), *American State Papers: Military Affairs*, vol. 2 (Washington: Gales and Seaton, 1834), 455–56.

Map 76. Distribution of Regular Army Troops: 1830

In the 1820s War Department plans called for a line of exterior posts along the Indian frontier from Sault Ste. Marie in the north to Fort Jesup in the south. But Secretaries of War John C. Calhoun and James Barbour believed that troops should be concentrated in a few centers rather than dispersed broadly, and in 1826 Jefferson Barracks was established a few miles below St. Louis to be a central depot for troops and supplies.

In 1830 the defense system followed a simple arrangement: small fortifications along the Atlantic, along the frontier of the Great Lakes, and at the mouth of the Mississippi; in the West, in addition to the concentration at Jefferson Barracks, small garrisons at selected points along the Indian border. A line of posts marked the Fox-Wisconsin waterway between the Lakes and the Mississippi.

Distribution of the Army, 1830

State	Post	Number of troops
Alabama	Fort Mitchell	39
Connecticut	Fort Trumbull	105
Delaware	Fort Delaware	89
Florida	Fort Marion	51
Illinois	Fort Armstrong	94
	Fort Dearborn	95
Kansas	Cantonment Leavenworth	181
Louisiana	Cantonment Atkinson	50
	Baton Rouge	180
	Cantonment Jesup	149
	Fort Pike	50
	Fort St. Philip	48
	Fort Wood	41
Maine	Hancock Barracks	173
	Fort Preble	59
	Fort Sullivan	52
Maryland	Fort McHenry	105
	Fort Severn	48
	Fort Washington	47
Massachusetts	Fort Independence	154
Michigan	Fort Brady	118
	Fort Gratiot	114
	Fort Mackinac	111
Minnesota	Fort Snelling	160
Missouri	Jefferson Barracks	591
New Hampshire	Fort Constitution	48
New York	Fort Columbus	218
	Madison Barracks	108
	Fort Niagara	84
North Carolina	Fort Johnston	54
Oklahoma	Cantonment Gibson	243
Rhode Island	Fort Wolcott	56
South Carolina	Fort Moultrie	85
Virginia	Bellona Arsenal	57
	Fortress Monroe	340
Wisconsin	Fort Crawford	196
	Fort Howard	219
	Fort Winnebago	146

Source:
Tables C and D (dated November 20, 1830), Report of the Secretary of War, 1830, *Senate Document* no. 1, 21st Congress, 2d session, serial 203, pp. 88–91.

Map 77. Distribution of Regular Army Troops: 1839
The distribution of troops in 1839 reflected three significant events. One was Indian removal, principally of the Five Civilized Tribes (Cherokee, Creek, Choctaw, Chickasaw, and Seminole) from the southeastern states but also of many small tribes in the North. To protect them in the land assigned them west of Missouri and Arkansas, the federal government concentrated troops along the border. The second was the Florida War (the Second Seminole War), which broke out in 1835 and drained troops from regular garrisons in a futile attempt to force all the Seminoles out of Florida. The third was the so-called Patriot War of 1838–1840 along the Canadian frontier—one of the periodic outbreaks of agitation by self-styled patriots to free Canada from British rule and perhaps annex her to the United States. In addition to these main concentrations, troops remained at posts on the Great Lakes, the upper Mississippi, and the Fox-Wisconsin passageway.

Distribution of the Army, 1839

State	Post	Number of troops
Arkansas	Fort Smith	127
Florida	Troops in Seminole War	4,271
Kansas	Fort Leavenworth	436
Louisiana	Fort Jesup	323
Maine	Hancock Barracks	153
Maryland	Fort McHenry	69
Michigan	Fort Brady	97
	Detroit frontier	482
Minnesota	Fort Snelling	346
New York	Madison Barracks	591
	New York Harbor	52
	Niagara frontier	687
	Plattsburg	321
Oklahoma	Fort Gibson	596
	Fort Towson	339
	Fort Wayne	242
Wisconsin	Fort Crawford	187
	Fort Howard	86
	Fort Winnebago	166

Source:
Tables C and D (dated November 1839), Report of the Secretary of War, 1839, *Senate Document* no. 1, 26th Congress, 1st session, serial 354, pp. 68–73.

Map 78. Distribution of Regular Army Troops: 1843
After the Seminole difficulties ended and the patriots' agitation along the Canadian border died out, the distribution of troops returned to a more normal pattern.

Distribution of the Army, 1843

State	Post	Number of troops
Alabama	Fort Morgan	106
Arkansas	Fort Smith	110
Connecticut	Fort Trumbull	60
Florida	Fort Brooke	277
	Key West	96
	Fort Marion	248
	Pensacola (Fort Pickens, Fort McRee)	116
Georgia	Augusta Arsenal	56
	Oglethorpe Barracks	107
Iowa	Fort Atkinson	102
	Fort Des Moines	107
Kansas	Fort Leavenworth	381
	Fort Scott	195
Louisiana	Baton Rouge	102
	Fort Jesup	418
	New Orleans Barracks	110
	Fort Pike	52
	Fort Wood	62
Maine	Hancock Barracks	272
	Fort Preble	69
	Fort Sullivan	62
Maryland	Fort McHenry	123
	Fort Severn	58
Michigan	Fort Brady	74
	Detroit Barracks	312
	Fort Gratiot	112
	Fort Mackinac	135
Minnesota	Fort Snelling	195

State	Post	Number of troops
Missouri	Jefferson Barracks	956
New Hampshire	Fort Constitution	65
New York	Buffalo Barracks	231
	Madison Barracks	162
	New York Harbor (Fort Columbus, Fort Hamilton, Fort Lafayette)	519
	Fort Niagara	53
	Fort Ontario	61
	Plattsburg Barracks	80
North Carolina	Fort Johnston	64
	Fort Macon	65
Oklahoma	Fort Gibson	388
	Fort Towson	251
	Fort Washita	265
Pennsylvania	Carlisle Barracks	67
	Fort Mifflin	70
Rhode Island	Newport (Fort Adams, Fort Wolcott)	202
South Carolina	Charleston (Fort Moultrie, Castle Pinckney)	225
Virginia	Fort Monroe	418
Wisconsin	Fort Crawford	201
	Fort Winnebago	57

Source:

Table C (dated November 30, 1843), Report of the Secretary of War, 1843, *Senate Document* no. 1, 28th Congress, 1st session, serial 431, p. 67b.

Map 79. Distribution of Regular Army Troops: 1845

The arrangement of troops established by 1843 was seriously disrupted by the Mexican War, as large numbers of regular soldiers were sent to Texas. Some western posts were evacuated, and others were left with only skeletal garrisons. The defense installations along the Canadian border and on the Atlantic and Gulf coasts were retained, most with very few soldiers.

Distribution of the Army, 1845

State	Post	Number of troops
Arkansas	Fort Smith	64
Connecticut	Fort Trumbull	48
Florida	Fort Brooke	102
	Fort McRee	58
	Fort Marion	56
	Fort Pickens	77
Georgia	Augusta Arsenal	47
	Oglethorpe Barracks	48
Iowa	Fort Atkinson	58
	Fort Des Moines	64
Kansas	Fort Leavenworth	279
	Fort Scott	101
Louisiana	Fort Jesup	69
	Fort Pike	52
	Fort Wood	59
Maryland	Fort McHenry	106
Michigan	Fort Brady	53
	Detroit Barracks	86
	Fort Gratiot	50
	Fort Mackinac	51
	Fort Wilkins	48
Minnesota	Fort Snelling	89

State	Post	Number of troops
Missouri	Jefferson Barracks	357
New York	Fort Columbus	314
	Fort Hamilton	62
	Madison Barracks	97
	Fort Niagara	46
	Fort Ontario	52
	Plattsburg Barracks	48
Oklahoma	Fort Gibson	201
	Fort Towson	127
	Fort Washita	132
Pennsylvania	Carlisle Barracks	59
	Fort Mifflin	59
Rhode Island	Fort Adams	54
South Carolina	Charleston Harbor (Fort Moultrie, Castle Pinckney)	107
Texas	Army in Texas	4,079
Virginia	Fort Monroe	272

Source:

Tables C, D, and E (dated November 26, 1845), Report of the Secretary of War, 1845, *Senate Document* no. 1, 29th Congress, 1st session, serial 470, pp. 220 c-e.

Map 80. Distribution of Regular Army Troops: 1850

The rapid expansion of United States jurisdiction into the Trans-Mississippi West that came with the annexation of Texas in 1845, the settlement of the Oregon question in 1846, and the Mexican Cession following the Mexican War in 1848 meant that by 1850 the army had shifted its main effort to the region west of the ninety-eighth meridian. The tiny coastal fortifications and the posts along the Great Lakes were retained, but the western half of the continent became the scene of military activity, which steadily increased as emigrants, miners, and settlers caused Indian resistance and hostility. Thus new posts appeared along the Oregon Trail, on the frontiers of Texas, on the Rio Grande in New Mexico, in the Pacific Northwest, and in California.

Distribution of the Army, 1850

State	Post	Number of troops
California	Benicia	67
	Camp Far West	50
	Monterey Redoubt	38
	Presidio of San Francisco	24
	Mission of San Diego	85
	Post on the San Gabriel	71
	Mission of San Luis Rey	49
	Sonoma	37
	Camp Yuma	95
Connecticut	Fort Trumbull	50
Florida	Fort Casey	56
	Key West Barracks	51
	Fort Marion	53
	Fort Meade	55
	Fort Myers	111
	Pensacola (Fort Pickens, Fort McRee)	57
	Fort Pierce	57
Georgia	Oglethorpe Barracks	17
Iowa	Fort Clarke	77
Kansas	Fort Atkinson	77
	Fort Leavenworth	388

State	Post	Number of troops
	Fort Scott	61
Louisiana	Baton Rouge Barracks	54
	New Orleans Barracks	45
Maine	Fort Preble	48
	Fort Sullivan	52
Maryland	Fort McHenry	158
	Fort Washington	94
Massachusetts	Fort Independence	111
Michigan	Fort Brady	30
	Detroit Barracks	74
	Fort Gratiot	37
	Fort Mackinac	41
Minnesota	Fort Ripley	83
	Fort Snelling	198
Missouri	Jefferson Barracks	385
Nebraska	Fort Kearny	101
New Hampshire	Fort Constitution	54
New Mexico	Abiquiu	64
	Albuquerque	114
	Ciboleta	54
	Dona Ana	117
	Las Vegas	113
	Rayado	81
	Santa Fe	346
	Socorro	101
	Taos	52
New York	New York Harbor	
	Fort Columbus	133
	Fort Hamilton	107
	Fort Lafayette	58
	Madison Barracks	54
	Fort Niagara	47
	Fort Ontario	48
	Plattsburg Barracks	48
Oklahoma	Fort Arbuckle	51
	Fort Gibson	192
	Fort Towson	51
	Fort Washita	94
Oregon	Camp Astoria	63
	Camp Drum	87
Pennsylvania	Fort Mifflin	53
Rhode Island	Fort Adams	196
South Carolina	Fort Moultrie	203
	Castle Pinckney	56
Texas	Austin	40
	Fort Brown	107
	Fort Croghan	98
	Corpus Christi	94
	Fort Duncan	216
	El Paso	91
	Fort Gates	92
	Fort Graham	91
	Fort Inge	98
	Fort Lincoln	141
	Fort McIntosh	133
	Fort Martin Scott	102
	Fort Merrill	118
	Ringgold Barracks	112
	San Antonio	173
	San Elizario	55
	Fort Worth	100
Virginia	Fort Monroe	128

State	Post	Number of troops
Washington	Columbia Barracks	256
	Steilacoom	69
Wisconsin	Fort Howard	77

Source:
Tables C, D, and E (dated November 30, 1850), Report of the Secretary of War, 1850, *Senate Executive Document* no. 1, pt. 2, 31st Congress, 2d session, serial 587, following p. 116.

Map 81. Distribution of Regular Army Troops: 1860
The number of western posts increased in the 1850s, and the coastal fortifications of the East were almost completely drained of their soldiers. On the eve of the Civil War nearly the entire regular army was west of the Mississippi.

Distribution of the Army, 1860

State	Post	Number of troops
Arizona	Fort Breckinridge	73
	Fort Buchanan	45
	Fort Defiance	256
	Fort Mojave	109
California	Alcatraz Island	43
	Benecia Barracks	61
	Fort Bragg	31
	Fort Crook	55
	Fort Gaston	50
	Fort Humboldt	52
	Nome Cult Indian Agency	24
	Presidio of San Francisco	65
	Fort Tejon	37
	Fort Ter-Waw	57
	Fort Yuma	95
Colorado	Fort Garland	52
Florida	Barrancas Barracks	52
	Key West Barracks	58
Kansas	Fort Larned	166
	Fort Leavenworth	379
	Fort Riley	89
Louisiana	Baton Rouge Barracks	40
Massachusetts	Fort Independence	69
Michigan	Fort Mackinac	64
Minnesota	Fort Ridgely	89
	Fort Ripley	184
Missouri	Jefferson Barracks	159
Nebraska	Fort Kearny	206
Nevada	Carson Valley Expedition	254
New Mexico	Albuquerque	115
	Cantonment Burgwin	19
	Fort Craig	27
	Fort Fillmore	56
	Los Lunas	59
	Fort Marcy	23
	Fort Stanton	77
	Fort Union	161
New York	New York Harbor (Fort Hamilton, Fort Lafayette)	65
	Plattsburg Barracks	61
North Dakota	Fort Abercrombie	141
Oklahoma	Fort Arbuckle	85
	Fort Cobb	273
	Fort Washita	23

State	Post	Number of troops
Oregon	Fort Dalles	72
	Fort Hoskins	108
	Fort Umpqua	17
	Fort Yamhill	67
South Carolina	Fort Moultrie	90
South Dakota	Fort Randall	341
Texas	Camp Barranca	59
	Fort Bliss	60
	Fort Brown	249
	Fort Chadbourne	107
	Fort Clark	92
	Camp Colorado	76
	Camp Cooper	87
	Fort Davis	138
	Fort Duncan	88
	Camp Hudson	54
	Fort Inge	47
	Fort Lancaster	79
	Camp McIntosh	81
	Fort Mason	124
	Fort Quitman	32
	Ringgold Barracks	127
	Camp Rosario	57
	San Antonio Barracks	65
	Fort Stockton	83
	Camp Verde	83
	Camp Wood	54
Utah	Camp Floyd	284
Virginia	Fort Monroe	410
Washington	Fort Cascades	55
	Camp Chehalis	59
	Fort Colville	166
	Fort Steilacoom	254
	Fort Vancouver	428
	Fort Walla Walla	276
	Escort to boundary commission	112
Wyoming	Fort Bridger	143
	Fort Laramie	333

Some dots on the map represent troops in the field or en route from Utah at the end of the Mormon War.

Source:

Tables C, D, E, F, G, H, and I (dated November 28, 1860), Report of the Secretary of War, 1860, *Senate Executive Document* No. 1, pt. 2, 36th Congress, 2d session, serial 1079, pp. 214–29.

Map 82. Distribution of Regular Army Troops: 1867

At the end of the Civil War, Indian disturbances in the West called for an extension of the military frontier, with posts manned to a large extent by veterans of the war. The resultant distribution of troops at new posts in Dakota, along the Powder River in Wyoming, and in the Southwest changed the configuration of troop distribution. At the same time a large number of small troop concentrations appeared throughout the South as part of the Reconstruction occupation.

The eastern posts and the southern occupation troops, although shown on the map, are not included in the list below. For Texas, only the Indian-related regular forts are listed.

Distribution of the Army in the West, 1867

State	Post	Number of troops
Arizona	Camp Bowie	46
	Camp Goodwin	141
	Camp Grant	165
	Camp Lincoln	94
	Camp Lowell	51
	Camp McDowell	225
	Camp McPherson	93
	Camp Mojave	248
	Camp at Tubac	143
	Camp Wallen	36
	Camp Whipple	44
California	San Francisco area	
	Alcatraz Island	228
	Angel Island	119
	Fort Point	83
	Presidio of San Francisco	297
	Point San Jose	110
	Camp Bidwell	101
	Camp Cady	36
	Drum Barracks	575
	Camp Gaston	130
	Camp Independence	106
	Camp Lincoln	119
	Camp Wright	67
	Fort Yuma	68
Colorado	Fort Garland	53
	Fort Lyon	211
	Fort Morgan	87
	Fort Reynolds	101
	Fort Sedgwick	206
Idaho	Fort Boise	54
	Fort Lapwai	65
	Camp Lyon	42
	Camp Three Forks Owyhee	179
Kansas	Fort Dodge	310
	Downer's Station	82
	Camp Grierson	76
	Fort Harker	398
	Fort Hays	560
	Camp Hoffman	82
	Fort Larned	309
	Fort Leavenworth	127
	Monument Station	105
	Fort Riley	198
	Fort Wallace	383
Minnesota	Fort Ripley	48
	Fort Snelling	85
Montana	Fort C. F. Smith	375
	Camp Cooke	438
	Fort Ellis	185
	Fort Shaw	363
Nebraska	Fort Kearny	72
	Fort McPherson	332
	Camp Sargent	231
Nevada	Fort Churchill	83
	Camp Halleck	54
	Camp McDermit	105
	Camp McGarry	51
	Camp Ruby	91
	Camp Winfield Scott	29
New Mexico	Fort Bascom	21

State	Post	Number of troops
	Fort Bayard	67
	Fort Craig	65
	Camp Plummer	77
	Fort Selden	164
	Fort Stanton	43
	Fort Sumner	424
	Fort Union	85
	Fort Wingate	142
North Dakota	Fort Abercrombie	215
	Fort Buford	371
	Fort Ransom	148
	Fort Rice	291
	Fort Stevenson	242
	Fort Totten	315
Oklahoma	Fort Arbuckle	208
	Fort Gibson	233
Oregon	Camp C. F. Smith	58
	Camp Klamath	89
	Camp Logan	39
	Camp Steele	65
	Fort Stevens	78
	Camp Warner	57
	Camp Watson	108
South Dakota	Fort Dakota	81
	Fort Randall	67
	Fort Sully	300
	Fort Wadsworth	238
Texas	Fort Belknap	72
	Brownsville	433
	Fort Chadbourne	396
	Fort Clark	88
	Fort Davis	278
	Fort Hudson	131
	Fort Inge	80
	Fort McIntosh	69
	Fort Mason	77
	Ringgold Barracks	282
	San Antonio	114
	Fort Stockton	313
	Camp Verde	176
	Camp Wilson	210
Utah	Camp Douglas	92
Washington	Camp Colville	52
	Camp Disappointment	79
	Camp Steele	60
	Fort Steilacoom	73
	Fort Vancouver	253
Wyoming	Fort Bridger	156
	Fort D. A. Russell	345
	Fort Fetterman	576
	Fort Laramie	1,023
	Fort Phil Kearny	408
	Fort Reno	328
	Fort Sanders	516

Source:

Tables C, D, E, F, and N (dated October 20, 1867), Report of the Secretary of War, 1867, *House Executive Document* no. 1, 40th Congress, 2d session, serial 1324, pp. 436–57, 470–73.

Map 83. Distribution of Regular Army Troops: 1870

By 1870 the military occupation of the South was about ended, and the main work of the regular army was again at posts scattered throughout the Indian regions of the West. There were especially heavy concentrations in the Central and Southern Plains.

The list below shows the posts beyond the first tier of states west of the Mississippi; the eastern posts, however, are shown on the map.

Distribution of the Army in the West, 1870

State	Post	Number of troops
Arizona	Camp Bowie	155
	Camp Crittenden	59
	Camp Date Creek	102
	Camp Goodwin	112
	Camp Grant	268
	Camp Hualpai	129
	Camp Lowell	47
	Camp McDowell	192
	Camp Mogollon	195
	Camp Mojave	118
	Camp Verde	234
	Fort Whipple	116
California	San Francisco area	
	Alcatraz Island	126
	Angel Island	59
	Benicia Arsenal	55
	Point San Jose	118
	Presidio of San Francisco	406
	Yerba Buena Island	103
	Camp Bidwell	57
	Drum Barracks	70
	Camp Gaston	108
	Camp Independence	75
	Camp Wright	83
Colorado	Fort Garland	157
	Fort Lyon	263
	Fort Reynolds	76
	Fort Sedgwick	210
Idaho	Fort Boise	86
	Fort Hall	67
	Fort Lapwai	84
	Camp Three Forks Owyhee	64
Kansas	Fort Dodge	286
	Fort Harker	166
	Fort Hays	246
	Fort Leavenworth	434
	Fort Riley	375
	Southeastern Kansas	229
	Fort Wallace	309
	In the field	650
Montana	Camp Baker	64
	Fort Benton	66
	Fort Ellis	158
	Fort Shaw	389
Nebraska	Fort Kearny	49
	Fort McPherson	500
	Omaha Barracks	620
Nevada	Camp Halleck	142
	Camp McDermit	53
	Camp Winfield Scott	66
New Mexico	Fort Bascom	133
	Fort Bayard	212
	Fort Craig	146
	Fort Cummings	69
	Fort McRae	292

State	Post	Number of troops
	Fort Selden	126
	Fort Stanton	134
	Fort Union	244
	Fort Wingate	51
North Dakota	Fort Abercrombie	99
	Fort Buford	296
	Fort Pembina	168
	Fort Ransom	103
	Fort Rice	264
	Fort Stevenson	97
	Fort Totten	182
Oklahoma	Fort Gibson	82
	Fort Sill	792
	Camp Supply	638
Oregon	Camp Harney	199
	Fort Klamath	59
	Fort Stevens	61
	Camp Warner	238
South Dakota	Cheyenne Agency	189
	Crow Creek Agency	120
	Grand River Agency	187
	Lower Brule Agency	107
	Fort Randall	207
	Fort Sully	235
	Fort Wadsworth	152
	Whetstone Agency	130
Texas	Austin	88
	Fort Bliss	50
	Fort Brown	437
	Fort Clark	340
	Fort Concho	516
	Fort Davis	427
	Fort Duncan	217
	Fort Griffin	345
	Jefferson	104
	Fort McIntosh	184
	Fort McKavett	332
	Fort Quitman	317
	Fort Richardson	593
	Ringgold Barracks	351
	San Antonio	168
	Fort Stockton	221
	Waco	104
Utah	Camp Douglas	173
	Fort Rawlins	90
Washington	Fort Cape Disappointment	47
	Fort Colville	56
	San Juan Island	80
	Fort Vancouver	57
	Vancouver Arsenal	26
Wyoming	Fort Bridger	177
	Camp Brown	63
	Fort D. A. Russell	647
	Fort Fetterman	149
	Fort Fred Steele	241
	Fort Laramie	295
	Fort Sanders	297
	Fort Stambaugh	154

Source:
Tables C, D, and F (dated October 20, 1870), Report of the Secretary of War, 1870, *House Executive Document* no. 1, pt. 2, 41st Congress, 3d session, serial 1446, pp. 66–73, 76–77, 84–87.

Map 84. Distribution of Regular Army Troops: 1878

The 1870s were years of Indian wars, with the Red River War on the Southern Plains and the Sioux War (including Custer's defeat) on the Northern Plains. The map for 1878 shows the heavy concentration of troops in the area of the Little Bighorn and at Fort Clark on the Rio Grande, where marauding Indians caused great concern.

The list below shows only the posts in the West, although the map includes the eastern posts as well.

Distribution of the Army in the West, 1878

State	Post	Number of troops
Arizona	Camp Apache	234
	Camp Bowie	110
	Camp Grant	204
	Camp Huachuca	135
	Camp Lowell	21
	Camp McDowell	95
	Camp Mojave	41
	Camp Thomas	90
	Camp Verde	229
	Fort Whipple	105
California	San Francisco area	
	Alcatraz Island	85
	Angel Island	115
	Benicia Barracks	182
	Fort Point	81
	Presidio of San Francisco	113
	Point San Jose	46
	Camp Bidwell	110
	Camp Gaston	42
	San Diego	38
Colorado	Fort Garland	87
	Fort Lyon	157
Idaho	Fort Boise	109
	Camp Coeur d'Alene	76
	Fort Hall	162
	Fort Hall Agency	116
	Fort Lapwai	227
Kansas	Fort Dodge	124
	Fort Hays	113
	Fort Leavenworth	312
	Fort Riley	188
	Fort Wallace	85
Montana	Camp Baker	101
	Fort Benton	51
	Fort Custer	507
	Fort Ellis	323
	Fort Keogh	807
	Camp at Marias Crossing	262
	Fort Missoula	163
	Fort Shaw	322
Nebraska	Fort Hartsuff	37
	Fort McPherson	109
	Omaha Barracks	126
	Red Cloud Agency	150
	Camp Robinson	68
	Sidney Barracks	38
Nevada	Camp Halleck	119
	Camp McDermit	43
New Mexico	Fort Bayard	241
	Fort Marcy	40
	Fort Stanton	175
	Fort Union	123

State	Post	Number of troops
	Fort Wingate	137
North Dakota	Fort Abraham Lincoln	216
	Fort Buford	340
	Fort Pembina	96
	Fort Rice	61
	Standing Rock Agency	237
	Fort Stevenson	108
	Fort Totten	128
Oklahoma	Fort Gibson	41
	Fort Reno	217
	Fort Sill	328
	Camp Supply	147
Oregon	Camp Harney	251
	Fort Klamath	39
	Fort Stevens	43
South Dakota	Cheyenne Agency	230
	Lower Brule Agency	77
	Fort Randall	112
	Rosebud Agency	140
	Camp Ruhlen	171
	Fort Sisseton	48
	Fort Sully	45
Texas	Fort Bliss	114
	Fort Brown	424
	Fort Clark	1,039
	Fort Concho	353
	Fort Davis	330
	Fort Duncan	213
	Fort Elliott	201
	Fort Griffin	58
	Fort McIntosh	225
	Fort McKavett	279
	Ringgold Barracks	315
	San Antonio	269
	San Diego	55
	San Felipe	104
	Fort Stockton	236
Utah	Fort Cameron	84
	Camp Douglas	148
Washington	Fort Canby	79
	Fort Colville	139
	Fort Townsend	33
	Fort Vancouver	177
	Fort Walla Walla	350
Wyoming	Camp Brown	68
	Fort D. A. Russell	64
	Fort Fetterman	124
	Fort Fred Steele	106
	Fort Laramie	114
	Fort McKinney	808
	Fort Sanders	82

Source:
Tables C and E (dated October 14, 1878), Report of the Secretary of War, 1878, *House Executive Document* no. 1, pt. 2, 45th Congress, 3d session, serial 1843, pp. 12–17, 22–25.

Map 85. Distribution of Regular Army Troops: 1885

By 1885 the active field operations of the army in the West were about at an end, and the many small garrisons scattered through the West were consolidated into fewer and larger posts. The rapid extension of the railroads aided the process, for railroads made possible the deployment of troops from concentrated centers.

The list below includes only those posts beyond the first tier of states west of the Mississippi.

Distribution of the Army in the West, 1885

State	Post	Number of troops
Arizona	Fort Apache	248
	Fort Bowie	183
	Fort Grant	397
	Fort Huachuca	261
	Fort Lowell	162
	Fort McDowell	165
	Fort Mojave	51
	San Carlos	222
	Fort Thomas	198
	Fort Verde	179
	Whipple Barracks	144
California	San Francisco area	
	Alcatraz Island	83
	Angel Island	148
	Benicia Barracks	87
	Fort Mason	41
	Presidio of San Francisco	270
	Fort Winfield Scott	116
	Fort Bidwell	107
	Fort Gaston	45
	San Diego Barracks	42
Colorado	Fort Lewis	425
	Fort Lyon	245
	Cantonment on the Uncompahgre	69
Idaho	Boise Barracks	117
	Fort Coeur d'Alene	280
Kansas	Fort Hays	136
	Fort Leavenworth	628
	Fort Riley	396
Montana	Fort Assinniboine	548
	Fort Custer	521
	Fort Ellis	144
	Fort Keogh	429
	Fort Maginnis	258
	Fort Missoula	175
	Camp Poplar River	101
	Fort Shaw	211
Nebraska	Fort Niobrara	271
	Fort Omaha	399
	Fort Robinson	222
	Fort Sidney	224
Nevada	Fort Halleck	44
	Fort McDermit	42
New Mexico	Fort Bayard	305
	Fort Marcy	48
	Fort Selden	54
	Fort Stanton	283
	Fort Union	219
	Fort Wingate	404
North Dakota	Fort Abraham Lincoln	191
	Fort Buford	335
	Fort Pembina	83
	Fort Totten	186
	Fort Yates	273
Oklahoma	Fort Gibson	96
	Fort Reno	428

State	Post	Number of troops		State	Post	Number of troops
	Fort Sill	264			Fort Huachuca	272
	Fort Supply	403			Whipple Barracks	300
Oregon	Fort Klamath	116		California	San Francisco area	
South Dakota	Fort Bennett	47			Alcatraz Island	131
	Fort Meade	575			Angel Island	298
	Fort Randall	182			Benicia Barracks	206
	Fort Sisseton	88			Fort Mason	68
	Fort Sully	189			Presidio of San Francisco	705
Texas	Fort Bliss	97			San Diego Barracks	73
	Fort Brown	165		Colorado	Fort Logan	677
	Fort Clark	619		Idaho	Boise Barracks	123
	Fort Concho	308			Fort Sherman	359
	Fort Davis	207		Kansas	Fort Leavenworth	830
	Camp Del Rio	66			Fort Riley	810
	Fort Elliott	225		Montana	Fort Assinniboine	405
	Fort McIntosh	159			Fort Custer	377
	Camp Pena Colorado	56			Fort Keogh	334
	Camp Rice	57			Camp Merritt	61
	Fort Ringgold	203			Fort Missoula	305
	San Antonio	280		Nebraska	Fort Niobrara	476
	Fort Stockton	149			Fort Omaha	571
Utah	Fort Douglas	498			Fort Robinson	516
Washington	Fort Canby	77		New Mexico	Fort Bayard	424
	Fort Spokane	209			Fort Stanton	71
	Fort Townsend	55			Fort Wingate	299
	Vancouver Barracks	580		North Dakota	Fort Buford	252
	Fort Walla Walla	357			Fort Yates	313
Wyoming	Fort Bridger	220		Oklahoma	Fort Reno	427
	Fort D. A. Russell	343			Fort Sill	452
	Fort Fred Steele	189		South Dakota	Fort Meade	516
	Fort Laramie	292		Texas	Fort Bliss	173
	Fort McKinney	423			Fort Brown	134
	Fort Washakie	144			Fort Clark	588
					Eagle Pass	65
					Fort Hancock	71
					Fort McIntosh	198
					Fort Ringgold	212
					Fort Sam Houston	756
				Utah	Fort Douglas	566
					Fort Duchesne	127
				Washington	Fort Canby	129
					Fort Spokane	200
					Vancouver Barracks	632
					Fort Walla Walla	250
				Wyoming	Fort D. A. Russell	512
					Fort Washakie	75
					Fort Yellowstone	143

Source:

Tables D and E (dated October 10, 1885), Report of the Secretary of War, 1885, *House Executive Document* no. 1, pt. 2, 49th Congress, 1st session, serial 2369, pp. 82–91.

Map 86. Distribution of Regular Army Troops: 1895

The distribution of regular army troops by 1895 no longer reflected frontier needs. A large number of posts had been given up, and those that remained, for the most part, were simply used to house the peacetime army. New posts like Fort Sheridan, north of Chicago, and Fort McPherson, at Atlanta, were just as important as Fort Riley or Fort Sill.

The following list does not include the eastern or central posts.

Distribution of the Army in the West, 1895

State	Post	Number of troops
Arizona	Fort Apache	322
	Fort Grant	410

Source:

Table B (dated November 5, 1895), Report of the Secretary of War, 1895, *House Document* no. 2, 54th Congress, 1st session, serial 3370, pp. 82–89.

SECTION IX
Aspects of the Indian Frontier

Map 87. Indian Frontier: 1785–1800

This map follows the map "The Military Frontier: 1785–1800," in Francis Paul Prucha, *The Sword of the Republic: The United States Army on the Frontier: 1783–1846* (New York: Macmillan Company, 1969), 22. It shows the military posts in both the Northwest Territory and the South, the chief military engagements, and a few significant settlements. The line of posts in the North-west Territory established for the military thrust against the Indians is clearly shown.

Map 88. Detroit Theater in the War of 1812

This map follows the map "The Detroit Theater in the War of 1812," in Prucha, *Sword of the Republic*, 109. The important Indian engagement was the Battle of the Thames.

Map 89. Southern Frontier: 1813–1818
This map follows the map "The Southern Frontier: 1812–1818," in Prucha, *Sword of the Republic,* 116. It shows the main places associated with Andrew Jackson's military activities in the South and the Creek cession that Jackson acquired in 1814 at the Treaty of Fort Jackson.

Map 90. Black Hawk War
This map follows the map "The Black Hawk War," in Prucha, *Sword of the Republic,* 221, which was based on a map in *Black Hawk (Ma-Ka-Tai-Me-She-Kia-Kiak): An Autobiography,* ed. Donald Jackson (Urbana: University of Illinois Press, 1955).

Map 91. Emigration Routes in the Removal of the Southern Indians
After the passage of the Removal Act in 1830, the Five Civilized Tribes each signed a removal treaty with the United States. This map shows in general the routes by which the Cherokees, Creeks, Choctaws, Chickasaws, and Seminoles moved to lands assigned them in what is now Oklahoma. Some of the routes were overland, others were by water.

A careful compilation of data on the various routes was made by Grant Foreman, and a sketch based on the data was published in his *Indian Removal: The Emigration of the Five Civilized Tribes of Indians* (Norman: University of Oklahoma Press, 1932), following p. 384. It was redrawn, with clearer labels for the routes of the different tribes, for the 1972 edition of *Indian Removal,* 396–97. I follow this information, in much simplified form, here.

Other cartographic representations of the routes all seem to be based on Foreman's original map.

See Maps 23–26 for the eastern land cessions of the Five Civilized Tribes; see Maps 58–60, 92 for the locations of the tribes in the Indian Territory.

Map 92. Location of Indians in the Indian Territory after Removal
The removal treaties with the Five Civilized Tribes in the 1830s allotted territory to them in what is now Oklahoma. At the same time small tribes in the North also moved to the West. The location of the tribes west of Arkansas and Missouri is shown on this map.

I have been guided by the map "Indian Territory before 1854" in Arrell Morgan Gibson, *The American Indian: Prehistory to the Present* (Lexington, Mass.: D. C. Heath and Company, 1980), 313. But ultimately much

of the information comes from two government maps:

"Map of the Western Territory &c [1834]," in "Regulating the Indian Department," *House Report* no. 474, 23d Congress, 1st session, serial 263, following p. 132. This map, in reduced size, is reprinted in Grant Foreman, *Indian Removal: The Emigration of the Five Civilized Tribes of Indians* (Norman: University of Oklahoma Press, 1932), following p. 240.
"Map Showing the Lands Assigned to Emigrant Indians West of Arkansas & Missouri [1836]," in "Colonel Dodge's Journal," *House Document* no. 181, 24th Congress, 1st session, serial 289, following p. 36. It is reprinted, in reduced size and in color, in *Historical Atlas of the United States* (Washington: National Geographic Society, 1988), 46.

Beyond these contemporary maps, one must rely on the maps in Charles C. Royce, *Indian Land Cessions in the United States,* Eighteenth Annual Report of the Bureau of American Ethnology, 1896–1897, part 2 (Washington: Government Printing Office, 1899). They show the lands of the various tribes as they were later ceded to the United States (see plates 22, 27, and 41).

Map 93. Second Seminole War: 1835–1842
The Second Seminole War began in 1835 when the Indians forcibly resisted movement to the Indian Territory under the provisions of the Treaty of Payne's Landing, which the federal government determined to enforce at all costs. It was not an easy task to force the Indians out, and the war dragged on until 1842, by which time all but a small remnant of the Seminoles had been killed or removed. In the process, Florida (together with southeastern Georgia) was dotted with many forts. Some of them, like Fort King, Fort Drane, and Fort Brooke, antedated the hostilities, but most of them were only temporary establishments, which sometimes were merely numbered, not named. A list of the named forts (more than 150) is given in Francis Paul Prucha, *A Guide to the Military Posts of the United States, 1789–1895* (Madison: State Historical Society of Wisconsin, 1964), 139–41.

Geographical data on the Second Seminole War appear in great detail on two manuscript maps in the Cartographic Branch of the National Archives, Records of the Office of the Chief of Engineers, Record Group 77:

"Map of the Seat of War in Florida, compiled by order of Bvt. Brigr. Genl. Z. Taylor, principally from the surveys & reconnaissances of the Officers of the

U.S. Army, by Capt. John Mackay and Lieut. J. E. Blake, U.S. Topographical Engineers, Head Quarters, Army of the South, Tampa Bay, Florida, 1839."
"Map of the Seat of War in Florida, compiled by Capt. J. McClellan and Lieut. A. A. Humphreys, U.S. Topographical Engineers, from examinations made by Officers of the U.S. Topographical Engineers, Ordnance, Dragoons, Artillery, Infantry, and Navy. Bureau of Topographical Engineers, 1843, with late corrections from Surveys under the direction of Brigadier General W. I. Worth."

A simplified printed version of the Mackay and Blake map is the following: *Map of East Florida, Reduced from the Map compiled by Capt. John Mackay & Lieut. J. E. Blake, and published by order of the Senate of the U. States for the Monthly Chronicle, 1840.* It is reprinted in Prucha, *Guide to the Military Posts of the United States,* 142, from a copy in the Library of Congress.

Two earlier maps of a portion of Florida are printed in *House Document* no. 78, 25th Congress, 2d session, serial 323, pp. 407 and 768. They are entitled "Copy of a Map of the Seat of War in Florida, forwarded to the War Department by Major Genl. W. Scott, U.S.A. [1836]," and "A Map of the Seat of War in Florida, 1836."

Map 93 follows the simplified map: "Florida—1835–1842," drawn by J. E. Massey, 1962, which is published in John K. Mahon, *History of the Second Seminole War, 1835–1842* (Gainesville: University of Florida Press, 1967), inside back cover. The county boundary lines of 1840 are taken from *Historical U.S. County Outline Map Collection, 1840–1980,* senior editor, Thomas D. Rabenhorst (Baltimore: Department of Geography, University of Maryland Baltimore County, 1984), 1940. The boundary of the reservation established by the Treaty of Moultrie Creek, September 18, 1823, and later extensions is given in Charles C. Royce, *Indian Land Cessions in the United States,* Eighteenth Annual Report of the Bureau of American Ethnology, 1896–1897, part 2 (Washington: Government Printing Office, 1899), plate 14, Royce Area no. 173.

Map 94. Pacific Northwest: 1850–1880
The three decades after 1850 were full of significant Indian events, beginning with the treaties signed with the tribes in 1854–1855 by Isaac I. Stevens, the first governor of Washington Territory. There were wars with the Indians in the 1850s and 1870s. I have relied to some extent on the map "The Mountain Wars, 1850–1880," in Robert M. Utley, *The Indian Frontier of the American West,*

1846–1890 (Albuquerque: University of New Mexico Press, 1984), 194–95. See also the map "The Northwest: Frontier and Indian Wars, 1860–90," in *The American Heritage Pictorial Atlas of United States History* (New York: American Heritage Publishing Company, 1966), 246–47.

Map 95. Southwest Indian Frontier: 1860–1890

The Indians of the Southwest were the last to be subdued by the military forces of the United States, and the area has scattered battle sites. I have taken some of the material from the map "The Southwest and the Southern Plains," in Utley, *Indian Frontier of the American West*, 68–69. See also the map "The Southwest: Frontier and Indian Wars, 1860–90," in *American Heritage Pictorial Atlas of United States History*, 248–49. The Navajo data came from Map 7, "The Long Walk of the Navajo Indians," in Francis Paul Prucha, *The Great Father: The United States Government and the American Indians*, 2 vols. (Lincoln: University of Nebraska Press, 1984), 1:454.

Map 96. Enlargement of the Navajo Reservation

The Navajo Reservation, unlike many reservations that were steadily reduced in size, grew as the Navajo population increased. This map shows the original Navajo Reservation established in 1868 when the Indians returned from exile at the Bosque Redondo and areas added within specified periods. I have simplified Map 28, "Evolution of the Navajo Reservation," in James M. Goodman, *The Navajo Atlas: Environments, Resources, People, and History of the Diné Bikeyah* (Norman: University of Oklahoma Press, 1982), 56. Goodman's piece-by-piece enlargement of the reservation is very similar to Map 1, "Boundaries of the Navajo Reservation," in Lawrence C. Kelly, *The Navajo Indians and Federal Indian Policy, 1900–1935* (Tucson: University of Arizona Press, 1968), 18–19.

Map 96 shows the Hopi executive order area of 1882, the restricted Hopi Reservation within it, and the Hopi-Navajo Joint Use Area. For division of the Joint Use Area, see Map 97.

Map 97. Division of the Hopi-Navajo Joint Use Area: 1977

The rectangular area of this map shows the Hopi Reservation determined in an executive order of December 16, 1882 (printed in Charles J. Kappler, *Indian Affairs: Laws and Treaties*, 5 vols. [Washington: Government Printing Office, 1904–1941], 1:805). The wording of the order was ambiguous about allowing other tribes to settle in the area, and many Navajos moved in.

Shown on the map is the Hopi Reservation (Land Management District no. 6) with the boundaries determined in 1943. The United States District Court for the District of Arizona on September 28, 1962, confirmed that this area was exclusively Hopi but declared that in the rest of the 1882 reservation, the so-called Joint Use Area, both tribes had a joint interest (*Healing v. Jones, Federal Supplement*, 210:125–92).

Continuing conflicts between the Hopis and the Navajos led to an act of December 22, 1974 (*United States Statutes at Large*, 88:1712–23), which provided for a partition of the Joint Use Area. The mediator called upon to make the partition submitted a report, "Hopi-Navajo Land Dispute: Mediator's Report and Recommendations," which was accepted by the court and issued by Judge James A. Walsh on February 10, 1977. The mediator's report includes as Exhibit A a summary map showing the partition line, which is the basis for Map 97. The report is reproduced in "Relocation of Certain Hopi and Navajo Indians," *Hearing before the United States Senate Select Committee on Indian Affairs, Ninety-fifth Congress, Second Session, on S. 1714* (1978), 919–1037; the map is on p. 927. In a "Summary Judgment on the Boundary Issue and Judgment of Partition," dated April 18, 1979, the United States District Court for the District of Arizona issued a final decree confirming the partition line, including in Hopi land the areas marked A and B on the mediator's map. This judgment is reproduced in "Relocation of Certain Hopi and Navajo Indians," *Hearing before the Select Committee on Indian Affairs, United States Senate, Ninety-sixth Congress, First Session, on S. 751 and S. 1077* (1979), 183–85.

Some small changes have been made in the partition line since 1977.

SECTION X
A Portfolio of Maps by Rafael D. Palacios

Maps 98–109.

These maps are a selection from the maps drawn by Rafael D. Palacios to illustrate Ralph K. Andrist, *The Long Death: The Last Days of the Plains Indians* (New York: Macmillan Company, 1964), 33, 71, 100, 156, 173, 194, 220, 250, 309, 322, 339, 349. The maps are reproduced here slightly enlarged and are used with permission of the Macmillan Company.

Index

Indexing of military posts: In general a post is indexed as Fort ——, even though it may at one time have been designated a camp or cantonment. Those that were always called Camp —— or Cantonment —— are so indexed. Garrisoned sites that were not formally designated as forts or camps are indexed as garrisons, for example, Abiquiu garrison.

Indexing of Indian names: The common or usual name is used in the index for the most part, even though variant spellings appear on the maps and in Notes and References.

Arkansas Post Factory, 55
Armstrong Male Academy, 63
Army, United States, 83–110
Assiniboine Indians, 5, 6, 7
Asylum. *See* Canton Insane Asylum
Atakapa Indians, 5
Atchison, Topeka, and Santa Fe Railroad, 132, 135
Atka (Alaska Native village), 81
Atkasook (Alaska Native village), 81
Atlanta SMSA, 146
Atmautluak (Alaska Native village), 81
Atoka, Oklahoma, 72
Attakapas garrison, 93, 96
Auburn Health Center, 67
Auburn Rural Tribal Health Program, 67
Augusta, Georgia, 113
Augusta Arsenal, 163, 164, 165
Augustine Reservation, 44, 152
Austin garrison, 93, 166, 169
Austin SMSA, 146
Autosee, Creek Nation, 115

Bad Axe, battle of, 116
Badlands, 136
Bad River Reservation, 39, 50, 156
Bakersfield SMSA, 146
Bakersfield Urban Health Program, 67
Baltimore SMSA, 146
Banning Rural Tribal Health Program, 67
Bannock Indians, 5
Baptist agencies, 59
Baraga Health Center, 67
Barbour, James, 163
Barona Rancheria, 44, 152
Barracks. *See* Forts
Barrancas Barracks, 166
Barrow (Alaska Native village), 81
Barrow Hospital, 67
Baton Rouge Barracks, 93, 96, 162, 163, 164, 166
Battles and engagements: Adobe Walls, 121; Apache Pass, 121; Bad Axe, 116; Bear Paw Mountains, 134; Beecher Island, 129; Big Dry Wash, 121; Big Hole, 120, 134; Big Meadows, 120; Birch Coulee, 126; Birch Creek, 120; Burnt Corn, 115; Camas Meadows, 134; Camp Grant, 121; Camp Izard, 119; Canyon Creek, 134; Canyon de Chelly, 121; Chakalka's Island, 119; Cibeque Creek, 121; Clearwater, 120, 134; Clinch's, 119; Dry Lake, 131; Fallen Timbers, 113; Four Lakes, 120; Horseshoe Bend, 115; Kanapaha Prairie, 119; Land's Ranch, 131; Little Bighorn, 133; Lockahatchee, 119; McClellan Creek, 121; Okeechobee, 119; Palo Duro Canyon, 121; Pecatonica River, 116; Rosebud, 133; Salt River Canyon, 121; Sand Creek, 121, 127; Soldier Spring, 121; Spokane Plain, 120; Steptoe, 120; Stillman's Run, 116; Thames, 114, 172; Tinaja de las Palmas, 121; Washita, 121, 129; White Bird, 134; White Bird

Canyon, 120; Wisconsin Heights, 116; Wood Lake, 126; Wounded Knee, 136, 137
Bayfield Health Center, 67
Bay Mills Reservation, 50, 156
Beardstown, Illinois, 116
Bear Paw Mountains, battle of, 134
Beaver (Alaska Native village), 81
Beecher Island, battle of, 129
Belcourt Hospital, 67
Belkofsky (Alaska Native village), 81
Belle Fontaine Factory, 55
Belle Fontaine garrison, 163
Bellingham Health Center, 67
Bellingham SMSA, 146
Bellona Arsenal, 164
Benicia Barracks, 86, 165, 166, 169, 170, 171
Benton Paiute Reservation, 44, 152
Bering Strait Eskimo tribal area, 77
Bering Straits Native Corporation, 80, 81
Berry Creek Rancheria, 44, 152
Bethel (Alaska Native village), 81
Bethel Agency, 61
Bethel Hospital, 67
BIA area offices, 61, 158
BIA off-reservation boarding schools, 64, 159
BIA on-reservation boarding schools, 64, 159
BIA post-secondary schools, 64, 159
Big Bend Rancheria, 44, 152
Big Cypress Reservation, 52, 157
Big Dry Wash, battle of, 121
Big Foot's camp, 136, 137
Big Hole, battle of, 120, 134
Bighorn campaign, 133
Big Lagoon Rancheria, 44, 152
Big Meadows, battle of, 120
Big Pine Rancheria, 44, 152
Big Sandy Rancheria, 44
Big Valley Rancheria, 44
Billings Area Office, 61, 158
Billings SMSA, 146
Billings Urban Health Program, 67
Bill Moore's (Alaska Native village), 81
Birch Coulee, battle of, 126
Birch Creek (Alaska Native village), 81
Birch Creek, battle of, 120
Bishop Hospital, 65
Bishop Rancheria, 44, 152
Bishop Rural Tribal Health Program, 67
Bismarck, North Dakota, 133, 135
Bismarck School, 63
Bismarck SMSA, 146
Black Bob Reservation, 39
Blackfeet Agency, 58, 59, 60, 61
Blackfeet Community College, 64
Blackfeet Indians, 5, 6, 7, 130; land cessions, 34, 149–50
Blackfeet Reservation, 39, 41, 45, 153
Blackfeet Sanatorium, 65
Blackfeet School, 62, 63
Black Hawk War, 116, 172
Black Hills, 136

Black Mesa, 123
Blood Indians, 149–50
Bloomfield School, 63
Boarding schools, 62–64, 158, 159
Boise Barracks, 84, 170, 171
Bois Forte Band, 7
Bois Forte Reservation, 39, 41, 50, 155
Bosque Redondo, 121
Boston SMSA, 146
Bowleg's Town, Florida, 115
Bowler Health Center, 67
Box Elder Health Center, 67
Bozeman, Montana, 128, 133, 134
Bozeman Trail, 128
Brazos Agency, 58
Bremerton SMSA, 146
Brevig Mission (Alaska Native village), 81
Bridgeport Rancheria, 44, 152
Brighton Reservation, 52, 157
Brimley Health Center, 67
Bristol Bay Native Corporation, 80, 81
British traders, 162
Broken Bow Health Center, 67
Browning Hospital, 67
Brownsville garrison, 168
Buckland (Alaska Native village), 81
Buffalo Barracks, 165
Buffalo range, 130
Buffalo SMSA, 146
Burney Rural Tribal Health Program, 67
Burns Paiute Colony, 43, 152
Burnt Corn, battle of, 115
Butte Urban Health Program, 67
Bylas Health Center, 67

Cabazon Reservation, 41, 44, 152
Cachil Dehe Rancheria, 152
Caddo Indians, 5, 7, 160
Cahuilla Indians, 5
Cahuilla Reservation, 41, 44, 152
California: land cessions in, 148; reservations in, 39, 41, 44, 152–53
California culture area, 4
California Indians, 6, 7
Calhoun, John C., 157, 162, 163
Calista Corporation, 80, 81
Calusa Indians, 5
Camas Meadows, battle of, 134
Camp Alvord, 84
Camp Anderson, 84, 86
Camp Antelope Rural Tribal Health Program, 67
Camp Arbuckle, 91, 93
Camp Armistead, 96
Camp Astoria, 84, 166
Camp Atkinson, 93, 164
Camp at Marias Crossing, 169
Camp Babbitt, 86
Camp Baker, 168, 169
Camp Barranca, 167
Camp Beales Springs, 87
Camp Beecher, 91
Camp Brown, 169, 170
Camp C. F. Smith, 84, 168

Chignik Lagoon (Alaska Native village), 81
Chignik Lake (Alaska Native village), 81
Chilkat (Alaska Native village), 81
Chilocco Hospital, 65
Chilocco School, 62, 63
Chinle Agency, 61
Chinle Hospital, 67
Chinle School, 63, 64
Chinook Indians, 5, 7
Chippewa Agency, 58, 60
Chippewa and Munsee Reservation, 39, 41
Chippewa Indians, 5, 6, 7, 130; agreement with, 21; land cessions, 34; reservations, 34. *See also* Lake Superior Chippewa Indians
Chiricahua Apache Indians, 5, 6, 7
Chistochina (Alaska Native village), 81
Chitimacha Indians, 5
Chitimacha Reservation, 49, 155
Chitina (Alaska Native village), 81
Choctaw Agency, 56, 57, 59, 61
Choctaw Central School, 64
Choctaw-Chickasaw Sanatorium, 65
Choctaw Indians, 5, 6, 117, 160; land cessions, 32, 149; treaties with, 149, 160
Choctaw Nation, 70, 71, 72
Choctaw Reservation. *See* Chickasaw and Choctaw Reservation
Christian Church agencies, 59
Chugach Natives, Inc., 80, 81
Chumash Indians, 5
Churches, assignment of agencies to, 59, 157–58
Chuska / Tobatchi School, 64
Cibeque Creek, battle of, 121
Cibecue Health Center, 67
Ciboleta garrison, 166
Cincinnati, Ohio, 113
Cincinnati SMSA, 146
Circle (Alaska Native village), 81
Citizen Potawatomi Indians, 160
Claremore Hospital, 67
Clark's Point (Alaska Native village), 81
Clatsop Indians, 5, 7
Clearwater, battle of, 120, 134
Cleveland SMSA, 146
Clewiston Health Center, 67
Clinch's Battle, 119
Clinton Hospital, 67
Clontarf School, 62
Cloquet Health Center, 67
Clovis Rural Tribal Health Program, 67
Cochiti Pueblo, 39, 47, 154
Cocopah Reservation, 46, 154
Coeur d'Alene Hospital, 65
Coeur d'Alene Indians, 5, 7
Coeur d'Alene Reservation, 39, 41, 45, 153
Cold Springs Rancheria, 44, 152
Coleraine garrison, 97, 113
Colerain Factory, 55
Colonies. *See* Reservations
Colonization of Indians, 37
Colorado, reservations in, 39, 41, 47, 154
Colorado River Agency, 59, 60, 61

Colorado River Hospital, 65
Colorado River Reservation, 39, 41, 44, 46, 152, 154
Colorado River School, 62, 63
Colorado Springs SMSA, 146
Columbia Barracks, 166
Columbia Indians, 5
Columbia Reservation, 39
Columbia River District Agency, 58
Columbus Barracks, 94
Columbus SMSA, 146
Colusa Rancheria, 44
Colville Agency, 59, 60, 61
Colville Indians, 5, 7
Colville Reservation, 39, 41, 43, 151
Comanche Agency, 58
Comanche Indians, 5, 6, 7, 130, 160
Comanche, Kiowa, and Apache Reservation, 72
Community colleges, 64, 159
Compton Urban Health Program, 67
Concentration of Indians, 37
Concho Agency, 61
Concho Health Center, 67
Congregational agencies, 59
Connecticut, reservations in, 51, 156
Contract off-reservation boarding schools, 64, 159
Contract schools, 158, 159
Cook Inlet Region, Inc., 80, 81
Cooperative boarding schools, 64, 159
Coos Indians, 5
Copper Center (Alaska Native village), 81
Coquille Indians, 7
Corpus Christi garrison, 93, 166
Cortina Rancheria, 44, 152
Cosmit Reservation. *See* Inaja-Cosmit Reservation
Costanoan Indians, 5
Council Bluffs. *See* Fort Atkinson (Nebraska)
Council Bluffs Agency, 57
Council Bluffs Subagency, 57
Counties, Indian population of, 11–16, 73, 74, 144, 160
Coushatta Reservation, 49, 155
Covelo Rural Tribal Health Program, 67
Covington garrison, 162
Cow Creek Reservation, 43
Cowlitz Indians, 5, 6, 7
Coyote Valley Rancheria, 44, 152
Craig (Alaska Native village), 81
Crandon Health Center, 67
Craney Island garrison, 163
Creek Agency, 56, 57, 59
Creek and Seminole Reservation, 118
Creek Indians, 5, 6, 7, 117, 160; land cessions, 31, 115, 148; treaties with, 148, 160
Creek Nation, 70, 71, 72
Crooked Creek (Alaska Native village), 81
Crook's column, 133
Cross Lake School, 63
Crow Agency, 59, 60, 61
Crow Agency Hospital, 67

Crow Creek Agency, 60, 61
Crow Creek Agency garrison, 169
Crow Creek High School, 64
Crow Creek Hospital, 65
Crow Creek Reservation, 39, 41, 48, 136, 155
Crow Creek School, 62, 63
Crow Hospital, 65
Crow Indians, 5, 6, 7, 130; agreements with, 150; land cessions, 34, 150; treaty with, 150
Crownpoint Hospital, 67
Crownpoint School, 64
Crow Reservation, 39, 41, 45, 153
Crow School, 62, 63
Crow Wing River Subagency, 57
Crystal School, 64
Culture areas, 3, 5, 77, 161; definition of, 141
Cushman Hospital, 65
Cushman School, 63
Custer, Montana, 133
Cuyapaipe Reservation, 44, 152

Dade's Battle, 119
Dakota Territory, reservations in, 39
Dallas–Fort Worth SMSA, 146
Dallas SMSA, 146
Dallas Urban Health Program, 67
Dania Reservation, 52. *See also* Hollywood Reservation
Darlington, Oklahoma, 72
Darlington Agency, 132
Day schools, 62–64, 158, 159
Deer Creek Reservation, 41, 50, 155
Deering (Alaska Native village), 81
Delaware Agency, 58
Delaware and Shawnee Agency, 56
Delaware and Wyandot Reservation, 118
Delaware Indians, 5, 7, 160
Demography, 142
Dennehotso School, 64
Denominations, assignment of agencies to, 157–58
Denver, Colorado, 127, 129, 130, 135
Denver-Boulder SMSA, 146
Denver SMSA, 146
Detroit, Michigan, 113, 114
Detroit Barracks, 164, 165, 166
Detroit Factory, 55
Detroit garrison, 89, 94, 163
Detroit SMSA, 146
Detroit Subagency, 56
Detroit theater in the War of 1812, 114, 171–72
Detroit Urban Health Program, 67
Devils Lake Agency, 59, 60
Devils Lake Reservation, 39, 41
Dilkon School, 64
Dilkon Health Center, 67
Dillingham (Alaska Native village), 81
Dillingham Hospital, 67
Distribution of regular army troops, 98–110, 162–71
Division of Hopi-Navajo Joint Use Area, 123

Muckleshoot Reservation, 41, 43, 151
Munsee Indians, 5
Munsee Reservation, 39. *See also* Chippewa
　and Munsee Reservation; Stockbridge
　and Munsee Reservation
Muskegon–Norton Shores–Muskegon
　Heights SMSA, 147
Muskogee Area Office, 61, 158

Naknek (Alaska Native village), 81
Nambe Pueblo, 7, 39, 47, 154
NANA Regional Native Corporation, 80, 81
Nanticoke Indians, 5
Napaimute (Alaska Native village), 81
Napakiak (Alaska Native village), 81
Napaskiak (Alaska Native village), 81
Narragansett Indians, 5
Narragansett Reservation, 51
Nashville, Tennessee, 113, 115, 117
Nassau-Suffolk SMSA, 147
Natchez, Mississippi, 113
Natchez Indians, 5
Natchitoches Factory, 55
Natchitoches garrison, 93, 162
Navajo Agency, 58, 59, 60. *See also* Eastern
　Navajo Agency; Western Navajo Agency
Navajo Area Office, 61
Navajo-Hopi Joint Use Area, 122, 173
Navajo Hospital, 65
Navajo Indians, 5, 6, 7
Navajo Long Walk, 121, 173
Navajo Mission Academy, 64
Navajo Mountain School, 64
Navajo Reservation, 39, 41, 46, 47, 121, 122,
　154, 173
Navajo Sanatorium, 65
Navajo School, 62, 63
Nazlini School, 64
Neah Bay Agency, 59, 60
Neah Bay Health Center, 67
Neah Bay treaty council, 120
Nebraska, reservations in, 39, 41, 48, 155
Nebraska College, 64
Negro Fort, 115, 119
Nelson Lagoon (Alaska Native village), 81
Nenahnezad School, 64
Nenana (Alaska Native village), 81
Neopit Mills Hospital, 65
Neosho Agency, 59
Neosho Subagency, 57
Nespelem Health Center, 67
Nespelem Indians, 7
Nett Lake Health Center, 67
Nett Lake Reservation. *See* Bois Forte Reser-
　vation
Nevada, reservations in, 39, 41, 44, 153
Nevada Agency, 60. *See also* Eastern Nevada
　Agency; Western Nevada Agency
Nevada School, 62
Newark SMSA, 146, 147
New England, reservations in, 51, 156
Newhalen (Alaska Native village), 81
"New" Indians, 145
New Madrid garrison, 91, 96

New Mexico, reservations in, 39, 41, 47, 154
New Orleans, Louisiana, 113, 117
New Orleans Barracks, 164, 166
New Orleans garrison, 93, 96, 162
New Orleans SMSA, 147
Newport Barracks, 89, 94, 96, 162, 165
New Stuyahok (Alaska Native village), 81
Newtok (Alaska Native village), 81
New Town Health Center, 67
New Ulm, Minnesota, 126
New York, reservations in, 51, 156
New York City, Indians in, 9
New York Harbor, 163, 164, 165, 166
New York Indians Reservation, 118
New York Liaison Office, 61
New York SMSA, 146, 147
New York Subagency, 57
New York Urban Health Program, 67
Nez Perce Agency, 59, 60
Nez Perce Indians, 5, 6, 7
Nez Perce Reservation, 45, 134, 153
Nightmute (Alaska Native village), 81
Nikolai (Alaska Native village), 81
Nikolski (Alaska Native village), 81
Ninilchik (Alaska Native village), 81
Niobrara Reservation, 39, 41
Nisenan Indians, 5
Nisqually Indians, 7
Nisqually Reservation, 39, 41, 43, 151
Noatak (Alaska Native village), 81
No Man's Land, 71, 72
Nome Agency, 61
Nome Cult Indian Agency garrison, 166
Nome Hospital, 67
Nome Lackee Agency, 58
Nome Lackee garrison, 84, 86
Nondalton (Alaska Native village), 81
Non-Indian land holdings, 151
Nonreservation boarding schools, 62, 63,
　158, 159
Nooksack Indians, 7
Nooksack Reservation, 43, 151
Noorvik (Alaska Native village), 81
Norfolk Harbor, 163
Norfolk–Virginia Beach–Portsmouth
　SMSA, 147
North Alaska tribal area, 77
North Carolina, reservation in, 51, 156
North Dakota, reservations in, 41, 48, 155.
　See also Dakota Territory
Northeast culture area, 4
Northern Arapaho Indians, 6, 7
Northern California Agency, 61
Northern Cheyenne Agency, 61
Northern Cheyenne Indians, 6, 7
Northern Cheyenne Reservation, 41, 45,
　153
Northern Idaho Agency, 61
Northern Pacific Railroad, 135
Northern Paiute Indians, 5, 6, 7
Northern Pueblos Agency, 61
North Platte, Nebraska, 129, 130
North Platte Station, 90
Northway (Alaska Native village), 81

Northwest Coast culture area, 4, 77, 161
Northwestern Shoshone Reservation, 46
Nuiqsut (Alaska Native village), 81
Nulato (Alaska Native village), 81
Nunapitchuk (Alaska Native village), 81
Nunivak Eskimo tribal area, 77
Nuyaka School, 63

Ocmulgee Old Fields Factory, 55
Off-reservation boarding schools, 158
Oglala Lakota College, 64
Oglethorpe Barracks, 97, 164, 165
Ohio Subagency, 57
Ohogamiut (Alaska Native village), 81
Oil Springs Reservation, 156
Ojo Caliente garrison, 87
Ojo Encino School, 64
Okanogan Indians, 7
Okeechobee, battle of, 119
Okeechobee Health Center, 67
Okeefenokee Swamp, 119
Okemah Hospital, 67
Okihumpky, Florida, 119
Oklahoma, 69–74, 160–61; historic Indian
　areas of, 74, 145, 155, 160–61; Indian
　population, 73, 74, 144, 160, 166; reser-
　vation in, 49, 155
Oklahoma City, Indians in, 9
Oklahoma City SMSA, 73, 146, 147
Oklahoma City Urban Health Program, 67
Okmulgee, Oklahoma, 72
Okmulgee Agency, 61
Okmulgee Health Center, 67
Old Bent's Fort, 127
Old Harbor (Alaska Native village), 81
Old Town Health Center, 67
Old Winnebago Reservation, 39
Olympia SMSA, 147
Olympic Peninsula Agency, 61
Omaha, Nebraska, 129
Omaha Agency, 58, 59
Omaha and Winnebago Agency, 60
Omaha Barracks, 168, 169
Omaha Indians, 5, 6
Omaha Reservation, 39, 41, 48, 118, 155, 156
Omaha School, 62
Omaha SMSA, 146, 147
Omaha Urban Health Program, 67
Oneida Indians, 5
Oneida Health Center, 67
Oneida Hospital, 65
Oneida Reservation (New York), 51
Oneida Reservation (Wisconsin), 39, 41, 50,
　156
Oneida School, 62, 63
Onondaga Indians, 5
Onondaga Reservation, 51, 156
Ontonagon Reservation, 39, 41, 50, 156
Opelousas garrison, 93, 96
Oregon, reservations in, 39, 41, 43, 152
Oregon Country, 58
Oregon question, 165
Oregon Trail, 127, 128, 165
Orlando SMSA, 147

Oroville Rural Tribal Health Program, 67
Orthodox Friends agencies, 59, 158
Osage Agency, 56, 60, 61
Osage Hospital, 65
Osage Indians, 5, 6, 7, 118, 160
Osage Reservation, 49, 72, 155
Osage River Subagency, 57
Osage School, 62, 63
Osage Subagency, 57
Oscarville (Alaska Native village), 81
Otoe Agency, 58, 59, 60
Otoe and Missouri Indians, 5, 7, 160
Otoe and Missouri Reservation, 39, 72, 118
Otoe School, 62, 63
Ottawa, Illinois, 116
Ottawa Indians, 7, 160
Ottawa Reservation, 72, 118
Ouachita garrison, 93, 96
Ouray School, 62
Ouzinkie (Alaska Native village), 81
Ownership status of reservation lands, 151
Owyhee Hospital, 67
Oxnard–Simi Valley–Ventura SMSA, 147
Oxnard-Ventura SMSA, 146
Ozette Reservation, 41, 43, 151

Pacific Eskimo tribal area, 77
Pacific Northwest frontier, 120, 172–73
Paimiut (Alaska Native village), 81
Paiute Agency, 59
Paiute Indians, 5. See also Northern Paiute
    Indians; Southern Paiute Indians
Paiute Reservation, 46
Palacios, Rafael D., maps by, 125–37, 173
Pala Reservation, 41, 44, 153
Palatka, Florida, 119
Palm Springs Field Agency, 61
Palo Duro Canyon, battle of, 121
Palouse Indians, 5, 7
Pamlico Indians, 5
Panamint Indians, 5
Papago Agency, 59, 61
Papago Indians, 5, 6, 7
Papago Reservation, 39, 41, 46, 154
Parker Hospital, 67
Paschal Sherman School, 64
Pascua Yaqui Reservation, 46, 154
Passamaquoddy Indians, 5, 6
Passamaquoddy Reservation, 51
Pass Christian garrison, 93, 96, 163
Patriot War, 164
Patwin Indians, 5
Pauloff Harbor (Alaska Native village), 81
Pauma Reservation, 44, 153
Pawhuska, Oklahoma, 72
Pawhuska Health Center, 67
Pawnee Agency, 58, 59, 60, 61
Pawnee Health Center, 67
Pawnee Hospital, 65
Pawnee Indians, 5, 6, 7, 118, 160
Pawnee Reservation, 72
Pawnee School, 62, 63
Payne's Landing, Florida, 119
Payson Community Reservation, 46, 154

Peace policy, 157–58
Peach Springs Health Center, 67
Pecatonica River, battle of, 116
Pechanga Reservation, 44, 153
Pecos Pueblo, 5, 19
Pedro Bay (Alaska Native village), 81
Peliklakaha, Florida, 119
Pembina Band, 7
Pendleton Health Center, 67
Pend d'Oreille Indians. See Upper Pend
    d'Oreille Indians
Pennacook Indians, 5
Penobscot Indians, 5, 6
Penobscot Reservation, 51, 156
Pensacola, Florida, 115
Pensacola garrison, 163, 164
Pensacola SMSA, 147
Peoria, Illinois, 116
Peoria and Kaskaskia Reservation, 118
Peoria Indians, 5, 7, 160
Peoria Reservation, 72
Peoria Subagency, 56
Pequot Indians, 5
Pequot Reservation, 51
Peripheral dormitories, 159
Permanent Indian frontier, 37
Perris School, 62
Perry Health Center, 67
Perryville (Alaska Native village), 81
Petite Coquille garrison, 162, 163
Philadelphia Hospital, 67
Philadelphia SMSA, 146, 147
Phoenix Area Office, 61, 158
Phoenix Hospital, 65, 67
Phoenix Sanatorium, 65
Phoenix School, 62, 63
Phoenix SMSA, 146, 147
Phoenix Urban Health Program, 67
Piankeshaw Indians, 7
Picolata, Florida, 119
Picuris Pueblo, 39, 47, 154
Piegan Indians: agreements, 149–50; land
    cessions, 149–50
Pierre, South Dakota, 136
Pierre Hospital, 65
Pierre Indian Learning Center, 64
Pierre School, 62, 63
Pierre School Health Center, 67
Pierre Urban Health Program, 67
Pillager Band, 7
Pilot Station (Alaska Native village), 81
Pilot Point (Alaska Native village), 81
Pima Agency, 58, 60, 61
Pima and Maricopa Agency, 59
Pima and Maricopa Indians, 7
Pima Sanatorium, 65
Pima School, 62, 63
Pine Creek Reservation, 156
Pine Hill School, 64
Pine Point School, 62
Pine Ridge Agency, 61, 135
Pine Ridge Hospital, 65, 67
Pine Ridge Reservation, 41, 48, 135, 136, 155
Pine Ridge School, 62, 63, 64

Pine Springs School, 64
Pipestone Hospital, 65
Pipestone School, 62, 63
Piqua Agency, 56
Piro Indians, 5
Pitkas Point (Alaska Native village), 81
Pitt River Indians, 7
Pittsburgh Arsenal, 163
Pittsburgh garrison, 94, 163
Pittsburgh SMSA, 147
Pleasant Point Reservation, 156
Plains. See Central Plains; Great Plains;
    Southern Plains
Plateau culture area, 4
Platinum (Alaska Native village), 81
Plattsburg Barracks, 95, 163, 164, 165, 166
Poarch Creek Reservation, 52
Point Elliott treaty council, 120
Point Hope (Alaska Native village), 81
Point Lay (Alaska Native village), 81
Point No Point treaty council, 120
Point Petre, 162
Point San Jose, 167, 168, 169
Pojoaque Pueblo, 39, 47, 154
Polson Health Center, 67
Pomo Indians, 5
Ponca Agency, 58, 59, 60
Ponca Indians, 5, 6, 7, 160
Ponca Reservation, 39, 72
Ponca School, 62, 63
Poospatuck Reservation, 156
Poplar Health Center, 67
Population on Indian reservations, 43–52.
    See also Alaska Native population;
    Aleuts: population; Eskimos: popula-
    tion; Indian population
Portage Creek (Alaska Native village), 81
Porterville Rural Tribal Health
    Program, 67
Port Gamble Reservation, 43, 151
Port Graham (Alaska Native village), 81
Port Heiden (Alaska Native village), 81
Portland Area Office, 61, 158
Portland SMSA, 146, 147
Portland Urban Health Program, 67
Port Lions (Alaska Native village), 81
Port Madison Reservation, 39, 41, 43, 152
Port Orford Agency, 58
Post on Brazos River, 92
Posts, military, 83–110
Potawatomi Agency, 58, 59, 60
Potawatomi and Shawnee Reservation, 72
Potawatomi Indians, 5, 6, 7; land cessions,
    33, 149; treaties with, 149
Potawatomi Reservation, 39, 41, 48, 50, 118,
    155, 156
Potawatomi School, 62
Powhatan Indians, 5, 6
Prairie du Chien Agency, 56
Prairie du Chien Factory, 55
Prairie du Chien Subagency, 57
Prairie Island Reservation, 50, 155
Pratt, Richard Henry, 158
Presbyterian agencies, 59

189